Nature: Collabo-rations in Design

Andrea Lipps
Matilda McQuaid
Caitlin Condell
Gène Bertrand

Cooper Hewitt Design Triennial
co-organized with Cube design museum

Contents

Directors' Foreword

Nature is an enduring concern of design. Its properties and resources are a means of constant inspiration and a spur for innovation. Yet while nature's allure is as strong as ever for designers, it is now joined with a profound awareness that it is time to change the paradigm. Stirred by the conditions created by anthropogenic climate change and desiring more meaningful connections within our shared biosphere, design is seeking greater cooperation to assure that nature can continue to generate its bounty.

This publication and the accompanying exhibition, *Nature—Cooper Hewitt Design Triennial*, tracks the efforts of designers to create a more holistic and harmonious relationship with nature. Their multidisciplinary, collaborative process is inherently optimistic and aligns design with like-minded scientists, engineers, artists, and advocates who also want to learn from and sustain nature. Sixty-two projects are included, from the microscopic to the monumental. Soot collected from car emissions becomes water-resistant ink. Coral and seashells shape building materials. A fruit tree preserves dozens of rare varieties of cherries, apricots, plums, and peaches. And a canopy built with bamboo, rope, and recyclable mesh collects potable water from dew, mist, and rain. Many of the projects relate to climate change and human impact on the natural world, with both innovative solutions and thought-provoking conceptual statements: from discarded plastics transformed into new materials to a digital resurrection of the extinct male northern white rhino.

Cooper Hewitt established the Design Triennial in 2000 to surface emerging trends and ideas formed in dialogue with current social and cultural conditions. These exhibitions provoke important conversations concerning design's objectives and introduce audiences to designers from around the world working at the vanguard of their fields. *Nature* is Cooper Hewitt's sixth Design Triennial and inaugurates the triennial Cube Signature Series. An ambitious initiative more than two years in the making, the collaboration brings together America's design museum with the first museum in the Netherlands that places special focus on the design process, and culminates in an impactful exhibition presented simultaneously on both sides of the Atlantic. We are enormously grateful to the designers, our international advisory committee, and our two museum teams who elevated this endeavor into a groundbreaking demonstration of international accord. This book ensures the dialogue continues well into the future and reaches even greater audiences. It is our hope that *Nature* in all its locations and interpretations will contribute to the diversity of knowledge and approaches needed for global climate action.

Tremendous thanks and congratulations to Cooper Hewitt curators Caitlin Condell, Andrea Lipps, Matilda McQuaid, and Caroline O'Connell and Cube curators Gène Bertrand, Hans Gubbels, and Madeleine van Daele. Together, they enthusiastically embraced the challenge of organizing and mounting simultaneous exhibitions. Sincere thanks as well to Neil Donnelly Studio, which designed a striking graphic interpretation of *Nature* to emphasize the interdisciplinary practices therein. At Cooper Hewitt, we are deeply grateful to our Board of Trustees, dedicated supporters of our Triennial series and everything we do to share design's importance with the world. *Nature—Cooper Hewitt Design Triennial* is made possible by support from The Ainslie Foundation. Funding is also provided by Amita and Purnendu Chatterjee, the August Heckscher Exhibition Fund, the Esme Usdan Exhibition Endowment Fund, and the New York State Council on the Arts with the support of Governor Andrew M. Cuomo and the New York State Legislature. At Cube, we acknowledge gratefully the support from the government of the Province of Limburg, Fonds 21, and Prins Bernhard Culture Fund. Both institutions are grateful to the Creative Industries Fund NL for its generous support.

Caroline Baumann, Director, Cooper Hewitt,
Smithsonian Design Museum

Hans Gubbels, Director, Cube design museum

Introduction   Matilda McQuaid

Designers today are transforming our relationship with the natural world. As humans contend with the ecological condition of our planet, designers are thinking holistically about the consequences of our actions on the environment and are challenging the most basic assumptions and beliefs about humanity's relationship with nature. The designers in this publication and the exhibition, *Nature—Cooper Hewitt Design Triennial*, understand that we must enlist nature as a guide and partner to alter the imbalance of human impact on our world. The approach is transdisciplinary and involves scientists, engineers, advocates for social and environmental justice, artists, and philosophers, who apply their conjoined knowledge toward a more harmonious and regenerative future.

Why nature? Nature's intricate and interconnected ecosystems shape and support life. When the curators at Cooper Hewitt decided to tackle the topic of nature as an exhibition and publication, it was with the spirit of celebration and urgency demanded by our time. Co-organizing the exhibition with Cube design museum underscored the need for a global perspective that reflected diverse ideas and points of focus. To expand the reach of projects proposed for the exhibition, the curators formed an Advisory Committee comprised of individuals from different parts of the world as well as different disciplines: Aric Chen (curator-at-large, M+, Hong Kong and professor of Practice, College of Design & Innovation, Tongji University, Shanghai), Michael John Gorman (founder of BIOTOPIA in

Munich), Suzanne Lee (chief creative officer at Modern Meadow), Ravi Naidoo (founder and managing director of Interactive Africa, in Cape Town, SA), Simone Rothman (founder and CEO of FutureAir), and Barbara Stauffer (chief of community programs at Smithsonian Institution, Museum of Natural History). In addition, Emeka Okafor (organizer of Maker Faire Africa) advised on designers in Africa.

The sixty-two projects included in the exhibition reflect a desire to capture the sense of optimism with which many designers are practicing today. Optimism is imperative to finding solutions that enable humans to coexist with nature and the biosphere. Victor Papanek, whose long advocacy as a designer and educator for social and ecological responsibility, presciently explained in *The Green Imperative*, "These dangerous times for Earth call not just for passion, imagination, intelligence and hard work, but—more profoundly—a sense of optimism that is willing to act without a full understanding, but with a faith in the effect of small individual actions on the global picture."[1] Just as grassroots efforts have played an important role in social change, citizen scientists' investigative work and documentation have resulted in notable discoveries. These citizens are part of the teams of designers and other collaborators included in this publication and Triennial, who are stalwarts in their belief that we need to reimagine our relationship with nature.

Why now? As a design triennial, *Nature* is a snapshot of what is happening today and not a comprehensive look at the role of nature in design. What is different now is how scientific information is more accessible through open-source initiatives and a greater embracing of design thinking applied to non-design areas. Advances in biology and technology enable designers to partner with nature in their work like never before. Designers also benefit from today's broader societal and global network, which suits the collaborative nature of the design profession. And, of course, the urgency of climate change is felt by everyone involved in this exhibition.

The 2010 exhibition *Why Design Now?—Cooper Hewitt Design Triennial* emphasized socially and environmentally responsible design that, in many respects, led up to this current Triennial. Nine years later there has been a greater shift in the relationship between designers and nature and between designers, scientists, and technological innovators. It is no longer "natural versus artificial" or "human versus nature," but humanity as an integral part of nature with each mutually affecting the other. We *are* nature. Michael John Gorman in his conversation with Koert van Mensvoort (see p. 49) notes that with 95 percent of mammals and birds on the planet being either humans or livestock, it is impossible to think of humans as something outside of nature. How will we work together to change our world for the betterment of all?

Why collaboration? Design has always been an integrated discipline because it affects human experience directly. Increasingly scientists are recognizing the aims of design, developing applications and systems that confront problems from different perspectives. All sixty-two projects have been realized through a collaborative process of multidisciplinary creativity—designers, engineers, biologists, material scientists, philosophers, and artists working together to find meaningful alternatives for humanity to live in harmony with the natural world.

The challenges to our planet today are so complex that they cannot be solved by one discipline. Design is the bridge. It translates scientific ideas and discoveries into real-world applications. Both design and science are encompassing disciplines and have expanded their breadth with time, yet share common ground on many levels. In 1864 George Marsh, a pioneer of the American conservation movement, wrote about this in *Man and Nature*. He discussed the vastness of the natural sciences and how everyone must now be a specialist, confining him/herself to a very narrow circle of research for the rest of his/her life. Although specialization of professions and knowledge has emerged, so too has a greater understanding of the intricate interrelationships between all forms of life. Marsh explains that "every human movement, every organic act, every volition, passion, or emotion, every intellectual process, is accompanied with atomic disturbance and every such movement, every such act or process affects all the atoms of universal matter."[2] This fundamental idea is the underpinning of understanding nature. It is exquisitely visualized by artist and scientist Charles Reilly's Choreography of Life, where atoms attract and repel each other and eventually form communities similar to those of humans. Reilly's interpretation also represents the immense power of observation, a shared component of design and science that can be pursued by citizen scientists and the general public alike. This experience reveals new worlds, enabling all of us to understand the natural realm. Its inclusivity reflects the action of designing *with*.

How are designers collaborating with nature? More meaningful than the outcome is the process in which designers and scientists pursue their goal. The seven themes of the show, also the essays in this book—Understand, Simulate, Salvage, Facilitate, Augment, Remediate, and Nurture—explore how designers are collaborating *with* nature. The work ranges from the speculative to the practical, from microscopic to macroscopic, and represents an extraordinarily rich variety of disciplines. Interspersed between the essays are focused conversations with scientists, philosophers, educators, and designers that delve deeper into the intersections of their disciplines and some of the challenges and discoveries of collaborating.

Understand: Intrinsic to mutually beneficial relationships with others is an openness to learning about and discovering commonalities and differences with an underlying goal of empathy. Openness can manifest as the exploration of how it feels to be someone or something else, as in Thomas Thwaites's journey to become a goat. Or it can be in devising a system to grapple with the emotional and physical toll that a child's illness has on a family, as in Giorgia Lupi and Kaki King's <u>Bruises—The Data We Don't See</u>. Visualization organizes data that are too complicated for comprehension in their original form, requiring designers to interpret and communicate information, from the smallest microbiomes in our environment to the architecture of our cosmos. In the form of a video game, visualization can launch us into the past and into the mind and writings of naturalist and philosopher Henry David Thoreau, experiencing virtually the plants and animals of Walden Pond, and understanding the necessity to regain a balance with nature.

Simulate: With a greater knowledge of the non-human aspects of nature and how they work comes the desire to emulate certain properties and efficiencies found in nature. When designers simulate nature they use it as a guide and model for systemic approaches—from devising efficient structural applications such as Michelin's Visionary Concept Tire, which draws inspiration from coral, to the structure of Airbus's Bionic Partition that is generated from algorithms based on slime mold growth. Underscoring all of the projects in this section is the role of nature as teacher—we can learn from slugs about creating adhesives that will work on wet surfaces and we can utilize the behavioral patterns of ants and marine life for human applications.

Salvage: One of the most remarkable aspects of nature is the lack of waste. Decomposition, scavenging, and biodegradation are some of nature's processes to maintain a closed-loop life cycle. Can we learn to manage our own waste similarly? Many designers are looking at the problem of plastics and other pollutants as a resource for their work. Graviky Labs transforms captured pollution from cars into permanent ink for printing. For Shahar Livne, plastic waste becomes a new material for creating, complete with its own set of tools for extraction and manipulation. Others try to avoid plastics and other polluting materials altogether, seeking alternative biomaterials like algae or seaweed, which become nutrients for the Earth at the end of their life cycle. Designers are, in fact, redefining raw materials with their new perspectives and applications of traditional waste materials. They recognize the intrinsic value of these materials and remove them from the waste stream, adding creative potential and diversity and transforming them into resources.

Facilitate: Designers are supporting, guiding, and assisting growth using a variety of processes that enable nature in some way. The natural growing cycle of bamboo is uninterrupted in <u>Bamboo Theater</u> as villagers in rural China bend and interlace bamboo stalks to create a living structure for performances and communal gatherings. Some of the most groundbreaking work has been in the area of biofabrication—a manufacturing process in which bacteria, yeast, cells, and fungi are harnessed as factories to grow products. Taking advantage of the metabolic activity of bacteria has led to new nonpolluting and energy-efficient ways of "dyeing" textiles as well as growing cement bricks. Regardless of how they are produced or how much time is required to bring them to fruition, they share a reliance on nature's own creation process.

Augment: How can we develop materials, objects, and the built environment to enhance not just human existence, but nature itself? The Mediated Matter group at Massachusetts Institute of Technology (MIT) Media Lab has discovered the material intelligence of natural materials such as chitin (found in shrimp shells) and reformulated it to create responsive forms that can enhance our environment. Reformulation happens in other materials, such as silk fiber and volcanic rock, as designers working with scientists transform these materials into the unexpected: silk screws, glowing silk threads, and ceramic glaze. With tools such as the Crispr-Cas9 system, a naturally occurring programmable gene editor, scientists and designers test their hand at altering genomes at the level of DNA, while others question these technological approaches to life. The work of Oron Catts and Ionat Zurr probes the fetishization of manipulating biological systems, calling it "DNA chauvinism."

Remediate: With an imbalanced ecosystem, designers with their collaborators are exploring ways to bring it into alignment again by reforming attitudes, rehabilitating our mental and physical well-being, and regenerating local traditions and habitats. It can begin with changing behavior from how we think about death and burial to overcoming our reliance on fossil-fuel materials such as plastic. Open-source methods help to communicate this information, which empowers the users and those advocating for change. This process is essential to social scientists and activists like Max Liboiron, whose research into the ubiquity and devastation of microplastics to marine life shows the equally destructive forces on indigenous populations whose communities rely on fish for sustenance. Liboiron argues that "objects are as implicated in social relations as human beings, and thus demand close attention. Objects have agency. They influence the things around them in relation to each other."[3]

Nurture: Taking greater care of the living is a criterion that designers are integrating into their work, challenging us in large and small ways, to reevaluate the way we live. The act of feeding bacteria and plants in order to have light encourages a closer relationship between the living lights and their owners. Allowing and encouraging growth, such as moss and lichen, on building façades or integrating an abundance of trees and plants into a dense, urban space enhances the health of the community and, as architect Vo Trong Nghia explains, "helps people develop a sense of treasuring nature." Without this feeling of responsibility and ownership toward living matter, we are faced with extinction. Designer Alexandra Daisy Ginsberg reminds us of this reality with her project The Substitute, which resurrects the northern white rhino through artificial intelligence. Why are we trying to create new life forms when we consistently disregard existing species?

Nature: Collaborations in Design presents new materials, technologies, objects, buildings, and much more that are evocative of designers' multidisciplinary approach to generate work in harmony with nature. At the same time, this book and exhibition includes work that probes and pokes at a techno-utopianism to remind us that in the end, design is not a panacea. But *with* design, we have the ability to become active agents in our relationship with nature. *With* design, we elevate and materialize our priorities and ultimately choose the future we want for ourselves and this planet. The questions, speculations, provocations, and solutions put forth by the extraordinary design teams herein serve as encouragement for an enduring partnership with nature.

1

Victor J. Papanek, *The Green Imperative: Natural Design for the Real World* (New York: Thames and Hudson, 1995), 25.

2

George Marsh, *Man and Nature* (New York: Charles Scribner, 1865), 548.

3

Max Liboiron, "Redefining pollution and action: The matter of plastics," *Journal of Material Culture* 21, no. 1 (2016), 90.

Simulate
Salvage
Facilitate
Augmer
medi
Nurture
Understand
Simulate
Salvage
Facilitate
Augmer
Remediate
Nurture
Understand

Each day, as we rouse ourselves from sleep, we face the edge of our present understanding of the phenomena of the physical world. Over the course of the day, we run experiments, record data, perform calculations, take photographs and videos, and exchange communications. By day's end, our fundamental knowledge of the natural world and our role within it has changed: our understanding of nature has evolved.

This rapid pace of discovery and learning often evades easy grasp. Our longing to comprehend the nuances of nature is rooted in empathy. Humans seek connections with our natural world that shift our perspective. Design creates opportunities for reflection by offering methods of seeing nature anew. Through visualization, data become discernable.

In the spring of 2016, a team of scientists at the University of California, Berkeley radically expanded the tree of life, a diagram that shows the relationships between all known organisms, both living and extinct. The augmented rendering of the tree of life included more than one thousand new microbial species found in some of the most inhospitable environments around the world, from a salt flat in Chile's Atacama desert to the inside of a dolphin's mouth. The branches revealed that the vast majority of the Earth's biodiversity can be found in an enigmatic group of microorganisms invisible to the naked eye, upending our understanding of biology and the unseen life within and around us.[1] "This wasn't like discovering a new species of mammal," says microbiologist Laura Hug, one of the authors of the new tree of life. "It was like discovering that mammals existed at all, and that they're all around us and we didn't know it."[2]

The new tree of life incorporated more than fifteen years of research by Australian microbiologist Jill Banfield and the scientists of the Banfield Lab at UC Berkeley. Since 2001, the Banfield Lab has explored the microbiome, a vast landscape of microorganisms and their combined genetic material. To do this, they employ metagenomics, a powerful method of study that identifies every organism present in an environment at the time that a sample is taken. As Banfield and fellow researcher Brian Thomas describe it, this approach arms scientists "with an understanding of who the organism is, and what that organism is capable of. From this, you can make predictions about how to get it to grow in the lab, or what it's doing in the environment or how it's interacting with its neighbors."[3]

Microbial communities are found in terrestrial ecosystems, in the built environment, and within larger organisms. As the Banfield Lab continued to collect samples from this vast reserve and sequence the genomes of microbes, they amassed an overwhelming amount of data. The scientists struggled to make hypotheses because they lacked a tool to visualize the data from the microscopic samples.

The Banfield Lab turned to Stamen Design, a firm founded by Eric Rodenbeck that specializes in interactive design and data visualization, to develop software that would allow the lab to vary the way they could see DNA sequences of the organisms. The resulting collaboration, Metagenomic Data Visualization (2016), generates genome summaries from the data gathered in any given microbial sample. Stamen created three different types of visualizations from the same data, which allowed the researchers to "query the data in new ways."[4] A color-coded bar chart enables scientists to understand which genes are most expressive. A treemap allows scientists to identify the degree of confidence that a genetic sample matches one already identified. And a radial dendrogram uses text-based classification information to visualize the location of genomes within the tree of life. Advances in understanding the newly discovered microorganisms will likely have applications in agriculture, medicine, and biotechnology. These potentially significant outcomes highlight one other quality of the Metagenomic Data Visualization software—it processes information quickly, speeding up the pace of scientific discovery.

While Stamen was creating a tool for scientists exploring microscopic domains, German designer Kim Albrecht was busy translating an entire universe into a digital realm. Albrecht was a designer-in-residence at the Barabási Lab, whose work focuses on exploring how networks emerge, evolve, and impact "our understanding of complex systems." Among the complex systems being explored was the cosmic web—the system by which all the galaxies in the universe are held together by gravity.

To develop hypotheses about the structure of the cosmic web, physicist Bruno C. Coutinho and a team of researchers gathered data from twenty-four thousand galaxies and applied different algorithms to the data set. Albrecht built a web-based simulation, Visualizing the Cosmic Web (2016), that explored three possible models based on certain parameters: fixed length (based on distance), varying length (based on size), and nearest neighbors. The research team then studied both the observable data and the simulation. Their conclusion was that the nearest neighbors model, "which relies on spatial proximity only, captures the best correlations between the physical characteristics in nearby galaxies."[5]

Albrecht and the Barabási Lab decided to make their research tool accessible publicly so that internet users could toggle between the three models and explore for themselves. The simulation was published concurrently with a scholarly article. Overnight, the program became an internet sensation. Visualizing the Cosmic Web is a sophisticated scientific tool, and it is also extraordinarily beautiful, making it appealing to a wide audience, regardless of scientific background. Users all over the world can tour the universe and comprehend the underlying architecture of the cosmos.

As evidenced by the embrace of data visualization in both the Banfield and Barabási Labs, scientists are increasingly recognizing the value of information design as a tool for scientific discovery as well as for communication with the public. But few scientists have the training to design tools themselves. Australian scientist Charles Reilly defies easy classification, having navigated between the disciplines of biochemistry, art, commercial filmmaking, and computer animation for most of his career. Since joining the Wyss Institute for Biologically Inspired Engineering at Harvard University in 2014, Reilly has been able to use the "pursuit of an artistic agenda," as he calls it, to "lead to scientific insights."[6] This notion that creating scientific simulation might lead to scientific discovery is a radical rethinking of the experimentation process.

Reilly's recent work has led him to explore adenosine triphosphate (ATP) synthase, an enzyme that produces ATP. Reilly describes ATP as "essentially the energy currency of life."[7] He argues that in considering these biomolecules in isolation, subtle but significant dynamics between molecules are being overlooked. "We should consider every individual molecule as a dynamic system of systems, with each system contributing to the local environment in which another system is found. In other words," Reilly says with characteristic humor and clarity, "while we can think of the molecular world as a jiggling set of sticky balls that constantly bump into one another, it is my opinion that we should be giving more weight to the way these balls move with respect to one another."[8]

Reilly explores his hypothesis through the computer-generated animation Choreography of Life (2019). The film depicts a molecular scene of approximately five hundred thousand atoms, moving at a rate of femtoseconds (one millionth of one billionth of a second). Each atom has its own narrative, attracting and repelling its neighbors, developing relationships and, eventually, communities. As Choreography of Life proceeds, time accelerates and larger-scale structures of molecules appear, revealing the full mechanical motion of the ATP synthase enzyme.

If this simulation of molecular systems supports Reilly's hypothesis, the strategies revealed will influence his drug discovery and biophysics research. But Reilly believes that Choreography of Life may bear lessons that extend beyond the scientific. "Every component of life, no matter how small," Reilly notes, "contributes to the world at large. Life at the most fundamental of

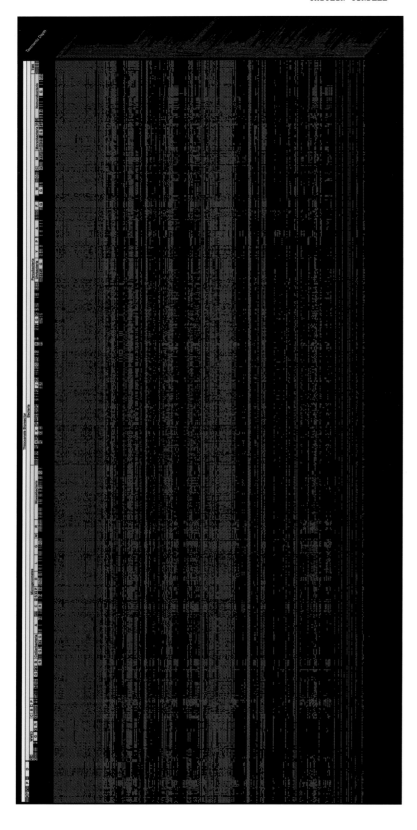

Metagenomic Data Visualization, 2016;
Eric Rodenbeck (American, b. 1970),
Kai Chang (American, b. 1987), Alec
Burch (American, b. 1990), Zan Armstrong
(American, b. 1982), and Greg Corradini
(American, b. 1978), Stamen Design (San
Francisco, California, USA, founded
2001) for Jill Banfield (Australian, b.
1959) and Brian Thomas (American, b.
1970), Banfield Laboratory, University
of California, Berkeley (Berkeley,
California, USA, founded 1990); d3,
Javascript, html, Canvas, Photoshop

↑
Bar chart enables scientists to understand which genes are most expressive.

↑ (Opposite)
Treemap allows scientists to identify the
degree of confidence that a genetic sample
matches one already identified.

↓ (Opposite)
Radial dendrogram uses text-based
classification information to visualize the location of genomes within the
tree of life.

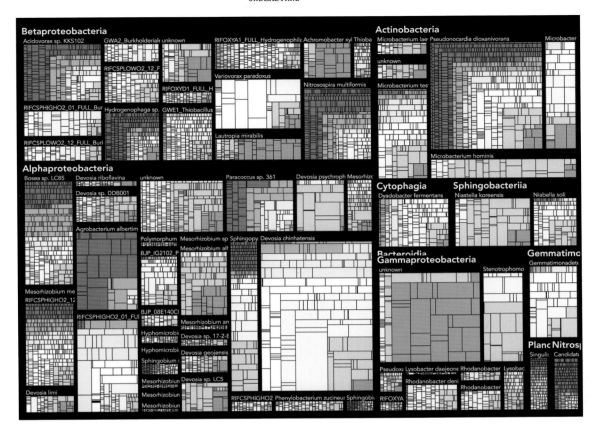

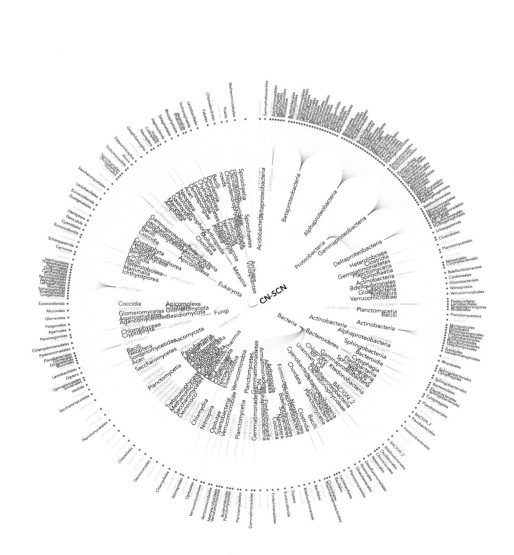

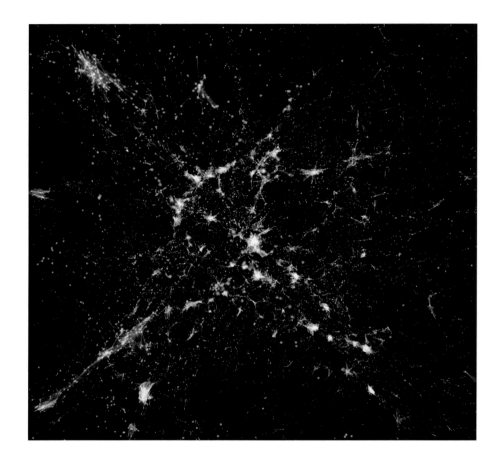

Visualizing the Cosmic Web, 2016; Kim
Albrecht (German, b. 1987), Barabási
Lab, Northeastern University (Boston,
Massachusetts, USA, founded 1995), based
on research from Bruno C. Coutinho and
Albert-László Barabási

↑
Fixed Length Model: All galaxies within
a set distance of l are connected by an
undirected link.

↑ (Opposite)
Nearest Neighbors Model: Each galaxy is
connected to its closest neighbors with
a directed link. In this model the length
of each link depends on the distance to
the nearest galaxy.

↓ (Opposite)
Varying Length Model: The length of each
link is proportional to the size of the
galaxy, l = a Ri1/2.

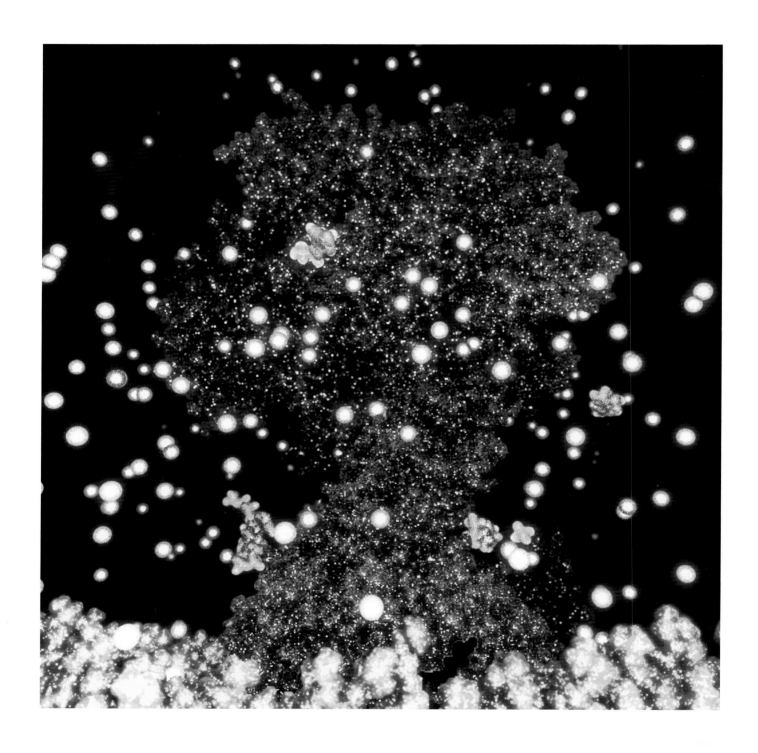

Choreography of Life, 2019; Charles
Reilly (New Zealander, b. 1983), Wyss
Institute for Biologically Inspired
Engineering, Harvard University (Boston,
Massachusetts, USA, founded 2009); Video,
4:00 minutes

←
Provisional render of the enzyme
adenosine triphosphate (ATP) synthase.
This large molecular machine harvests
metabolic energy and stores this energy
in the chemical bonds of ATP, a much
smaller molecule. ATP is found throughout all forms of life and is used to move
energy within cells. This process is an
essential component of life.

↑
Detail of a provisional render of
adenosine triphosphate (ATP) molecules
interacting with ATP synthase.

scales succeeds with constant interaction, relationships, and community; life is the opposite of isolation."[9]

The opportunity to use data to evoke empathy is at the core of Italian designer Giorgia Lupi's practice. "Data is almost never a perfect description of reality," notes Lupi.[10] Although data are often "treated like the keeper of infallible truths for our present and our future," Lupi believes that it is important to remember that data are human-made. Visualization of data enables us to "connect with ourselves and others at a deeper level."

Empathy was the impetus for one of Lupi's most personal projects, cocreated with American musician Kaki King. Lupi and King were friends and professional collaborators when, in the summer of 2017, King's three-year-old daughter Cooper began developing spontaneous bruises all over her body. Although Cooper did not feel sick, her body was covered in dark bruises and petechiae, small red dots that rise to the skin as a result of burst blood vessels. Cooper was soon diagnosed with the autoimmune disease Idiopathic Thrombocytopenic Purpura (ITP). ITP causes the body to attack its own platelets, which in turn limits the body's ability to clot blood. Over a period of weeks, Cooper was put on steroids and underwent a series of platelet transfusions and blood tests. King would later describe the period as one of "abject terror."[11]

While doctors were tracking Cooper's health, King was encouraged by Cooper's doctors to watch her daughter's skin for changes. King began recording notes on a daily basis, including changes visible on Cooper's skin, her platelet count, and her medication intake. At Lupi's urging, King also began recording notes on her own emotions, documenting her hopes, fears, and stresses. These daily observations, as Lupi would later recall, juxtaposed clinical data with "softer data" from King's life "to channel stress and anxiety into a semblance of control through meditative action."[12]

After four months, Cooper's health stabilized and King no longer needed to record the clinical data requested by the doctors, who now believe that Cooper may outgrow ITP. With the immediate terror behind them, King was still processing the experience. She and Lupi hoped that visualizing all of the data King had recorded might "activate us at an emotional level," and thus they developed Bruises—The Data We Don't See (2018). Lupi created a fluid timeline that charted one hundred and twenty days as pale petals, divided into groups of days between Cooper's various hospital admissions. Platelet counts are represented by red dots, and purple and green splotches vary in intensity in proportion to Cooper's bruises. Positive experiences for King are indicated by bright yellow spots, and her hope and fear levels are visualized through floating lines that frame the day. When Lupi had completed the hand-drawn visualizations, King composed a "musical map" of the data: one hundred and twenty measures in three-quarter time. The melody, a guitar line, tells the story of the bruises, while the bass drums signal the actual readings of Cooper's platelet levels.[13]

For a haunting three minutes and twenty-five seconds, the resulting video carries the viewer through the four-month journey of Cooper's illness. Each day emerges in the form of a delicate petal, and moments of fear and pain well up in the music, then subside. King described the process of composing as "playing my daughter's skin." The project has resonated deeply with viewers. Visualization offers a method for understanding health more holistically, correlating both the clinical and the emotional. King and Lupi have begun pilot projects with healthcare providers to explore broader applications. Bruises—The Data We Don't See suggests "a future where, instead of using data only to become more efficient, we will all use data to become more human."[14]

The full complexity of nature is rarely visible to the naked eye, and the advancing field of nanotechnology has driven interest in seeing nature as a model. Designers and engineers frequently turn to nature's existing solutions for guidance in how to approach their own innovations. American scientist James C. Weaver has pioneered new forms of imaging at the nanoscale with his Electron Micrographs (2019) at the Wyss Institute for Biologically Inspired Engineering at Harvard University. Scanning electron microscopy (SEM) reveals insights about the texture, structure, and chemical composition of a selected sample. A scanning electron microscope scans the surface of a sample using a focused beam of high-energy electrons. The electrons interact with the atoms in the sample, producing a variety of signals containing information about its topography and composition. SEM images have been used for decades to reveal physical properties of biological specimens. More recently, SEM has become a valuable tool in materials science and engineering, microchip assembly, and forensic investigation. Weaver has sought to push the spatial resolution limit of SEM, resulting in new imaging techniques.

Weaver's Electron Micrographs have captured the extraordinary complexity of individual organisms using three imaging techniques: stereo, polychromatic, and wide-field. The Electron Micrographs are astonishingly beautiful, but their primary purpose is to provide a better understanding of specific systems and structures for designers and engineers. In collaboration with American-Israeli designer Neri Oxman, who runs the Mediated Matter group at MIT Media Lab, Weaver imaged the skeletal structures of reef-building corals in the Indo-Pacific.[15] Weaver and Oxman have used the images to identify patterns formed by different species of corals and experimented with their potential application in architectural and design structures. Weaver has also collaborated with biologist George Lauder and bioengineer Li Wen to image the skin of different shark species. The detailed images have helped facilitate a better understanding of how denticles on sharks' skin reduce drag as water flows across their bodies. After careful study of the electron micrographs, the research team was able to produce a 3D-printed flexible biomimetic sharkskin sample and further explore the hydrodynamic properties of different shark species.[16] The design applications of such research are vast. From the hull of a ship to a swimsuit, improved hydrodynamic surfaces have the potential to save energy and increase speed. Seeing nature through the electron micrographs provides a greater understanding of microscopic biological production strategies, offering design strategies for the future.[17]

The desire to see that which we cannot see with our naked eye is also at the heart of Dutch designer Aliki van der Kruijs's textile project Made by Rain (2012–ongoing). Van der Kruijs believes that rainfall changes our experience of space.[18] We hear the rain, feel the rain, and see the rain. The falling rain beats a wet pattern onto surfaces, a pattern observed occasionally but obscured quickly as the water accumulates and then dissipates—seeping into the ground, running into streams and lakes, and evaporating into clouds.

When van der Kruijs was young, her grandfather recorded the weather from his home in Gemert, the Netherlands. He transcribed his observations perfunctorily in a preprinted calendar. After his death, van der Kruijs was given her grandfather's calendars. Weather patterns had changed over the course of van der Kruijs's lifetime, a fact she confirmed by examining the calendars. Van der Kruijs had the impulse to archive the weather in a more visual way.

Van der Kruijs developed a technique of drawing with rain she calls "pluviagraphy." The technique operates in two forms. In one, a layer of inked film is placed underneath a textile, and the two items are left in the rain. As raindrops fall, the ink seeps through to the surface of the textile, recording the form and pattern of raindrops. In the other, the textile is printed with a solid layer of ink, which bleeds upon contact with the raindrops.

To create Made by Rain, van der Kruijs traveled across the Netherlands mapping the rain. She silkscreened information about each recorded rainfall on the textiles, including the location, date, time interval, millimeters of rain, and weather conditions. Each textile became a "unique five minutes of drizzle."[19] Raindrops become their own archivists, making their mark on the textile and charting a map of the moment when they hit the earth. Made by Rain allows us to see in perpetuity that which we cannot otherwise see—the precise pattern of a rainfall.

Halfway around the globe, in rural Montana, the Spanish architecture firm Ensamble Studio has sought to see nature anew through architectural intervention. Located north of Yellowstone National Park, Tippet Rise Art Center occupies more than eleven thousand acres of a sheep ranch and serves as a place where art, music, poetry, and landscape come together. The rolling hills seem to stretch on endlessly toward the snowcapped Beartooth Mountains in the distance. When principals Débora Mesa and Antón García-Abril first

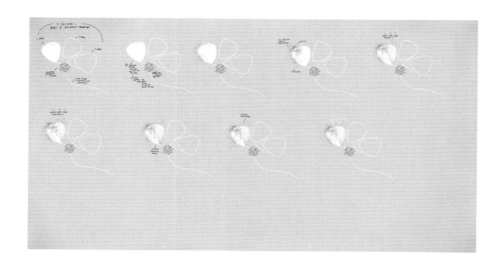

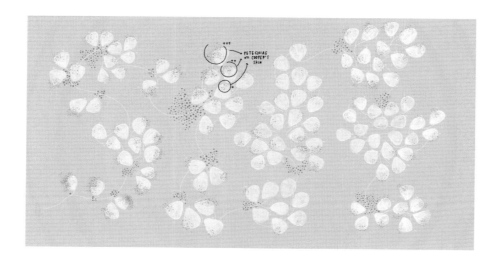

Bruises—The Data We Don't See, 2018;
Giorgia Lupi (Italian, b. 1981), Accurat
(New York, New York, USA and Milan,
Italy, founded 2011) and Kaki King
(American, b. 1979); Visualization:
Procreate, Photoshop; Musical score:
Fender guitar, Logic

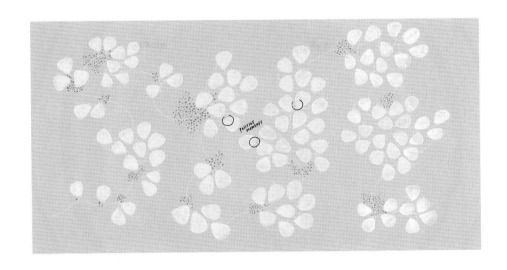

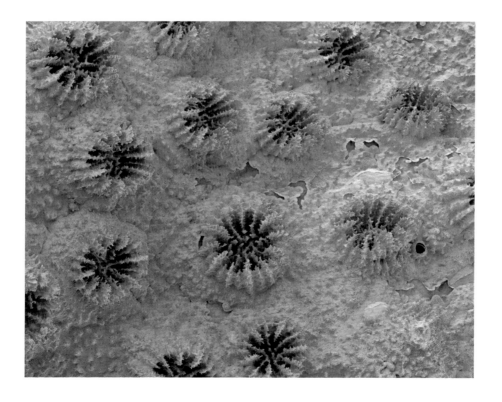

Electron Micrographs, 2019; James
C. Weaver (American, b. 1974), Wyss
Institute for Biologically Inspired
Engineering, Harvard University (Boston,
Massachusetts, USA, founded 2009);
Polychromatic scanning electron micro-
graphs of the skeletal details of corals

↑
Platygyra sp.
Field of view: 14 mm

↓
Cyphastrea sp.
Field of view: 11 mm

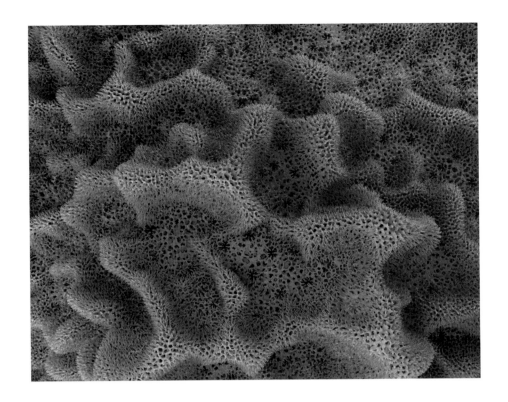

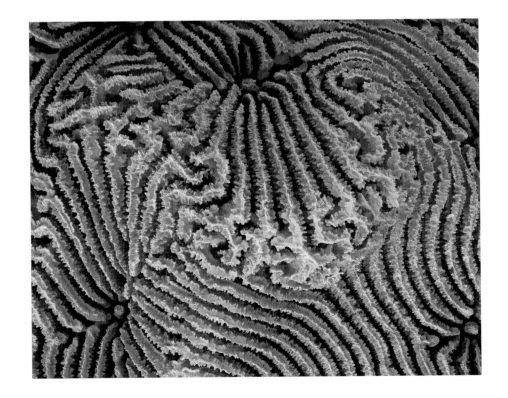

↑
Montipora sp.
Field of view: 16.5 mm

↓
Coscinaraea sp.
Field of view: 2.1 mm

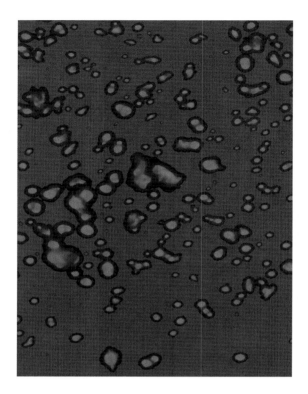

Made by Rain, 2012-ongoing; Aliki van der
Kruijs (Dutch, b. 1984); Digitally
printed silk, wetted by rain

↑
Model with Made By Rain scarf,
Amsterdam, 2013.

↓
Aliki van der Kruijs creating a Made by
Rain textile, Amsterdam, 2012.

visited the site with the center's founders Cathy and Peter Halstead, they were drawn to the remoteness of the landscape. They sought to create minimal but monumental interventions in the landscape that could serve as both markers for navigating the site and shelters for musical performances. Above all, the constructions would offer ways of grappling with the vast raw landscape.

The rawness of nature is both a source and a motif for designers at Ensamble Studio. They are preoccupied by the "slippery, blurry, ambiguous condition between architecture and landscape."[20] At Tippet Rise, Mesa and García-Abril found very few references that punctuated the vast space, and they began to think about "episodes" they could create in the topography. Structures of Landscape (2016–ongoing) includes the three built structures *Domo*, *Beartooth Portal*, and *Inverted Portal*, each taking the shape of interventions directly into the landscape on which they rest. Concrete was poured into a hole dug at each site, then excavated. The dirt was returned to the earthen molds, and the concrete forms were placed atop their sites. Their massive scale (*Domo* is 98 feet long and weighs 2.5 million pounds) is still, at times, dwarfed by the Montana landscape.

Ensamble Studio designers work with the "actions of nature," and they embrace the changes that exposure to harsh conditions will take on the structures. The weathered surfaces and the earthen forms suggest structures that have already stood the test of time. The effect is one of natural wonder— Structures of Landscape looks as if it has been there forever, formed by nature itself.[21]

What if architecture was "not obsessed with the act of building itself, but with what buildings allow us to enact in nature?"[22] What if the study of naturally occurring architecture can inform our understanding about our own built environment? Those are the questions that prompted Stella Mutegi and Kabage Karanja to found Cave in their native Nairobi, Kenya. The result of millions of years of geologic processes, caves are "ingrained in our prehistoric consciousness."[23] In thinking about the future of Nairobi, Mutegi and Karanja believe that a geological perspective on architecture, rooted in survey and study of the cave structures embedded within the city, will enable a more responsive mode of urban building.

Anthropocene Museum (2017–19)[24] is a design sited in the Mbai Cave network in Nairobi. Submitted as an unsolicited proposal to the National Museums of Kenya, the Anthropocene Museum is intended to foster "a broader consciousness to produce self-preserving, responsive ideas about the built environment." Cave surveyed the first "trunk" of the Mbai Cave network using 3D scanning technology, mapping the 2.5 million-year-old space for the first time. Through the course of the "waterfall walk," "nave," and "tube," visitors to the Anthropocene Museum would experience the structure of the naturally formed architecture as a space to reflect on the Anthropocene—the geological age that most scientists believe we are currently inhabiting, in which humans exert a dominant influence on the environment.

Cave's Anthropocene Museum would host theater performances, film screenings, and poetry sessions, in effect returning the Mbai Cave (also known locally as Paradise Lost) to a space of meditation. But the primary provocation of the proposal is the simple premise that careful study of an ancient naturally formed space is the ideal method for gaining perspective on our current geological age. "After all," Mutegi and Karanja say, "the Earth is resilient and independent enough to sustain itself with or without our presence."[25]

The independence of the geological landscape from human impact stands in contrast to the interdependence of living organisms. With their installation Curiosity Cloud (2015–19), Austrian design team mischer'traxler, Katharina Mischer and Thomas Traxler, sought a way to interpret the "dialogue between humans and nature" within the confines of a museum experience. They created an installation of several hundred glass bulbs, each filled with a single hand-fabricated insect that replicates an insect found in nature. Each bulb contains a thermal sensor connected to a motor. As a visitor moves closer to the bulbs, a soft, glowing light is emitted in the bulb and the insects become activated, fluttering around and softly clinking against the glass in which they are encapsulated. As the visitor moves away, the insects cease to move, and the installation falls silent.

mischer'traxler considered the purpose of a museum, to conserve, as they developed Curiosity Cloud. Housed within the glass, the insects are safe from the potential of destructive human touch, but they can only be animated by close proximity with visitors. Each insect species is carefully researched—some are commonly found in nature, others are newly discovered, and still others are species that have become endangered or have gone extinct. Curiosity Cloud unites species of insects that, as a group, would never coexist in a moment in time in the natural world. Through their harmonious simulation, mischer'traxler offer a celebration of biodiversity while offering a moment of meditation on our own role. "Species may disappear, yet new ones appear . . . We should not take nature for granted," write the designers, but also respect that "insects reoccur and develop further. Every aspect of a living creature has a *raison d'être*, working together in an endless cycle of dialogue and correlation."[26] Nature is nuanced and fragile, and we are just a part of it.

There are times when the crushing responsibilities and expectations of being mortal are just too overwhelming, and we seek solace in the notion that other creatures live simpler, worry-free lives. It was out of such malaise with being human that British designer Thomas Thwaites asked the question, "Wouldn't it be nice to be an animal just for a bit?"

Thwaites described his initial motivation as born out of a desire to escape "the angst in being human,"[27] and to experience the process of transforming himself into another creature. Thwaites's tongue-in-cheek query led to the undertaking of GoatMan (2014–16). GoatMan is part of a long history of striving toward understanding the nonhuman experience through scientific inquiry, observation, and imagination. We cannot fully know what it is like to be another organism, but through design and discovery, we can get a little closer to understanding how every living thing has a different relationship to nature.

After some consideration, Thwaites settled on becoming a goat, an animal "whose mental life would be simpler and more untroubled than his own."[28] First, there was the anatomy. To live as a goat, he had to construct an exoskeleton that would adapt his biped body into that of a quadruped. Then he had to create an artificial prosthetic rumen enabling him to live on a goat's grassy diet. Finally, he needed a way to retrain his senses of sight and hearing, morphing his experience of the world into that of a goat.

Thwaites's endeavor to "escape the constraints and expectations"[29] of his own biology led him to experts in many fields, including prosthetists, animal behaviorists, goatherders, neuroscientists, a shaman, as well as the writing of philosopher Martin Heidegger. Then, with his goat prosthesis, a helmet, and an artificial rumen, he set out to live as GoatMan for three days in the Swiss Alps.

The attempt to integrate himself into a goat herd had some success. He made a friend, and lived among the goats with little conflict. The life of a goat, he concluded, "consists of walking to a patch of grass and eating it for five minutes or so. Walking to another patch of grass, eating that. And so on and so forth."[30] But as Thwaites grazed, he began to observe distinctions in the natural world that he had not perceived before. There were subtle variations in the color of the grasses on which he grazed, and those color shifts corresponded to taste variations.

GoatMan proved to be about more than retrofitting a human being into a "goat" in order to temporarily escape the responsibilities that come with humanity. GoatMan reminds us of the limits of our own perspective on nature. "It's important to remember every now and again that we are animals," said Thwaites. "Being an animal would help us remember that there is no manifest destiny to the human species—we are just among all these other creatures."[31]

In the mid-nineteenth century, the transcendentalist writer Henry David Thoreau sought to immerse himself in nature and moved into a cabin beside Walden Pond, a small lake located in Concord, Massachusetts. "I went to the woods because I wished to live deliberately," Thoreau later wrote in *Walden*, the account of his time spent living at the pond. After Thoreau's death, *Walden* grew in popularity, and for decades it has been required reading for American teenagers.

Tracy Fullerton was raised not far from Concord, and she first read *Walden* when she was an adolescent. Over time it became one of her

Structures of Landscape, 2016-ongoing;
Antón García-Abril (Spanish, b. 1969) and
Débora Mesa (Spanish, b. 1981), Ensamble
Studio (Madrid, Spain and Brookline,
Massachusetts, USA, founded 2000); Earth,
reinforced concrete

↑
Domo, 2016; Fishtail, Montana, USA, completed 2016

↑
Beartooth Portal, 2016; Fishtail,
Montana, USA, completed 2016

↓
Inverted Portal, 2016; Fishtail, Montana,
USA, completed 2016

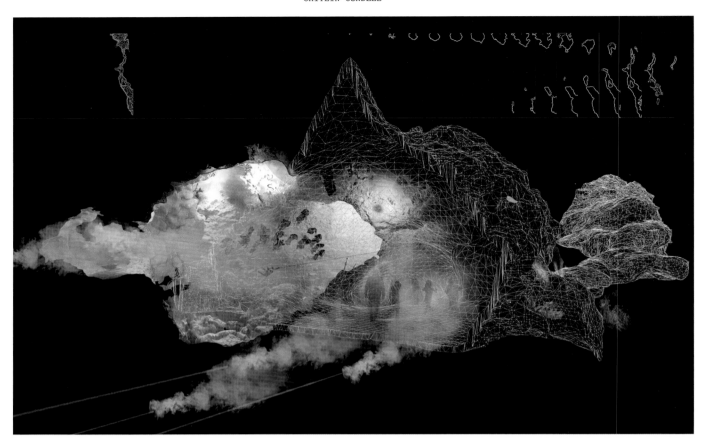

Anthropocene Museum, 2017-19; Mbai Cave,
Nairobi, Kenya, concept; Stella Mutegi
(Kenyan, b. 1979) and Kabage Karanja
(Kenyan, b. 1979), Cave (Nairobi, Kenya,
founded 2014)

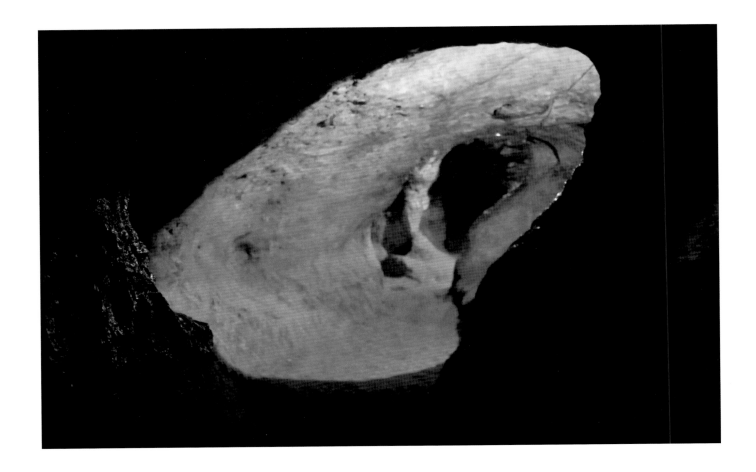

Curiosity Cloud, 2015-19; Katharina
Mischer (Austrian, b. 1982) and
Thomas Traxler (Austrian, b. 1981),
mischer'traxler Studio (Vienna, Austria,
founded 2009); Mouth-blown glass bulbs,
artificial handmade insects, aluminum hoods, custom-made circuit boards,
motors, LED lights, cables, ceiling
plate, sensors; Dimensions variable

GoatMan, 2014–16; Thomas Thwaites
(British, b. 1980); Wood, metal, plastic,
fiberglass, goat bones, fabric, leather;
Dimensions variable

↓
Thwaites developed different quadruped
exoskeleton designs before finalizing the
design for his GoatMan prosthetics.

favorite books. After years of working as a successful video game designer, Fullerton began to feel that she had gotten out of balance with nature. She reread *Walden* while on an extended camping trip and found that Thoreau's text helped reestablish her connection with the natural world. She began to envision a single-player video game in which the player could experience the life Thoreau described. The mechanics of playing would call into question whether or not the player was in balance with nature. Fullerton spent ten years researching and designing Walden, A Game (2017), "deconstructing the text" and "reconstructing the pond." The virtual world is populated with the plants and animals mentioned in Thoreau's text, and the sounds featured in the game were recorded at the present-day Walden Pond by sound designer Michael Sweet.

Walden, A Game begins in the summer, when berries are ripe on the bushes and twilight arrives late in the evening. Players can turn their gaze to flora and fauna for "inspiration," which is as essential for survival at Walden Pond as food or shelter. As the game proceeds, the seasons change, and with them come new challenges. At its core, Walden, A Game is a "deep survival simulator."[32] If a player has overexerted herself with work or not sought enough mindful connection with nature, the vibrant colors of the natural world begin to fade, and the player runs the risk of fainting. "Inspiration" can be found everywhere—one need only tread lightly when approaching a tentative rabbit and it will turn toward you to make sustained eye contact, filling you with enough "inspiration" to live a full day at Walden Pond. The need to be sustained as a player, with food, fuel, and shelter, is the hook that captures the player's attention. But as the game unfolds, it becomes clear that "the goal is to maintain balance, and to ensure that nature continues to inspire you."[33]

For some, building a virtual natural world to help others achieve balance with nature has seemed antithetical to the spirit of Thoreau's thinking. Fullerton and her codesigners do not believe that Walden, A Game should replace the physical experience of the natural world. But Fullerton does believe that the video game "encourage[s] us to slow down and reflect . . . the games we play are rehearsals for who we become."[34] Walden, A Game has become popular among educators and students seeking to gain insight into Thoreau's text, and also among those who are incarcerated and face limited opportunities to commune with nature. Fullerton has been surprised by the international popularity of the game, given its uniquely American roots. The longing for a connection to nature, Fullerton has discovered, transcends cultural barriers.[35]

1

Robert Sanders, "Wealth of Unsuspected New Microbes Expands Tree of Life," *Berkeley News*, April 11, 2016, https://news.berkeley.edu/2016/04/11/wealth-of-unsuspected-new-microbes-expands-tree-of-life/; Laura A. Hug et al., "A New View of the Tree of Life," *Nature Microbiology* 1 (2016): 1–6. http://nature.com/articles/doi:10.1038/nmicrobiol.2016.48.

2

Carrie Arnold, "The Never-Ending Quest to Rewrite the Tree of Life," *NOVA Next*, January 4, 2017, https://www.pbs.org/wgbh/nova/article/microbial-diversity/.

3

Eric Rodenbeck, "New Images of Complex Microbiome Environments Visualized by Berkeley Metagenomics Lab and Stamen Design." *Hi.Stamen.* September 26, 2016. https://hi.stamen.com/uc-berkeley-metagenomics-lab-releases-new-images-of-complex-microbiome-environment-discovered-a80000770c93.

4

Eric Rodenbeck, "The Banfield Lab," September 26, 2016, https://stamen.com/work/banfield/.

5

B. C. Coutinho et al., "The Network Behind the Cosmic Web," *arXiv* (2016): 4, arXiv:1604.03236.

6

Charles Reilly and Donald E. Ingber, "Art Advancing Science: Filmmaking Leads to Molecular Insights at the Nanoscale," *ACS Nano* 11, no. 12 (2017): 12156–66. doi:10.1021/acsnano.7b05266.

7

Charles B. Reilly, email correspondence with Caitlin Condell, February, 2018.

8

Charles B. Reilly, "The Choreography of Life," *The Biochemist* 40, no. 2 (2018): 10–13.

9

Reilly, email correspondence, February, 2018.

10

Giorgia Lupi, "Data is Beautiful," *Computer Arts* 265 (2017): 2.

11

Giorgia Lupi, "Bruises—The Data We Don't See," *Medium*, January 31, 2018, https://medium.com/@giorgialupi/bruises-the-data-we-dont-see-1fd-ec00d0036.

12

Ibid.

13

Ibid.

14

Ibid.

15

"Imaginary Beings: James Weaver's Electron Micrographs on Display in Paris," *Wyss Institute News*, June 1, 2012, https://wyss.harvard.edu/imaginary-beings-james-weavers-electron-micrographs-on-display-in-paris/.

16

Li Wen, James C. Weaver, and George V. Lauder. "Biomimetic Shark Skin: Design, Fabrication and Hydrodynamic Function," *The Journal of Experimental Biology* 217, no. 10 (2014): 1656–66. https://www.researchgate.net/publication/262341886_Biomimetic_Shark_Skin_Design_Fabrication_and_Hydrodynamic_Function; Yueping Wang et al., "A Biorobotic Adhesive Disc for Underwater Hitchhiking Inspired by the Remora Suckerfish," *Science Robotics* 2 (2017): 1–9. https://scholar.harvard.edu/files/yufengchen/files/science_robotics_suction_disk.pdf.

17

"James Weaver, Ph.D.," Coastal Marine Biolabs, Integrative Biosciences Program, http://coastalmarinebiolabs.org/bios/james.html.

18

Aliki van der Kruijs, "Made By Rain," video, December 31, 2016, https://vimeo.com/197594165.

19

Ibid.

20

Anton García-Abril, "Anton García-Abril Presentation," video, November 30, 2012, https://www.youtube.com/watch?v=7HY_T4DZFlk.

21

Kristin Hohenadel, "These Immense Concrete Sculptures Near Yellowstone Look Like They've Always Been There," *Slate*, July 8, 2016, https://slate.com/human-interest/2016/07/ensamble-studios-structures-of-landscape-are-giant-sculptures-at-tippet-rise-art-center-in-fishtail-montana.html.

22

Stella Mutegi and Kabage Karanja, "Cave Anthropocene," proposal submitted to Cooper Hewitt, Smithsonian Design Museum.

23

Balmoi Abe, Stella Mutegi, and Kabage Karanja, "Cave Manifesto," video, https://www.cave.co.ke/manifesto/.

24

Mutegi and Karanja, proposal, 2.

25

Ibid.

26

mischer'traxler, Curiosity Cloud Book (PDF) (Vienna: mischer'traxler Studio, September 2015), 6.

27

Thomas Thwaites, *GoatMan: How I Took a Holiday from Being Human* (New York: Princeton Architectural Press, 2016).

28

Joshua Rothman, "The Metamorphosis," *The New Yorker*, May 30, 2016, https://www.newyorker.com/magazine/2016/05/30/goatman-and-being-a-beast.

29

Thwaites, *GoatMan*.

30

Ibid.

31

Patrick Barkham, "No Kidding: What I Learned from Becoming GoatMan," *The Guardian*, May 15, 2016, https://www.theguardian.com/science/shortcuts/2016/may/15/no-kidding-what-learned-from-becoming-goatman.

32

Tracy Fullerton, interview by Caitlin Condell, August 2, 2018.

33

Eimear Lynch, "Has Tracy J. Fullerton Created the Year's Most Unexpected Video Game?" *Surface*, August 8, 2017, https://www.surfacemag.com/articles/walden-a-game-creator-tracy-j-fullerton/.

34

Ibid.

35

Fullerton, interview.

Walden, A Game, 2017; Tracy Fullerton
(American, b. 1965), Game Innovation Lab,
University of Southern California (Los
Angeles, California, USA, founded 2004)

Next Nature

How do our changing ideas of nature transform the role of designers? Michael John Gorman and Koert van Mensvoort explore how we can move beyond biomimicry and speculation to design new forms of cooperation with other species that expand our senses and foster empathy.

Prof. Dr. Michael John Gorman is Founding Director of BIOTOPIA, a new life sciences museum for Bavaria planned for Nymphenburg Palace, and Professor (Chair) in Life Sciences in Society at Ludwig-Maximilians-University Munich. Previously he was founder and CEO of Science Gallery International, dedicated to igniting creativity and discovery where science and art collide. Science Gallery spaces are open or in development in Dublin, London, Melbourne, Bangalore, and Venice. Before starting up Science Gallery, Gorman was lecturer in Science, Technology, and Society at Stanford University and has held postdoctoral fellowships at Harvard University, Stanford University, and MIT. He has written books on topics ranging from Buckminster Fuller's designs to seventeenth-century art.

Dr. Koert van Mensvoort is an artist and philosopher best known for his work on the philosophical concept of Next Nature, which revolves around the idea that our technological environment has become so complex, omnipresent, and autonomous that it is best perceived as a nature of its own. Van Mensvoort is director of the Next Nature Network, a twenty-first-century nature organization that wants to go forward—not back—to nature. Furthermore, he is a Next Nature fellow at the Eindhoven University of Technology, and also a board member at the Society of Arts of the Dutch Royal Academy of Sciences. Earlier, Van Mensvoort worked as a researcher at the Center for User-System Interaction (1998–2003), as a teacher at the Sandberg Institute (2002–2006), and as a Visionary in Residence at Art Center College of Design in Pasadena (2008). He is the author of numerous books and publications.

Michael John Gorman   We've been invited here today to the Cube design museum to discuss the question of design in nature. Why does it make sense to do an exhibition on this theme right now? Why is it important to look at design and nature? It seems like a really ancient theme.

Koert van Mensvoort   It is ancient, but also urgent because it's shifting over time. And I think now in the twenty-first century, we are living in a time in which humanity increasingly designs nature. Much of what we talk about as nature often has been designed, especially here in the Netherlands. Almost every tree that is here is based on a political decision. That's ancient! Already in the eighteenth century, the French philosopher Voltaire said, "God created the world except for the Netherlands. That they have done themselves." So this is an ancient theme, but because of all emerging technologies—the biotechnologies, nanotechnologies, information technologies—we are now digging deeper in the natural world. We're starting to reshape nature, but what will happen? Will we be the masters of it all? Or will strange natural things occur in places where we didn't expect it? I think that's an urgent and necessary discussion.

MJG   I think that the theme of nature is difficult for design for a number of reasons. You can look at the imitation of nature through design with, say, Leonardo da Vinci and his flapping-wing flying machines imitating bird flight, or the whole idea of biomimetic design, which has a very long history. But it seems that now we're at a different juncture. For me our current idea of nature was the conjoined twin born alongside technology during the industrial revolution. The idea of nature as this romantic picturesque place was such an important theme then it was almost the antithesis of technology. I think that, now, we are moving to a different phase when we need to move away from the idea of nature as something to be dominated, to be exploited, toward a reconfiguration of how we work with nature. And I too think our relationship with nature poses very urgent questions. A new "map of nature" has been published in May 2018 in the *Proceedings of the National Academy of Sciences of the United States of America*, and we now know what the biomass of the Earth looks like.[1] It forces us to completely reconfigure our ideas about our place in the Earth. Before we had the idea that humans could look at nature and observe it from the outside, and it was a beautiful antithesis to the satanic mills of the cities. Now, it turns out that 95 percent of the mammals and birds on the planet are either humans or livestock grown to feed and clothe humans. So it's no longer possible to think of humans as something outside of nature, and we are inextricably interconnected with the living systems around us. So that is why I think it's necessary for us to think of those living systems as something that we should find new ways to cooperate with, learn from, and benefit from rather than simply continue the previous few centuries of exploitation.

KvM   I agree because the traditional notion of nature is that it's untouched. And once humans get involved, then it's not natural anymore. But this is a wrong image, although you can understand how we got it. I think it also relates to biblical stories like Adam and Eve being expelled from Paradise, being antinatural against the beautiful natural paradise that was nature before, and once we touch it, we destroy it. But now we learn that we are part of it again, and we have to find a way to be with and in it.

MJG   What about speculative design in the context of nature? I think of some of your projects, like the Rayfish Footwear, for example, which was almost a prank project and got a lot of interest. The idea was that one could preorder genetically modified rayfish shoes by selecting the skin color and pattern of the fish one desired. And then, there was an attack on the business premises by animal rights activists followed by a release of the GM fish into the ocean . . . it was a wonderful project, very provocative. And there's been a lot of work by designers, such as Dunne and Raby, Daisy Ginsberg, Oron Catts, and other artists and designers whom we've both worked with, that are in this realm of provocation . . . particularly products related to the living world and to biology, or even "living products" that make people feel a little uncomfortable, in this boundary zone between what is ethically acceptable and what is not. We've had now a few years of this speculative design, engaging with biology and with medicine, and it's been extremely important in reframing the role of the designer. But is speculative design now over, in the era of fake news? Do we need to somehow flip from speculative design into a new kind of engagement for designers with nature. . . ?

KvM   In my view, a few things can happen because you have different types of speculative design. Personally, I shifted from injecting speculative designs into society at large into making more confined theatrical settings in which people know, "I'm now entering a space which is a theater. I understand it, I suspend my disbelief, and then I can dream in the design speculation," because I do think that speculative design and that quality of envisioning potential futures, making them tangible to have a better conversation about what future we want, that is very valuable. But the whole confusion about "I don't know what's real anymore," that is something that we need to move well away from because of these times. And something else is that maybe designers will move more into realization because technology is also catching up. Something that I myself work extensively on is envisioning futures around cultured meat. When we started doing that, the technology was not capable of making the things that we were envisioning and although it's still the case today, some of the dishes that we have envisioned around cultured meat, they have been made now. Like the victimless foie gras, for instance—you can make a foie gras, but you don't have to force-feed the goose anymore because you just take a cell and then you grow it.

MJG   But there are still some issues around cultured meat, right? In terms of the nutrients, the use of fetal calf serum, and so on. People talk about having found really good solutions to that, but I haven't really seen a lot of details yet. So I'm still a little bit skeptical of this being a potentially scalable solution. I mean, the problem that it's clearly addressing is perhaps the most critical problem for our engagement with the natural world, namely agriculture and land use. So I'm a hundred percent aligned in terms of the problem, but in terms of the cell-growth-based solutions that are being proposed, as opposed to, for example, the plant-based approach, I find what we've seen so far to be a little bit of smoke and mirrors.

KvM   Well, I agree partly on this because I know that the issue is that we grow meat from cells of animals, and then we don't have to slaughter the animal anymore, but then to feed the cells, we still have to use animal products because we need serum to do it. And everyone who is working on this knows that this has to be solved, or it will never be a success. And there are some people who say they have solved it. Like, for instance, the CEO of JUST, formerly Hampton Creek, he's a vegan, and he said, "I solved it. I'm just not telling you how because it's a secret of my company." So then we don't know if we have really solved the problem. Should we believe him? Or is he also a prankster and doing speculative design? It's really confusing. I do know that there are scientists in the Netherlands who have developed alternatives of plant-based serum. They are also using it to make milk, which doesn't need a cow. So that's vegan milk. It's being developed and they are making big steps. I think we need to explore all the options. So yes, people should eat more insects—becoming a vegetarian is wonderful—but also the option of cultured meat should be pushed further.

MJG   I completely agree. This whole area is a field that's rife with investment at the moment. Not just in terms of meat, and as you say milk, but also leather is a huge area with also very interesting design activity and new materials that go beyond leather, created with mushroom mycelium, pineapple leaves, or collagen.

KvM   Moving to the planetary scale, how is it for you to be alive in this era in which all these developments are happening and also mass extinction is ahead of us? How, as a human being, do you relate to that?

MJG   Well, I think it's a really challenging moment to exist in, because, as you say, we have a lot of evidence that we are in the middle of a mass extinction.

And Elizabeth Kolbert has made this case very convincingly in her book *The Sixth Extinction*.[2] As you know, the fifth mass extinction was the one that wiped out most of the dinosaurs sixty-six million years ago, and now it seems that number six is on its way. And it seems that this time, we humans are the asteroid. And there is a huge amount of evidence for this. And I'm surprised that people don't take this more seriously. In contrast, climate change gets more than eight times as much media attention as this question of mass extinction, which I think is arguably an even more serious problem. I mean, the clue is in the words, right? Mass extinction. It's not a happy situation. And you have amphibians disappearing at twenty-five thousand times the background rate. There's been a three-quarter drop in the number of insects in Germany in the last thirty years. This is a hugely pressing issue. How do you cope with this?

KvM   And how do you make people aware?

MJG   Well, it's difficult because as you know, if you raise these environmental issues, there's a big tradition of doing it through fear. If you discuss climate change, we're all going to die. Al Gore, the hockey stick chart, and so on. And fear has the tendency to paralyze. It creates awareness, undoubtedly. But then it also paralyzes. And I think that you will need to use a different way to get people aware. Emotion is key. I mean, we've seen that with Trump and populism. Facts don't persuade. Emotions persuade. And we are living in a moment now where we, the scientists, have a terrible history of being unwilling to connect with audiences emotionally because we feel it's against the nature of science. But now we need to bring science into the emotional arena. And what I think we need to do is to create a significant new perspective shift for people to create a new kind of empathy for other species. Empathy always involves shifting perspective, and empathy is an immediate emotional effect. A truly empathic relationship is if one appreciates, for example, that animals have emotions and are not just little machines, like Descartes said, but are actually emotional beings.

KvM   Yeah. And are very similar to us.

MJG   Yes. If one looks at primates, at birds or orcas, there is a huge amount of commonality with humans. So to create that connection is really a design challenge. We need new ways to allow people to make the perspective shift to create that empathic connection with other species. Now that could be with technology, such as sensor technologies, which allow us to see the world from the perspective of a different animal. But it could be also in recognizing ourselves as a habitat for other species—for example, the fact that only about 50 percent of our cells are human, and the rest are nonhuman. So I think the big challenge for design is to work with science to create emotional ways for people to develop empathy for other species. And only if we have empathy, then can we see, "Okay, eating beef is a problem." So eating beef is not just a problem factually in terms of its huge environmental footprint, but actually it's a problem because the animals that we are treating in this particular way are emotional beings. And so, I think that we have a role to play in bridging design and science to allow for this new perspective shift with nature.

KvM   Well, I like that suggestion of the importance of empathy a lot because then it's also about Earth. I think sometimes that in the end we not only have to save the polar bear and the panda, but all humans as well. We're all in it together because we represent this biological world, this biosphere that is now clashing with the technosphere that is emerging. All the technology. After the fifth mass extinction dinosaurs were wiped out, but mammals became successful. They filled the niche that was open there. But what will happen after the sixth extinction? Will we then only have a technosphere on the planet and no biosphere? I don't think that's a viable model that there will be only robots and no biological creatures anymore. I think it's also our job to balance these forces, and especially for humanity because we as humans, although we're not controlling it and it was also not our grand design, we are definitely a catalyst in this event. We somehow caused it, making us responsible, and so we have to be stewards that balance biology and technology in a way that they can merge. And, sure, it will be a different world. We cannot go back to the paradise that never really existed, but then I am not fearful. I'm actually hopeful that we can find a world in which biology and technology are more balanced and in which old creatures and new creatures can coexist and can share a space. And that's what I think we should aim for, that's what we should design for.

MJG   One interesting area is additive manufacturing—3D-printed houses down to organs and bioprinting individual cells. People have suddenly realized that nature did 3D printing first. So if you look at silkworms and spiders there are millions of years of evolution that have gone into developing these extraordinary ways to create structures from biology. And once you have that sudden realization, then you'll have a chance for that perspective shift where you see that we can benefit hugely from cooperating with this other intelligence. And one sees that happening now, with people working with spider silk from the artist Tomás Saraceno to companies like adidas making spider-silk shoes and so on. There are interesting things happening in that area. I think that harnessing natural intelligence also maybe can generate a new kind of respect for evolution and for the biodiversity around us. So I think that there is a chance there. But how do you create empathy for insects? This is critical and urgent because in certain cities in China, people have to pollinate fruit trees by hand. This is a solution that would be difficult to scale to the whole planet, but the rapid disappearance of insects is now established in Europe. There are so many scales at which you can look at this, but the urban scale is particularly important now. How could you redesign a city so it is as hospitable to nonhumans as to humans?

KvM   Our cities should become more natural. And then it is not a problem anymore that there is less rural area and that since 2007 already half of the global population lives in urban areas. So that means we humans, we are evolving into a species that lives in urban areas just like bees. They live in beehives. It's natural for bees to live in beehives. It's becoming natural for humans to live in urban areas. But then we should make sure that these areas also feel natural to us. Now it's often a mismatch if you live in a city, you are in the smog, it's unhealthy, it's noisy, it's basically extracting also from your humanity. It's pushing you as a human in . . . in a mold that doesn't fit you. So if we can design these areas better that they feel natural, that . . . that they fit to our senses, to our needs.
Toward the future, are you fearful or hopeful?

MJG   I am hopeful. I'm naturally an optimistic person, otherwise I cannot do any of the things that I do. I don't know if you've read *Enlightenment Now* by Steven Pinker?[3] He paints a quite convincing picture about why we should be optimistic about almost everything in the future. And much of it, I agree with, I have to say. But there are certain areas that I don't agree with. So he gives persuasive arguments about global health, reduction of extreme poverty, diminishing crime rates, and a decline of violence on a global scale, but when it comes to nature, he has only thirteen lines about the question of biodiversity, which I think is not really enough. And he basically says that nature will be fine. And this is an area where I think we really should be concerned and actively engaged to find solutions, where "business as usual" is not an option. And this, combined with the populism that's going on right now and the environment being a particular topic for attack by many of these more right-wing populist governments around the world, I think is something that we cannot be complacent about. So I'm still generally an optimist. And I believe in the amazing, inventive resourcefulness of humans, nature's ultimate ecosystem engineers, to deal with all sorts of problems, including those of our making. But nonetheless, I think this is an area of nature we really need to focus on. What about you, are you fearful or hopeful?

KvM   I'm not a utopist in the sense that all will be wonderful and great. No. I sense we are at a crossroads, and we can choose. And there's one road ahead—that on which the technologies we make may parasitize us, and parasitize the natural world. It will be a "next nature," but it's not a next nature in which human beings even have a good role anymore because we will then be boxed in, in small cities, and basically become the source of this technological superorganism. And because I'm a human, playing for Team Human, I want to go in the other direction, in which we are the intermediate between the biological world and the technological world, in which we balance biology and technology, and in which the technologies uplift us and maybe even can uplift some of the other species. If it's interconnected and interwoven in a sensible way, then I think there's a world where I can live and one I like, I'm actually looking forward to it. I'm craving it because I think the weird thing also about being human is that we kind of fell into this position. For centuries, humans were an insignificant species on the planet. The big predators, we were always worried about them. And we were not the dominant species. But then because of our cognition and our ability to manipulate our environment, we kind of jumped into this new setting where we're still children, and we don't know how to, still have to find our way to, cope with it. We're playing with tools that, in a way, we are not mature enough to play with. And I think in that sense, humanity is in its teenage time with a lot of friction. We have to mature in our role on the planet. I'm hopeful because I think if we can make the mind shift, understand, and look differently at the relationship between biology and technology, we can make the world better for all the species in it, make the world a truly natural place.

1

Yinon M. Bar-On, Rob Phillips, and Ron Milo, "The biomass distribution on Earth," *Proceedings of the National Academy of Sciences of the United States of America* 115, no. 25 (2018): 6506–11, https://doi.org/10.1073/pnas.1711842115.

2

Elizabeth Kolbert, *The Sixth Extinction: An Unnatural History* (New York: Henry Holt & Company, 2014).

3

Steven Pinker, *Enlightenment Now: The Case for Reason, Science, Humanism, and Progress* (New York: Viking, 2018).

Simulate

The evolutionary development of life on Earth has led to a diversity of species, intricate and interconnected ecosystems, and intelligence, all of which are part of nature. Over billions of years, the trials and errors of nature have yielded the world humans experience today. Successful and elegant—and sometimes odd—adaptations that impact and shape growth have evolved. Such adaptations enable and support life.

Humans have long recognized that nature contains optimal strategies, patterns, and forms to meet variable demands. We have therefore emulated nature, modeling systems, materials, and objects on biological structures. With advances in science, humans not only observe nature, but manipulate it. We decode nature's underlying forces, moving from a place of imitating nature to one of simulating. Designers translate such scientific and technological advancement into applicable products and buildings, looking to nature as a guide.

Humans have arguably pushed evolution more than any other species, impacting the Earth by exploiting it to accommodate human needs and desires. Estimates suggest that rates of species extinction are a thousand times higher than they would be without humans.[1] Among the species to have gone extinct in the past hundred years are flowering plants. Lost with them is the scent those flowers emitted into their environment. What if knowledge derived from scientific research could restore the smell of these extinct flowers?

Resurrecting the Sublime (2018–19) is a project that revives the smell of extinct flowers and places it in its lost, abstracted landscape. A collaboration between artist and designer Alexandra Daisy Ginsberg, smell researcher Sissel Tolaas, and the creative director of biotechnology company Gingko Bioworks, Christina Agapakis, the project triggers ideas of not just ephemeral beauty and ersatz nostalgia, but awe and enormous implications of nature coming from the lab. It searches for the sublime. Agapakis and Gingko scientists gathered flower specimens from Harvard University's Herbaria, in Cambridge, identifying those from which they could extract and sequence DNA. They selected three specimens for the project: the first from Hawaii, a species of *Hibiscus* closely related to one that went extinct in 1910; the next a species of *Orbexilum stipulatum* from the Kentucky river region that went extinct due to grazing buffalo and river conditions; and the third a species of *Leucadendron grandiflorum* from the Cape of Good Hope, on the Atlantic coast of the Cape Peninsula in South Africa. Gingko's scientists sequenced the DNA of each specimen and, working with paleogeneticists at the University of California, Santa Cruz, identified gene pathways to produce fragrance enzymes. They then synthesized those genetic sequences, inserted them into yeast, and cultured them to produce molecules that are extracted to simulate an approximation of the extinct smell. As Ginsberg, Tolaas, and Agapakis point out, "even the most advanced technology can only give an incomplete representation of nature."[2]

The project encourages consideration of the sensory heritage that vanishes with extinction. It questions the implications of reversing the natural order of time, life, and evolution through biotechnology, experienced as a lost smell. Nature here is abstracted, reduced to a diffusion of the resurrected scent and a representation of the landscape from which it was lost, only to be connected by the user. Like reaching the aesthetic state of the sublime that provokes both awe and terror, the designers contemplate the position of humankind within the overwhelming enormity of nature.

Other designers seek to simulate the ephemerality of natural phenomena. Ocean Memories (2017), a series of tables and benches by Mathieu Lehanneur, is a manifestation of the surface of the ocean, frozen in time. Lehanneur is fascinated by the tensions between different states of matter. He explores this in Ocean Memories "by offering a new state of matter,

Resurrecting the Sublime, 2018-19;
Christina Agapakis (American, b. 1984),
Alexandra Daisy Ginsberg (British and
South African, b. 1982), and Sissel
Tolaas (Norwegian, b. 1963), with support
from IFF Inc. and Ginkgo Bioworks Inc.;
Aluminum, plywood, neoprene, plasterzote,
LEDs, diffuser, motion sensor, smell solu-
tions, limestone boulder

For full caption information,
see page 239.

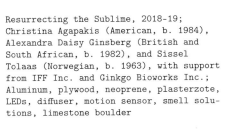

Circular Low Table XL, from the Ocean
Memories series, 2017; Mathieu Lehanneur
(French, b. 1974); Black marquina marble;
40 × 110 × 110 cm (15 3/4 × 43 5/16 ×
43 5/16 in.)

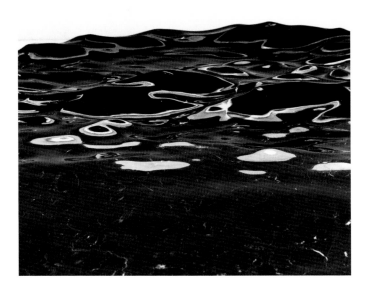

Circular Low Table XXL, from the Ocean
Memories series, 2017; Black marquina
marble; 40 × 170 × 170 cm (15 3/4 × 66
9/10 × 66 9/10 in.)

a state that nature and science have never been able to reproduce: the hybridization of water forms—visually liquid and structurally solid."[3] To replicate the ocean's textural topography, he adapted 3D special effects software that is used by the film industry to render CGI waves. Blocks of black marble are machine-cut following the digitally rendered forms and then hand-polished to a high gloss. These remarkable pieces of stone belie their material solidity to embody a snapshot of ocean turbulence.

In distinctive works recognizing changes in the land rather than the sea, Alexandra Kehayoglou, a Buenos Aires–based designer, creates hand-tufted carpets that depict landscapes either romantic or realistic, such as Patagonian glaciers or ecosystems impacted by deforestation. To study the landscapes, Kehayoglou uses drone photography and site analysis, then sketches on canvas before weaving a carpet. She uses natural sheep wool sourced from discarded thread from her family's factory and dyed to desired colors. Captured as bird's-eye views, the scenes are hauntingly distant yet politically poignant. The carpets portray not just blue rivers and plush growth, but the scars of human contact, parched earth and brush. The work lures viewers with a materially beautiful textile then confronts them with human impact on Earth. It is a conceptual, subversive, and thoroughly modern expression for the craft of carpet making.

Inspired by the geography of Argentina and her personal connection to its landscapes, Kehayoglou created Santa Cruz River (2017), a carpet that documents Argentina's last free-flowing, wild river where planned hydroelectricity dams will potentially and irrevocably alter the natural ecosystem. Studies for the carpet show her working through representations to immortalize and honor the river's landscape as it exists now. Seeing simulated aerial views of that landscape inherently makes one feel small. As Kehayoglou explains, "If we finally understand that we are not the centre of the Earth, but just a tiny part of it . . . our decision-making and behavior will lead us to a more environmentally conscious life."[4]

Most patterns in design are elements or shapes repeated in a predictable manner. In nature, patterns often seem chaotic, but science and mathematics enable the search for regularities and the ability to ascribe functions to them. For fashion designers Gabriel Asfour, Angela Donhauser, and Adi Gil of threeASFOUR, patterns in natural morphology are foundational in many of their garments. They explore intricate geometries and patterning systems as methods of wrapping a body, enabled by 3D-printing technologies. Their Harmonograph Dress (2016),[5] created with architect Travis Fitch and fabricated by Stratasys, was modeled after the geometry and intersections of wave oscillations like those that can be created with a harmonograph. The design of the dress was rendered digitally following a harmonograph simulation and 3D printed in a rubber mesh, its form like a Fibonacci spiral wrapped around the body and patterned with a complex web of oscillating curves.

For the Pangolin Dress (2016), threeASFOUR was inspired by a pangolin's unique plated armor, which consists of large hardened scales arranged in an overlapping pattern. The scales slide over each other for free movement, while also allowing the pangolin to curl up to protect itself when threatened. To create the dress, the design team was challenged by not only interpreting the pattern and physical structure, but also by researching digital production technologies that would enable high precision coupled with material variability during the 3D-printing process. They again collaborated with Fitch and Stratasys in the design and fabrication of the dress, which took five hundred hours to print on ten printers running simultaneously, followed by an intensive assembly process. The resulting dress yields alternating states of transparency and opacity due to color gradation and transformations in the porosity and flexibility of the material. It is akin to a plate-like sheath that protects the human body.

Nature-informed algorithms enable designers to simulate biological growth patterns. The aircraft manufacturer Airbus collaborated with architectural firm The Living and design software company Autodesk to optimize aircraft parts using two algorithms: one mimics the growth of slime mold, a single-celled organism that efficiently connects disparate points (or locations of food); and the other replicates the growth properties of mammal bones by removing mass where strength is not needed. They applied the algorithms to generate an optimal aircraft partition, which is the inch-thick dividing wall that separates the cabin from the galley of the plane and holds the crew's folding seats. Partitions must meet strict constraints, including weight, force threshold, and displacement in the event of a crash.

The team set the partition's parameters—a 30 percent weight reduction and structural performance (specifically, shifting no more than 7.8 inches in a 16g crash test)—and the algorithms did the rest, digitally rendering thousands of permutations based on the set constraints. Using big-data analytics, they mapped the results against weight, strength, and stress factors to identify the optimal form to prototype. The resulting Bionic Partition (2016–ongoing)[6] was 3D printed from Scalmalloy, its latticed, seemingly random structure made using the least amount of material possible while maintaining strength. It is 45 percent lighter than conventional partitions, which translates to more than seven thousand pounds of fuel saved per partition each year and a reduction of up to one hundred eighty-three tons of carbon dioxide emissions per plane each year. For a humble plane part, that's a big impact. Nature provided the underlying principles for generating its form.

Other mobility companies are using nature as a guide to optimizing structures. Michelin, the French tire company, integrated various research initiatives to create its Visionary Concept Tire (2016–19), whose form and internal structure are based on coral growth. Development of the tire was overseen by Michelin designer Mostapha El-Oulhani, whose team generated the form using advanced modeling software to ensure internal solidity but surface flexibility, enabling the performance required of an auto tire. The open structure of the tire is airless and not susceptible to blowout or explosion, and is 3D printed from biodegradable materials. The tread is adaptable and can be reapplied, also using 3D printing, to meet road conditions or when it wears down.

Just as growth patterns can be simulated in the design of objects, so too can biological behaviors be simulated. The design team at Festo, a German automation company whose robots are modeled on organisms found in nature, was inspired by the cooperative behavior of ants when creating the BionicANT (2018). Ants act independently but are subordinate to the goals of the colony. The BionicANT is a robot that has been designed similarly to make autonomous decisions while coordinating its actions in communication with other BionicANTs. It is through collective behavior that they are able to complete tasks, such as moving heavy objects. They can adjust their behavior cooperatively and flexibly as needs arise to reach their goal.

Festo's work exemplifies a knowledge transfer from the world of nature to the world of automation in behavior and form. The BionicANT's anatomy is based on an ant, just bigger. An optical mouse sensor (like those on computer mice) on the underside of the BionicANT's thorax provides position tracking. Piezo-ceramic transducers actuate its legs. Stereo cameras in its eyes allow the BionicANT to "see," and a radio module on its abdomen communicates with other BionicANTs. Antennae connect it to a charging station. Conductive tracks are printed directly on its body, allowing engineers to attach computer components. Festo sees the BionicANT as an important technology platform for future factories that require flexible robotic production, in which decentralized machines are networked to achieve tasks collectively.

Jellyfish also serve as models for Festo's designs of self-controlled, collective robots. The AquaJellies 2.0 (2008–ongoing) are aquatic robots that propel themselves in water by emulating the movements of jellyfish tentacles. A translucent hemisphere contains the control board, sensors (to prevent collisions when in motion), and a processor that controls the drive system. The drive unit moves plates in the AquaJelly's pressurized body, which set the eight tentacles in simultaneous, mesmerizing motion. Although jellyfish are ancient creatures, for Festo, jellyfish could also signal the future. AquaJellies 2.0 can be used for diagnostics and data collection in water management, pointing to automation technology that simulates models from nature.

For David Mooney and his team of researchers from the Wyss Institute for Biologically Inspired Engineering and the Harvard John A. Paulson School of Engineering and Applied Sciences (SEAS), a slug's

Study, Santa Cruz River I, 2017;
Alexandra Kehayoglou (Argentinian, b.
1981); 100% natural hand-tufted wool;
450 × 250 cm (14 ft. 9 3/16 in. × 8 ft.
2 7/16 in.)

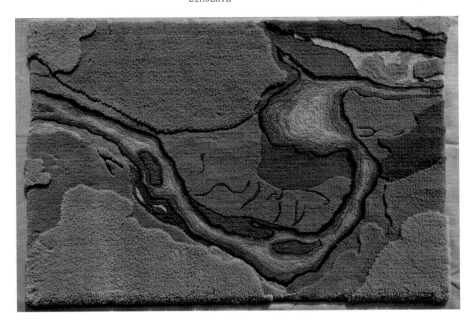

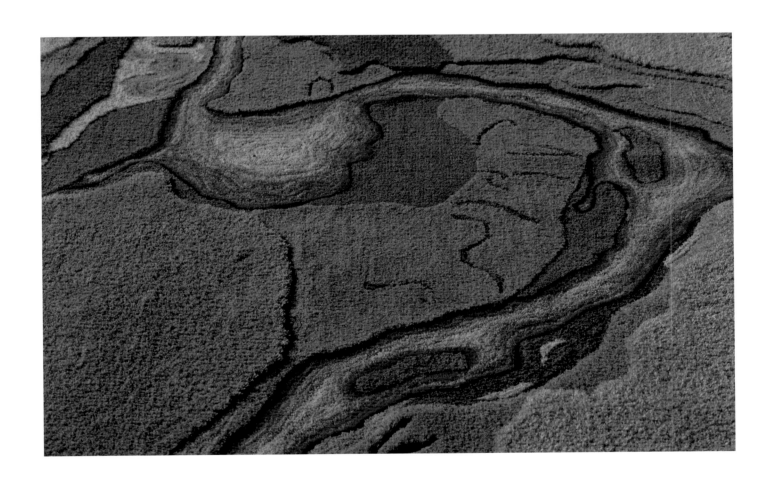

Study, Santa Cruz River II, 2017;
Alexandra Kehayoglou (Argentinian, b.
1981); 100% natural hand-tufted wool;
205 × 150 cm (6 ft. 8 11/16 in. ×
59 1/16 in.)

Harmonograph Dress, Biomimicry
Collection, 2016; Gabriel Asfour
(Lebanese, b. 1966), Angela Donhauser
(Tajikistani, b. 1971), and Adi Gil
(Israeli, b. 1974), threeASFOUR (New
York, New York, USA, founded 2005)
with Travis Fitch (American, b. 1987);
Produced by Stratasys (Eden Prairie,
Minnesota, USA, founded 1989); Agilus
30 multi material black 3D print, black
nylon powder mesh

Pangolin Dress, Biomimicry Collection,
2016; Gabriel Asfour (Lebanese, b.
1966), Angela Donhauser (Tajikistani,
b. 1971), and Adi Gil (Israeli, b.
1974), threeASFOUR (New York, New
York, USA, founded 2005) with Travis
Fitch (American, b. 1987); Produced by
Stratasys (Eden Prairie, Minnesota, USA,
founded 1989); Agilus 30 multi mater-
rial full color 3D print, black nylon
powder mesh

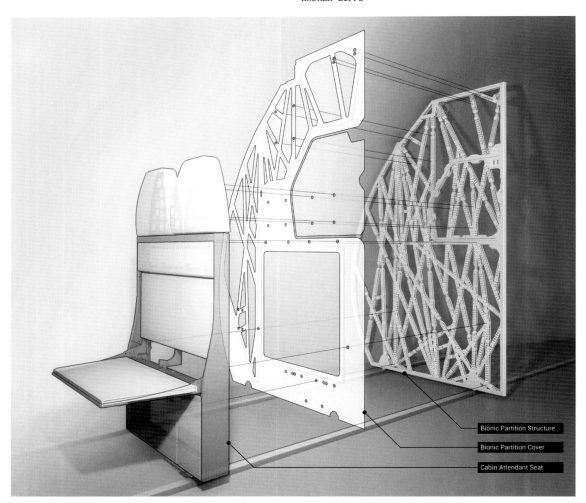

Bionic Partition Structure

Bionic Partition Cover

Cabin Attendant Seat

Bionic Partition, 2016-ongoing; Bastian
Schaefer (German, b. 1980), Airbus
(Toulouse, France, founded 1970); David
Benjamin (American, b. 1974), The Living
(New York, New York, USA, founded 2008);
Autodesk (San Rafael, California, USA,
founded 1982) and AP Works (Taufkirchen,
Germany, founded 2013); Metal
Scalmalloy®; 208.28 × 167.64 × 5.08 cm
(82 × 66 × 2 in.)

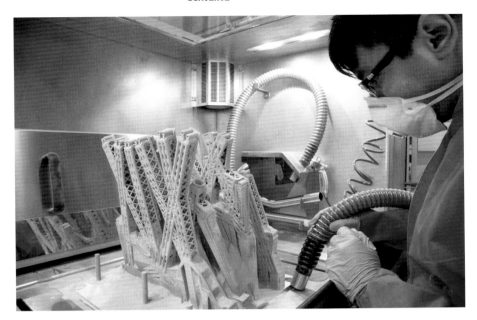

↑
Parts emerge from the 3D printer in a
cluster before being cleaned and detached
for assembly.

Visionary Concept Tire, 2016-19; Michelin
(Clermont-Ferrand, France, founded 1889);
Bio-sourced and recycled materials with
biodegradable, 3D-printed tread; 15 ×
70.8 cm (5 7/8 × 27 7/8 in.)

72

BionicANT, 2018; Sebastian Schrof
(German, b. 1989), Elias Knubben (German,
b. 1975), Jochen Spohrer (German, b.
1990), and Mart Moerdijk (Dutch, b.
1988), Festo AG & Co. KG (Esslingen,
Germany, founded 1925); Laser-sintered
polyamide, steel, gold plate, batteries,
sensor, processor, radio module, stereo
camera; 4.3 × 15 × 13.5 cm (1 11/16 × 5
7/8 × 5 5/16 in.)

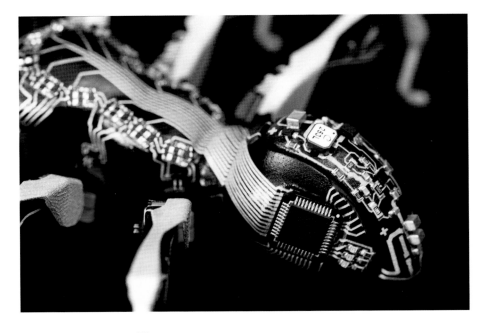

74

AquaJellies 2.0, 2008-ongoing; Rainer
Mugrauer (German, b. 1968) and Markus
Fischer (German, b. 1966), Festo AG & Co.
KG (Esslingen, Germany, founded 1925);
Polyamide, polycarbonate; H × diam.: 45 ×
35 cm (17 11/16 × 13 3/4 in.)

self-defense mechanism is a model for internal bandages. A Band-Aid® is great for external wounds, but what about internal ones? When startled, the slug known as the Dusky Arion (*Arion subfuscus*) secretes a watery, sticky mucus. The slug's glue, which it uses to adhere itself to a rock or branch so it can't be carried off by a predator, is incredibly strong—two to five times stronger than Super Glue or medical adhesives. Using this ancient adaptation as inspiration, Mooney and his team are developing flexible, super-strong, and biocompatible medical adhesives that can stick to dynamically moving tissue, like a beating heart. Their Sea Slug Bandages (2017–ongoing) could potentially assist with human tissue repair, wound dressings, and surgical sutures, used on wet surfaces like biological tissue to replace stitches, even in the presence of blood.

One layer is a sticky surface that contains a polymer and, similar to the proteins in the slug's glue, creates strong chemical bonds to the underlying tissue. The other layer is a stretchable, strong hydrogel. The Sea Slug Bandages can be formed into sheets or custom shapes to meet different needs. The adhesion could be as strong as natural cartilage binding to bone, a remarkable feat inspired by the Dusky Arion. As Mooney points out, "This particular slug has largely solved what we wanted to solve."[7]

Humans continue to probe and learn from nature, the ultimate teacher. Research and development in biotechnology is enabling researchers to simulate tissues and materials found in the animal kingdom for a range of applications, from optimized medical treatments to more environmentally sensitive materials. Among the research, scientists in the fields of tissue engineering and regenerative medicine are developing specialized biocompatible environments, called scaffolds, that can support new cell growth to induce tissue and bone regeneration. Ramille Shah and Adam Jakus are among them. They led a research team in the development of 3D-Painted Hyperelastic Bone™ (2018),[8] a versatile and scalable biomaterial that simulates bone to promote new bone growth.

The Hyperelastic Bone is made principally from a naturally occurring mineral called hydroxyapatite, a form of calcium found in bone and already used in reconstructive surgeries. Hydroxyapatite is extremely hard and brittle, but the team made it more flexible by mixing it with a polymer. The synthetic bone is then 3D printed to fabricate custom bone implants and complex shapes, such as spinal sections or jawbones. As Shah describes, "The first time that we actually 3D printed this material, we were very surprised to find that when we squeezed or deformed it, it reverted right back to its original shape."[9] The material is porous and absorbent yet robust, critical for in vivo applications because it encourages blood vessel growth and bone regeneration. Its unique properties enable it to be trimmed, folded, rolled, and shaped during a procedure. Early tests demonstrate its success in regenerating bone and integrating with existing tissue without inflammation or immune responses.

Other materials found in—and on—the body provide inspiration for designers. Hair-like structures are among the most multifunctional devices found across animal kingdoms, from human inner-ear cilia and their sensory properties, to the bristles on a worm's body that aid it in locomotion, to the dense, thick fur that keeps a bison warm in the winter. A group of researchers at the MIT Media Lab, led by Jifei Ou and under the direction of Hiroshi Ishii in the Tangible Media Group, has developed a computational method to 3D-print hair structures called Cilllia (2017–19). With it, they effectively design and fabricate hair geometries at a resolution of fifty micrometers. (By comparison, a strand of human hair is usually about seventy-five micrometers in diameter.)

In order to print a structure at a fifty-micrometer scale, the team developed a voxel-based printing method that approximates the geometry of natural hair. The researchers can arrange the voxels to change the shape of each hair, or they can tilt the angle of the hair to induce actuation and control the direction of movement. At that scale, the team can customize individual strands to create a superfine dense fur, to program functions such as adhesion or sensing, or to embed texture or optical effects. The results range from surprisingly soft synthetic furs, structurally complex 3D-printed textures, and even actuators that move objects.

What if leather didn't need to come from animal skin? Scientists and designers at biotechnology company Modern Meadow are harnessing biology to grow animal-free leather from yeast. The bioleather, called Zoa™ (2018–ongoing), is grown to mimic the texture and performance of animal leather. To make it, the team developed a fermentation-based technology that genetically engineers yeast to produce collagen, the protein in skin, rather than producing alcohol, when the yeast is fed sugar. The technique is exemplary of biofabrication, using biology to manufacture materials.

Biologically, Zoa is the same as traditional leather, but without the animal. It could one day be possible to grow alligator, calfskin, or ostrich-like leather in the lab without using animals. Zoa bioleather also transcends leather's physical constraints. It can be manufactured in a liquid state for spray applications, poured into molds to take on new shapes and patterns, used as a binder for fabric, or integrated with other fibers to make composite materials. Zoa pushes not just the fabrication process for an industry that is thousands of years old, but the performance and function of the material itself, with nature at its roots.

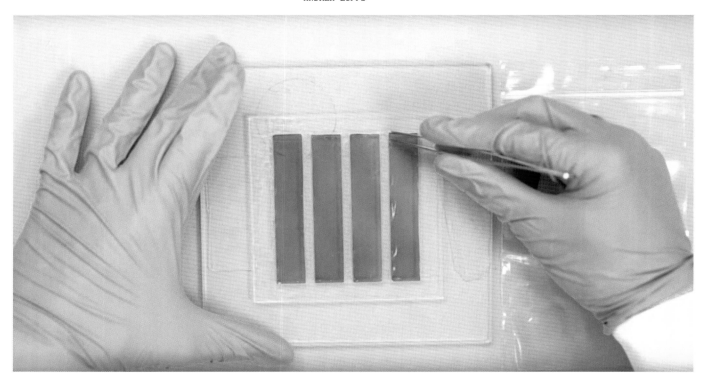

Sea Slug Bandages, 2017–ongoing; David
Mooney (American, b. 1964), Ben Freedman
(American, b. 1989), and Jianyu Li,
(Chinese, b. 1988), Mooney Lab for
Cell and Tissue Engineering (Cambridge,
Massachusetts, USA, founded 2004),
John A. Paulson School of Engineering
and Applied Sciences (Cambridge,
Massachusetts, USA, founded 1847), and
Wyss Institute for Biologically Inspired
Engineering, Harvard University (Boston,
Massachusetts, USA, founded 2009);
Hydrogel; 2.54 × 6.35 × 3.81 cm (1 × 2
1/2 × 1 1/2 in.)

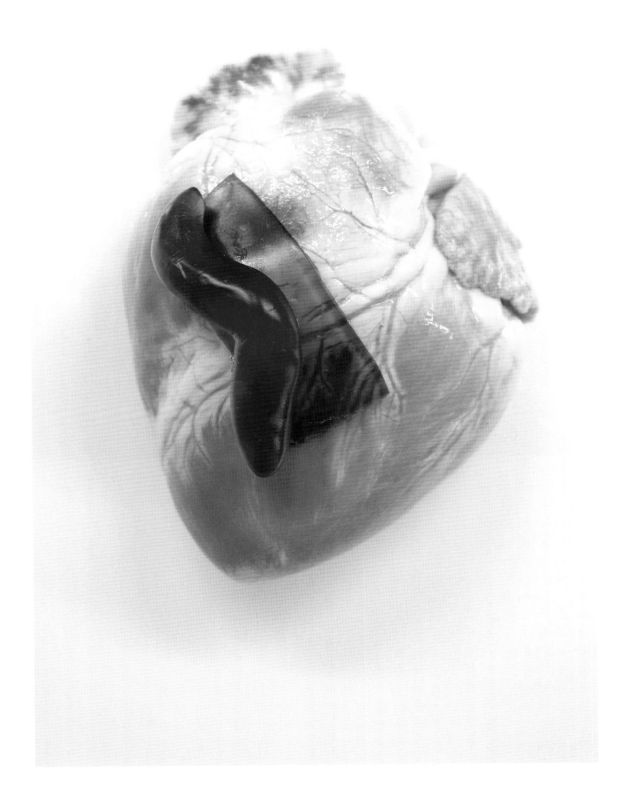

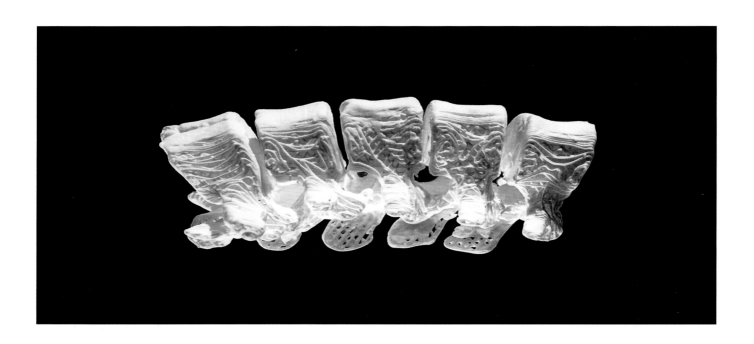

↑
Human spinal segment, 3D-Painted
Hyperelastic Bone®, 2015-18; Adam E.
Jakus (American, b. 1986), Dimension
Inx LLC (Chicago, Illinois, USA,
founded 2017); Hydroxyapatite;
Dimensions variable

→
Mandible, 3D-Painted Hyperelastic Bone®,
2018; Adam E. Jakus (American, b. 1986),
Dimension Inx LLC (Chicago, Illinois,
USA, founded 2017); Hydroxyapatite;
Dimensions variable

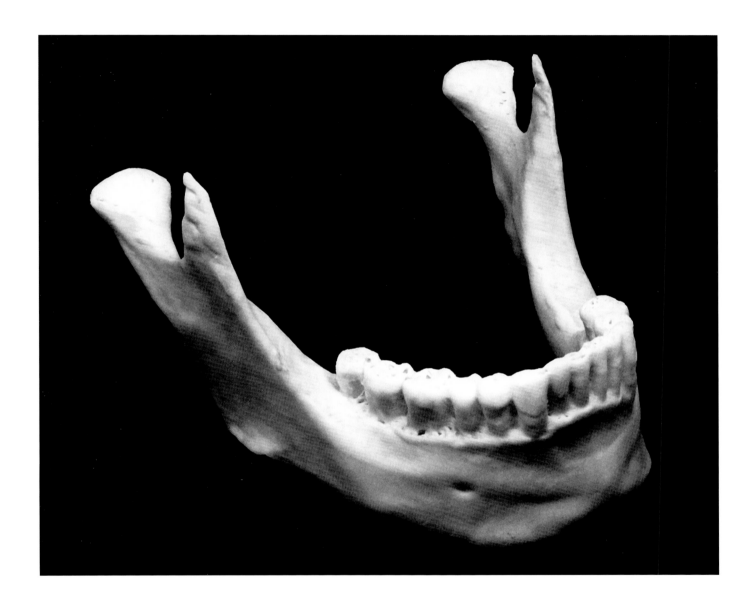

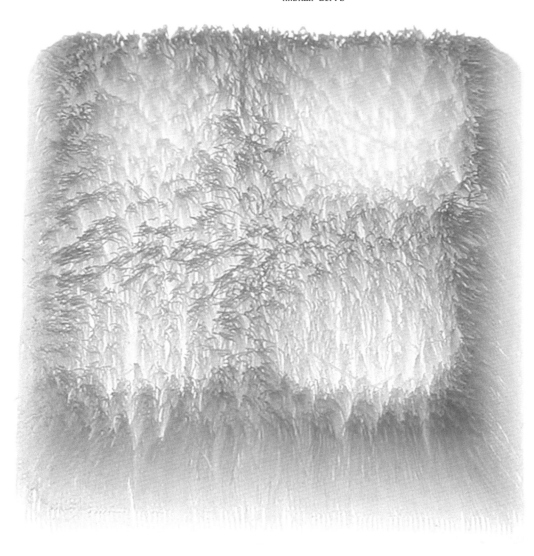

Cilllia, 2017-19; Jifei Ou (Chinese, active in USA, b. 1984) and Hiroshi Ishii (Japanese, active in USA, b. 1956), Tangible Media Group, MIT Media Lab (Cambridge, Massachusetts, USA, founded 1997); Contributing Team Members: Fabian Meumann and Sen Dai; Photopolymer, cornstarch, nylon; Dimensions variable

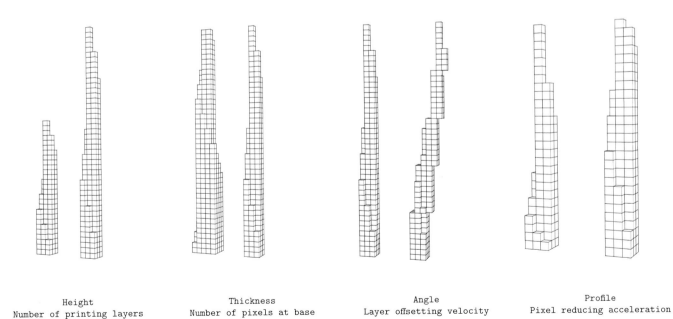

| Height
Number of printing layers | Thickness
Number of pixels at base
and tip layers | Angle
Layer offsetting velocity | Profile
Pixel reducing acceleration |

↓
Voxel-based design parameters: By arrang-
ing the voxels, the design team varies
the shape and performance of the printed
hair geometries.

Zoa™ Biofabricated Leather, 2019; Modern
Meadow (Nutley, New Jersey, USA,
founded 2011); Zoa-biofabricated
materials; Dimensions variable

1

Christine Dell'Amore, "Species Extinction
Happening 1,000 Times Faster Because of Humans?"
National Geographic, May 30, 2014, https://news.
nationalgeographic.com/news/2014/05/140529-
conservation-science-animals-species-endangered-
extinction/.

2

Alexandra Daisy Ginsberg, Sissal Tolaas, and
Christina Agapakis, Ginkgo Bioworks, "Resurrecting
the Sublime," proposal submitted to Cooper Hewitt,
Smithsonian Design Museum, May 18, 2018.

3

Carla Colón and Andrey Furmanovich, press contacts,
"Mathieu Lehanneur Q & A," Mathieu Lehanneur,
Ocean Memories, September 19–October 27, 2017
(New York: Carpenters Workshop Gallery Press Kit).

4

P. G. Hanna-Amanda, "To Freeze the Time through
Tapestry—Retrieving Memories through Carpet
Landscapes: Alex Keha," *Savant*, May 30, 2016,
http://www.savant-magazine.com/magazine/2016/5/
30/alexandrakehayoglou.

5

A simple harmonograph is an apparatus with two
pendulums that swing in different directions. For
example, when a pen held in one of the pendulum's
swinging arms meets a writing surface held by the
other swinging pendulum, the device records the
two oscillations as a single curve, creating harmony
in seemingly chaotic geometries and expanding
symmetries.

6

Scalmalloy is a blend of scandium, aluminum, and
magnesium developed by AP Works specifically
for the Additive Layer Manufacturing (ALM)
3D-printing process. Bastian Schaefer and David
Benjamin, meeting with Andrea Lipps and Matilda
McQuaid, September 26, 2018.

7

Teresa Carey, "Forget Stitches. These Slug-Inspired
Adhesives Could Soon Heal Your Wounds," *PBS
News Hour*, July 27, 2017, https://www.pbs.org/
newshour/science/forget-stitches-slug-inspired-
adhesives-soon-heal-wounds.

8

Adam E. Jakus et al., "Hyperelastic 'Bone': A Highly
Versatile, Growth Factor–Free, Osteoregenerative,
Scalable, and Surgically Friendly Biomaterial,"
Science Translational Medicine 8, no. 358
(2016): 358ra12728, http://stm.sciencemag.org/
content/8/358/358ra127.

9

James Vincent, "3D-Printed 'Hyperelastic Bone'
Could Be the Future of Reconstructive Surgery,"
The Verge, September 28, 2016, https://
www.theverge.com/2016/9/28/13094642/
hyperelastic-bone-graft-substance-unveiled.

Salvage

Salvage   Gène Bertrand

Human Nature

When looking at the photo series created by the Canadian photographer
Edward Burtynsky, we notice, as Burtynsky so poignantly puts it, "the indelible marks left by humankind on the geological face of our planet."[1] The photos
clearly show the impact of humankind on landscapes (Fig. 1), oceans, and the
air; in short, the habitats of everything that lives on our planet. The influence
on the ecosystems, whether positive or negative, is portrayed in a manner that
emanates beauty and vulnerability. At the same time, a story is told that leaves
a far greater impression than tables, figures, and facts. The photos reveal that a
change in perspective has a major impact in raising awareness of the considerable influence of humans on their environment. A changing perspective is one
of the key starting points for modern designers who incorporate nature in their
design concepts. To salvage nature is to discover new possibilities that emerge
from rescuing or reusing various raw materials that are found in nature. Even
the redefinition of what is meant by a natural raw material is taken as a starting
point in some cases. In this interpretation, reclaiming raw materials refers to
the search for new perspectives, applications, or products in which the tackling of ingrained opinions and the proper care of our lives and our planet form
the connecting factor. Diversity is a crucial principle for maintaining balanced
ecosystems, whether large or small. Over the past few billion years, this
balance has been disrupted regularly, often with serious consequences for existing ecosystems. Our planet has been changing constantly for 4.5 billion years,
a process that continues without interruption today. Under the influence of a
changing climate, natural ecosystems have been displaced, existing species have
evolved, and new entities have developed.

For the first part of our Earth's history—the Hadean eon that
occurred 4.5 to 4 billion years ago—there is no proof of life. The first conclu-
sive proof of life on Earth dates to around 3.7 billion years ago. This proof
consists of stromatolites from the Precambrian period, sedimentary rock
that was formed by the capturing and depositing of sediment by bacteria
and cyanobacteria. The first traces of these stromatolites were found in the
oldest rocks of Greenland, which became exposed as a result of the persistent
thaw in 2016.

Every period of the geologic timescale has its peculiarities. The first
mollusks in the sea appeared during the Cambrian period, and the first insects
emerged during the Devonian period, when carbon was responsible for the
development of vast areas of mangrove vegetation and river deltas. These
forests and marshes disappeared around 290 million years ago due to the influence of the changing climate. The climate became drier and hotter, which led
to desertification. Carbon laid the foundation for the later development of coal,
limestone developed during the Cretaceous period, and the end of the last ice
age was important for the evolution of algae, which made it possible for life
forms such as seaweed to develop.

During the entire history of humankind, humans have been capable of using the raw materials of each specific geologic period, whether as
fuel, as a basis for new products, or even to create completely new materials.
Scientific and technological developments have played an important role in the
extraction, processing, and use of these raw materials. As mentioned earlier,
many of these raw materials were the result of climate changes, whereby
longer periods of warm weather alternated with relatively short periods of cold
weather known as the ice ages. These changes were largely caused in the past
due to the shifting of the continents and changes in the composition of the
atmosphere. Major natural disasters such as volcanic eruptions or falling mete-
orites have also had an influence on Earth's changing climate.

Fig. 1   Clearcut #1, Palm Oil Plantation,
Borneo, Malaysia, 2016

Anthropocene

The term "Anthropocene" was introduced eighty years ago by the geologist Alexie Pavlov, and gained more prominence thanks to the ecologist Eugene F. Stroemer and the Dutch Nobel prize–winning atmospheric chemist Paul Crützen. According to this theory, the Holocene epoch, which started around twelve thousand years ago, made the transition into a new geological period, the Anthropocene, under the influence of human activity. The Anthropocene is characterized by the enormous impact of human activity on the Earth, its climate, and its atmosphere. In this regard, there are particularly important roles for the phenomenal growth in population, the strong increase in carbon dioxide concentration in the atmosphere, and the extinction of numerous species. All of these factors trigger far-reaching changes in the atmosphere, lithosphere, biosphere, cryosphere, and oceans. There has been a significant change in the concentration of certain substances in the atmosphere due to deforestation, combustion of fossil fuels, and widespread agricultural practices, all of which have led to the development of the greenhouse effect and, with it, global warming.

Earth Ecosystem

One form of evidence of the drastic influence of humankind on our living environment is the vast amount of plastic in the oceans. This so-called "plastic soup" can be found at several locations in the oceans and on beaches. One consequence of this is that sediments are containing more and more plastic. In Hawaii, for example, sandy beaches polluted with plastic are being transformed through hot lava flows into a new type of stone called Plastiglomerate.[2] This "new raw material" is regarded by many scientists as a potential feature of the Anthropocene.

The theory surrounding the Anthropocene and the development of Plastiglomerate play a central role in the speculative design project Metamorphism (2017–ongoing).[3] This project, created by the Israeli-born designer Shahar Livne, is based on the theme of Plastiglomerate and explores the possibilities of using this stone as a raw material for designing new products. The blurring of what is seen as natural and what is synthetic fascinates Livne in her research. She uses Plastiglomerate as a basis to create a new clay-like material that she calls Lithoplast. This speculative design project is based on her assumption that plastic will disappear in our modern world and that future generations will regard the plastic waste as a new natural resource that can be extracted in underground mining and used as a rare commodity for the production of new objects. In the creation of these new objects, craftsmanship and traditional production techniques play an important role. According to Livne, traditional craftsmanship will disappear along with the traditional raw materials of today. Through her project, she questions our definition of nature and culture within the context of this disappearing craftsmanship.

Sand consists of tiny hard or soft loose and granular particles of rock, and is one of the most common natural substances on Earth. It is formed by the erosion of rocks (such as mountains and boulders), and also consists of organic material (shells, coral) and minerals. This means that sand can originate from many different geological eras. In a collaborative project by Lonny van Ryswyck and Nadine Sterk of Atelier NL,[4] this more traditional resource is used, but with the designers taking a more personal, innovative approach.

As part of this project, entitled A World of Sand (2010–ongoing),[5] people are invited to send sand from every conceivable location in the world in order to make tangible the infinite riches under our feet, in both physical as well as digital form. Along with their bottle or container of sand, participants are also invited to submit their stories: stories about the sand's origin, the special meaning of where the sand was found, and what the people experienced there. A digital map of the stories and locations will be drawn up and made available online and the sand will be fused into glass objects to create a physical world "sand map." Dazzling colors are revealed when this sand, which originates from numerous different places on our planet, is heated to form

Metamorphism, 2017-ongoing; Shahar Livne
(Israeli, b. 1989); Plastic, minestone,
marble dust; Dimensions variable

A World of Sand, 2010-ongoing; Nadine
Sterk (Dutch, b. 1977) and Lonny van
Ryswyck (Dutch, b. 1978), Atelier NL
(Eindhoven, Netherlands, founded 2007);
Sand, glass

glass. These colors range from very light to deep dark green and to brown and even turquoise tints. This creates an alternative to the traditional glass industry, which may cause sand quarries to become exhausted at some point in the future. The entire project is characterized by a physical and digital approach, which contributes to the impact of A World of Sand.

Another material that originates from eroded rock is clay. Clay is made from sand that is transported by water to the lower parts of a landscape. This is why clay is usually found in the deltas of large rivers or in troughs in the landscape from which it cannot drain away. One of the purest types of clay is porcelain clay, of which kaolin or china clay is used most often. The designer Kirstie Van Noort considers herself to be part designer and part researcher. Her work is conceptual in many cases and she prefers to tell stories via the process rather than via the search for the perfect shape. As part of her project Latitude for Uniqueness Series (2014–ongoing),[6] she conducted a study into porcelain production in the Japanese village of Arita, where almost pure kaolin is used to produce the finest porcelain. She discovered tiny amounts of dark residual material that could not be used to make delicate white kaolin porcelain. Van Noort developed a new line based on the brown-black residues left over from normal production in Arita. This approach produced sufficient quantities of clay that could eventually be used to create a series of porcelain objects, including the use of a new palette of seven colors that are characteristic for Arita.

Air Ecosystem

According to the World Health Organization (WHO), 91 percent of the world's population lives in conditions that exceed WHO guidelines for air pollution, with the consequence that 4.2 million people in the world die per year as a result of poor air quality. These figures show just how important it is to find practical solutions that improve air quality, particularly in large cities.

A major consequence of human activity that influences air quality is the emission of carbon dioxide into our atmosphere. This is a huge challenge that designers are tackling in a variety of ways. The high concentrations of carbon dioxide in major cities are caused mainly by the incomplete combustion of fossil fuels. This theme forms the basis of the AIR-INK™ (2013–ongoing)[7] project set up by Anirudh Sharma, cofounder of Graviky Labs, which had its beginnings at MIT Media Lab in Massachusetts. The idea to convert carbon dioxide air pollution into ink was born when soot from exhaust gases landed on the white T-shirt that Sharma was wearing.

The project involves collecting the fine particulate matter from cars in Asia for subsequent use in production of water-resistant ink. The emissions from cars and, for example, diesel generators are collected using a filter device called Kaalink, which is attached to the exhaust pipe. The collected soot is then purified and what remains is almost pure carbon pigment. This pigment is used to manufacture the ink, which is now being used by more than one thousand international artists to create their works of art and murals.

The next step in the project is to supply Kaalink devices to bus and taxi companies who can store the captured soot emissions in "carbon banks." These containers are then collected by Graviky Labs and processed into ink. A thirty-milliliter bottle of AIR-INK is the equivalent of forty-five minutes of air pollution caused by a car. The approach taken by Graviky Labs is a good example of tinkering, a process in which goals are achieved through experimentation and trial and error, with prototyping playing an important role.

Water Ecosystem

Our oceans are the most important ecosystem on Earth. They are crucial for the survival of all known life forms on our planet and are also one of the most important biotopes. For designers, the oceans are a rich source of inspiration for new products and applications, which are of paramount importance now that the oceans are under severe threat from the influence and consequences of human activity.

The vast amount of plastic in our oceans shows clearly that we need to change the way we think if we still wish to have any influence on the impending extinction of animals and the presence of minuscule plastic particles in our food and seafood chain. This forms the starting point for a collaboration between the global sports manufacturer adidas and environmental collaboration network Parley for the Oceans.[8] Following Parley's AIR strategy (Avoid, Intercept, Redesign), their goal is to bring about a change in thinking and producing in which design is integrated at all different stages. Both partners hope this strategy will achieve an end to marine plastic pollution and its destructive consequences for animals, plants, and humanity. Parley regards plastic as a design failure that must be remedied as quickly as possible by reinventing the material itself.[9] In this approach, "Avoid" refers to the avoidance of using plastic where possible. "Intercept" is the removal of immediate plastic threats from nature. "Redesign" represents Parley's ultimate objective, which is presenting alternatives to plastic based on sustainable and reusable materials. To achieve this AIR goal, they are working on intercepting and "upcycling" plastic from the oceans. Upcycling is a principle that also plays an important role in the Cradle to Cradle design movement.[10] This refers to the fact that marine plastic is collected from the sea and reused in the manufacturing of new products, creating a closed circle in which no new plastic is incorporated.

This method creates an important role for consumers and designers. If people want to bring about change, then it is necessary to change the mindset of consumers. One of the results of this adidas × Parley collaboration is the introduction of the UltraBOOST Shoe (2016–ongoing), of which a total of five million pairs have been sold. These running shoes largely incorporate the plastic that was collected from remote shorelines and coastal areas such as the Maldives via the Parley "Intercept" activities. The shoe has a woven upper made from a mixture of Ocean Plastic™ (95 percent) and recycled polyester (5 percent). The heel cap, heel webbing, heel lining, and sock liner covers are also made from recycled materials. Appropriately, the design of the shoe has been inspired by ocean waves.

As an ecosystem, the sea contains many different forms of life that provide more and more inspiration for new concepts and products. A great starting point is provided by algae or seaweeds that can be found in various forms in the sea, ranging from single-cell to multicellular organisms. Their common feature is that during their growth they absorb carbon and emit oxygen.

The collaboration between Studio Eric Klarenbeek, Maartje Dros, and Atelier LUMA is an example of a design group that focuses on researching and designing new applications without losing sight of the past. They cooperate not only with designers, but also with chemists, color experts, fuel experts, and representatives of the regional salt industry. The Algae Lab (2018)[11] researches the possibilities of a circular concept by applying bioproduction in a decentralized setup, using equipment such as 3D printers. In doing so, the group explores the possibilities of cultivating living microorganisms from algae cultures that occur naturally along the coast. The salt flats along the French coast are particularly suitable for the growing of algae. This approach also makes it possible for "algae farms" to be set up in places such as industrial estates. The ultimate goal is to replace plastic produced from fossil fuel. According to the designers, it will be possible to replace all plastic with organic material in the future. One way they hope to achieve this is by setting up a network of "3D bakeries" to provide the opportunity to print objects from biodegradable materials at any of the locations. The Algae Lab is the winner of the Dutch New Material Award 2018.

Seaweed is based on various groups of nonrelated types of algae, which originated somewhere in the region of 3.5 billion years ago. Seaweed itself made an appearance approximately 1.2 billion years ago and has survived many geological changes, including events that led to the extinction of dinosaurs. Seaweed appears in many different forms and varieties and has been used for thousands of years, especially in Asian countries, usually as food. In Japan, for example, seaweed is dried into sheets of nori that are mainly used to make sushi.

Latitude for Uniqueness Series, 2014-
ongoing; Kirstie Van Noort (Dutch, b.
1986); Porcelain, raw kaolin, black
Amakusa stone waste; Dimensions variable

AIR-INK, 2013-ongoing; Anirudh Sharma
(Indian, b. 1988), Graviky Labs
(Bangalore, India, founded 2016);
Particulate carbon matter, glass
vial, brushes

15MM CHISEL TIP
APPROX 130 MINS
OF DIESEL CAR
POLLUTION

50MM WIDE TIP
APPROX 130 MINS
OF DIESEL CAR
POLLUTION

2MM ROUND TIP
APPROX 50 MINS
OF DIESEL CAR
POLLUTION

0.7MM ROUND TIP
APPROX 40 MINS
OF DIESEL CAR
POLLUTION

200ML REFILL
APPROX 830 MINS
OF DIESEL CAR
POLLUTION

**APPROX 19.6 HOURS
OF DIESEL CAR POLLUTION**

UltraBOOST Shoe, 2016-ongoing; adidas
(Herzogenaurach, Germany, founded 1949)
and Parley (New York, New York, USA,
founded 2012); Ocean plastics, synthetic
textiles, rubber; Dimensions variable

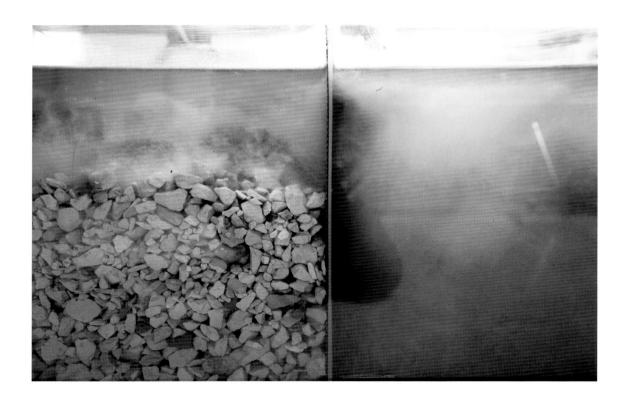

Algae Lab, 2018; Studio Klarenbeek & Dros
(Zaandam, Netherlands, founded 2004) with
Atelier Luma (Arles, France, founded
2016); Biomaterial made of locally grown
microalgae, sugar-based biopolymer;
Dimensions variable

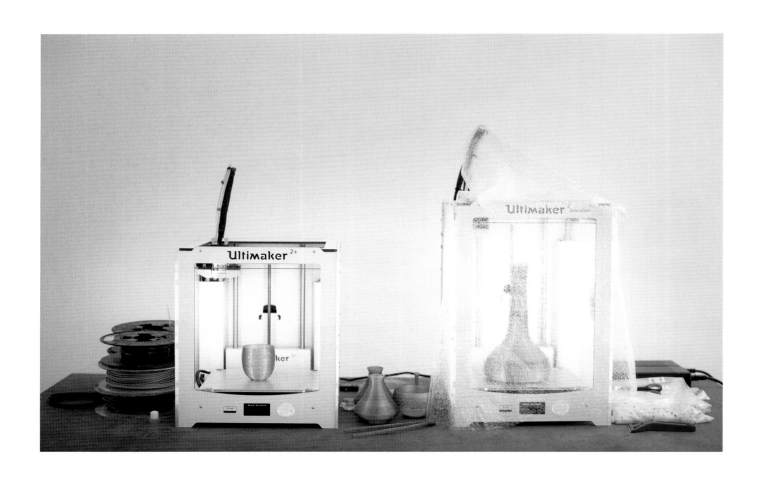

Algae Lab, 2018; Studio Klarenbeek & Dros
(Zaandam, Netherlands, founded 2004) with
Atelier Luma (Arles, France, founded
2016); Biomaterial made of locally grown
microalgae, sugar-based biopolymer;
Dimensions variable

Designers are often on the lookout for new materials or new material properties. The search for new materials and applications calls for an openness in interpreting the design trade, from which it is evident that a theoretical approach alone does not produce the desired results. Hands-on experience and the use of one's senses are important components on the road to success. Julia Lohmann is somebody who fully embraces this approach. She has combined experimenting, researching, and designing as her main mode of operation, giving an entirely unique interpretation to her profession. She became inspired by seaweed while visiting a fish market in Japan and turned this fascination into a project called <u>Department of Seaweed: Living Archive</u> (2018–ongoing)[12]— a mobile, multidisciplinary research environment that offers makers, designers, researchers, and architects the opportunity to conduct research, based on speculative design principles, into possible environmentally friendly and socially sustainable visions for our future. The objective of this environment is not purely and simply to exhibit the work that has been created, but also to provide the public with insight into her methods and approach. In her work with seaweed and particularly kelp, Lohmann is inspired by the properties of other materials, such as the translucency of glass, the structure of wood, and the strength and flexibility of leather. At the same time she is investigating whether seaweed could be used as an alternative for these materials, as a veneer, leather, or parchment, or as a replacement for oil-based products such as plastic. The objectives of the Department of Seaweed projects are to increase awareness of the origin of materials that we use and to restore the connection between our modern way of life and the plant and animal kingdoms. Lohmann experiments with seaweed from various parts of the world. She discovered that seaweed from Japan has very different properties than seaweed from Iceland. This difference in properties has consequences for products and the processing technology.

<u>Sea Me</u> (2017–ongoing) from Nienke Hoogvliet takes a different approach to generating awareness around the pollution of our seas and the resources we find in water ecosystems. Hoogvliet has developed a yarn out of natural sea algae, using seaweed pigments as dye. Sea algae grows more quickly and needs less nutrition than more traditional materials used in textiles, such as cotton. She combines the yarn with waste found in oceans, such as plastic fishing nets, to create handmade rugs.

The designers that are being explored in Salvage share a clear vision of nature as well as the passion to have meaningful impact and find solutions to crucial issues. All of the projects emphasize the importance of awareness and activating people. They look for alternatives to materials that have an impact on our climate or have a polluting effect on our environment. This search is one of the driving forces for some of today's generations of designers. In the projects described, we have seen that all applications and possibilities are examined and that the young generation of designers is not concerned exclusively with designing beautiful products. There is also an awareness that people are responsible for the consequences of using materials. Indeed, research into new applications and the consequences of the application fall under the designer's responsibilities.

The projects illustrate clearly that the design discipline is undergoing drastic changes. A multidisciplinary approach, the practice of tinkering, a multimedia concept, and the combination of design and research can be seen in many of the projects. All of the designers look at the bigger picture; they work on concrete solutions and applications but, at the same time, regard this as a starting point for building networks and communities.

The projects detailed in Salvage show that not only do people cause "the indelible marks left by humankind on the geological face of our planet"[13] but they also can prevent these scars from appearing in the first place.

1
Edward Burtynsky, "Anthropocene," accessed
February 13, 2019, https://www.edwardburtynsky.
com/projects/photographs/anthropocene/.

2
"Plastiglomerate," in *Wikipedia, the free encyclopedia*,
September 25, 2018, accessed November 2018
https://en.wikipedia.org/wiki/Plastiglomerate.

3
Trudie Carter, "Shahar Livne Uses Waste Plastic to
Create Lithoplast, a Precious Material of the Future,"
Dezeen, October 28, 2017, accessed November
2018, https://www.dezeen.com/2017/10/28/
shahar-livne-metamorphism.

4
"Creating Stronger Ties between the Earth's
Materials and Living Communities," Atelier NL,
accessed November 2018, http://www.ateliernl.com/
about.

5
"To See a World in a Grain of Sand," Atelier NL,
accessed November 2018, https://aworldofsand.com/.

6
Kirstie van Noort, "Latitude for Uniqueness:
Research, 2014–2016," accessed November 2018,
https://www.kirstievannoort.com/portfolio/
latitude-for-uniqueness.

7
"AIR-INK™," Graviky Labs, accessed November
2018, http://www.graviky.com/air-inktrade.html.

8
"Parley A.I.R. Strategy. The Plan that Can End
Plastic Pollution," adidas, accessed November 2018,
https://www.adidas.co.uk/parley.

9
"Facing Plastic Pollution," Parley, accessed
November 2018, https://www.parley.tv/oceanplastic.

10
"Cradle-to-Cradle Design," in *Wikipedia, the free
encyclopedia*, December 13, 2018, accessed November
2018, https://en.wikipedia.org/wiki/Cradle-to-cradle.

11
"Algae Lab. Can We Use Design to Bridge the Worlds
of Culture, Science and the Industry?" Atelier Luma,
accessed November 2018, https://atelier-luma.org/en/
projects/algae-lab.

12
"The Department of Seaweed Is a Trans-disciplinary
Platform for the Exploration of Seaweed as a
Sustainable Resource," Department of Seaweed,
accessed November 2018, https://www.department-
of-seaweed.com/.

13
Burtynsky, "Anthropocene."

Department of Seaweed: Living Archive,
2018-ongoing; Julia Lohmann (German, b.
1977), Violaine Buet (French, b. 1977),
and Jon Lister (New Zealander, b. 1977);
Seaweed and rattan; Dimensions variable

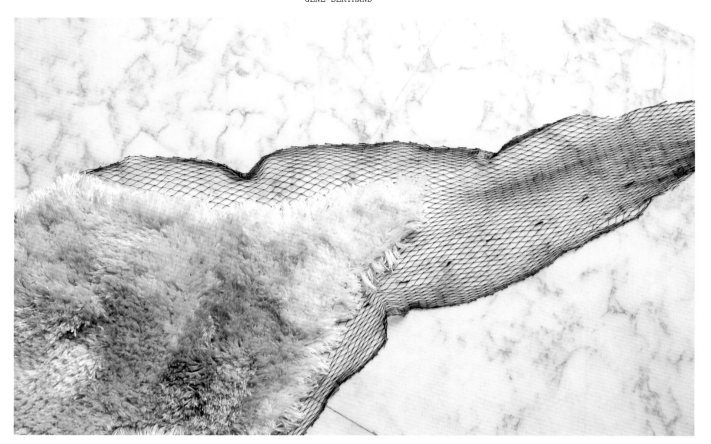

Sea Me, 2017-ongoing; Nienke Hoogvliet
(Dutch, b. 1989), Studio Nienke Hoogvliet
(Hague, Netherlands); Sea algae
yarn, fishing net; 60 × 140 cm (23.6 ×
55.12 in.)

Facilitate

In 1917, D'Arcy Thompson published his opus, *On Growth and Form*, a compendium of his studies of morphology. Thompson was a mathematical biologist. He analyzed the geometries of biological forms, theorizing that physical forces were more impactful to morphology than evolution. Forms found in nature could be understood by the mathematical principles that guided their growth. His descriptions and analysis, ranging from biological symmetries and cell division to Fibonacci spirals and fractals that shape natural forms, remain elegant and seminal across disciplines today, used as a core text in landscape architecture, biology, architecture, anthropology classes, and more. As architect Philip Beesley points out, "Thompson conceived of form not as a given, but as a product of dynamic forces that are shaped by flows of energy and stages of growth."[1]

Designers today are embracing the forces that facilitate growth, orienting and directing growth in the development of architecture, objects, and materials. The approaches are varied. Some are guiding growth itself—replete with biological rhythms and timescales—using cultivation, deposition, proliferation, and regeneration of living materials to grow architecture and objects. Others wield computational tools and parametric software that replicate natural growth processes—and hence natural forms—in order to create optimal structures that support ecosystem biodiversity. Still others partner with life scientists and tissue engineers to develop new materials and production processes using biological growth as a fabrication platform. If the methods differ, the intentions are the same: to enable nature.

On Guiding Growth and Form

Are we at the onset of an era in which objects become more grown than made? Where the industrial era largely eschewed biological growth and change in products and the built environment (its materials were concrete, steel, aluminum—impervious and impermeable to the forces of nature), the biological era embraces it. This isn't merely a turn of aesthetics, privileging the aesthetics of nature over the aesthetics of the machine. Designers are moving beyond nature as just an inspiration for form-giving and surface decoration, and are instead interested in facilitating nature itself by guiding and enabling growth. More than form-making or form-giving, the process is akin to form-guiding. It is a subtle and nuanced shift that at its foundation underscores the partnership between nature and designer. Nature isn't a mere resource. It is a collaborator.

The Bamboo Theater (2016) is a living structure hidden in the mountains of Hengkeng Village in remote China, about a six-hour drive southwest of Shanghai. With a rammed earth floor and seats made of stones, the open-air theater has walls of living bamboo that villagers bend and weave inward to form a vaulted space. The design uses the Mao Zhu bamboo of the mountain forest, which is known for its strength and resiliency. The Mao Zhu root system grows horizontally and interconnects underground to act like a building foundation. The bamboo shoots grow tall and bend under tension, but do not break. As new bamboo shoots grow along the perimeter, villagers weave them into the structure. Older bamboo shoots are removed. It is a lovely act of cultivation and pruning, tending to architecture.

The local Songyang County government commissioned architect Xu Tiantian, founder of the Beijing-based firm DnA_Design and Architecture, to create architectural interventions in many of the county's four hundred villages as part of its rural revitalization efforts. Xu spent years surveying the villages and talking with residents and officials to gather a deep understanding of each village's character. She describes her interventions as architectural

114

acupuncture, favoring small projects over large development to catalyze organic, local growth. The philosophy reflects the scale of the villages. The forms and materials are evocative of the local visual language rather than asserting a contemporary design aesthetic foreign to the landscape.

Xu found the Hengkeng Village itself, the location of the Bamboo Theater, to be like an organic system. Village residents work closely with nature and the resources that surround them—the bamboo forest, the craggy rocks from the mountains, the earth. Their ceremonies and theater traditions honor the elements and follow seasonal rhythms. Xu sought a gentle intervention, elevating the landscape and connecting to the village's history and identity. Facilitated by nature, the Bamboo Theater celebrates theater space and the importance of collective life in the village. It points to the balance that exists in treating nature like a partner rather than a resource, embracing its metabolism rather than fighting it to accommodate human needs. More than a static monument, the Bamboo Theater is an organic architecture, respecting the Earth and the materials it offers, embracing livingness, motion, and rhythm in a built structure.

From living bamboo architecture to salt stools, design can evoke nature's processes. Erez Nevi Pana's series of Bleached stools (2018) are effectively grown from salt. Nevi Pana is an Israeli designer who, having been raised on the grounds of a plant nursery, studied biology in school before attending the Design Academy Eindhoven in the Netherlands. His work treads lightly on the Earth. To create the stools, Nevi Pana crafts an improvisational stool from wood, covers it in loofah, and submerges it in the Dead Sea, which is so salinous it cannot support most forms of life (hence its name). The salt from the sea crystallizes on the loofah, a dense, fibrous nest of pockets and pathways, solidifying around the structure. The salt accumulates on the loofah over weeks that converge into months to become a jarring, beautiful evocation of the organic as ornate.

As a designer, Nevi Pana honors nature's own rhythms and processes in the creation of new work. With the Bleached stools, he acts as a guide for the mineral that is his source of exploration, not pushing the salt to do anything more or less than what it would when greeted with a substrate. Salt—once a mineral that was treated with reverence—now amasses in neglected white mountains in the desert, as Nevi Pana describes it,[2] the byproduct of the production of potash (a fertilizer) and bromine (a fire retardant) from the Dead Sea. The Bleached stools imbue the mineral with new value—as a crystalline totem. In Nevi Pana's hands, it is again revered.

Creating scaffolds to facilitate growth in objects is a gentle act. Designers guide form rather than assert it, accepting inconsistency and imperfection in the outcome. The practice stands in opposition to the rigors, perfection, and regimentation necessitated by industrial production, which stamps out copy after identical copy. Industrialization seemed largely to suppress nature, that force it displaced. Designers today are seeking the reverse: nature embraced.

Amy Congdon is a textile designer who grows cells over textile scaffolds, working at the intersection of tissue engineering and textile design. Inspired by Ellis Developments' embroidered implants for reconstructive shoulder surgeries (Figs. 1 and 2), Congdon's Tissue Engineered Textiles (2015–ongoing) explore how textile techniques—such as embroidery, crochet, and lace making—can be used to create scaffolds to guide cell growth. She has collaborated with Dr. Lucy Di Silvio, Professor of Tissue Engineering at King's College in London, to develop embroidered textiles on top of which bone or skin cells grow.

Tissue engineering is a field of study that applies biology and engineering to the growth of substitute and replacement tissue. A key focus of research is the design and fabrication of scaffolds that support new cell growth to rebuild a piece of organ or tissue. For instance, a surgeon could attach ligaments and tissue to various eyelets in the embroidered implant to orient cell growth. The implant would become populated with cells, which grow through, around, and between the embroidered fiber nest. Embroidered or crocheted fibers mimic fibrous arrays, such as protein matrices, found naturally in animals.

Fig. 1 Bioimplantable Device For Reconstructive Shoulder Surgery, 2004; Designed by Simon Frostick (British, b. 1956) and Alan McLeod (British, b. 1964); Textile designed by Peter Butcher (British, b. 1947); Developed by Ellis Developments Ltd. (Nottinghamshire, England, UK); Manufactured by Pearsalls Ltd. (Taunton, Somerset, England, UK); Polyester; Diam: 14.3 cm (5 5/8 in.); Cooper Hewitt, Smithsonian Design Museum; Gift of Ellis Developments Ltd., 2004-15-1

Fig. 2 Bioimplantable Device, 2004; Designed by Lars Neumann, W. Angus Wallace, and Dr. Alan McLeod; Textile designed by Peter Butcher (British, b. 1947); Developed by by Ellis Developments Ltd. (Nottinghamshire, England, UK); Manufactured by Pearsalls Ltd. (Taunton, Somerset, England, UK); Polyester; 10.3 1.7 cm (4 1/16 11/16 in.); Cooper Hewitt, Smithsonian Design Museum; Gift of Ellis Developments Ltd., 2004-15-3

Bamboo Theater, 2015-ongoing; Hengkeng
Village, Songyang County, Zhejiang
Province, China, completed 2015; Designed
by Xu Tiantian (Chinese, b. 1975), DnA_
Design and Architecture (Beijing, China,
founded 2004); Bamboo

Bleached (III), 2018; Erez Nevi Pana
(Israeli, active in Austria, b. 1983);
Salt-crystallized loofah over a wooden
structure; 65 × 58 × 58 cm (25 9/16 × 22
13/16 × 22 13/16 in.)

Bleached (II), 2018; Salt-crystallized
loofah over a wooden structure; 77.5 × 55
× 56 cm (30 1/2 × 21 5/8 × 22 1/16 in.)

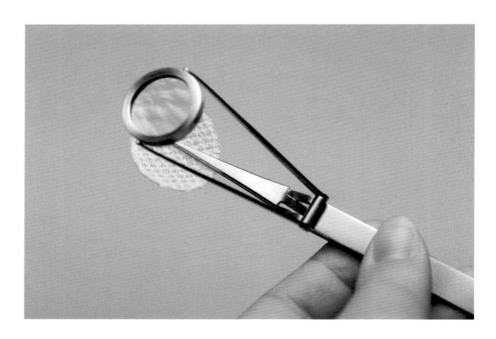

Tissue Engineered Textiles, 2015-
ongoing; Amy Congdon (British, active
in USA, b. 1986); Fixed mammalian
cells, silk, cellulose, acrylic, steel,
glass; Dimensions variable; With special
thanks to the Tissue Engineering and
Biophotonics Department, King's College
London, Design and Living Systems Lab and
Central Saint Martins UAL, Pelling Lab
University of Ottawa, and Modern Meadow

As Congdon tells us, "cells love structure to wind around and space to grow"[3]—whether inside or outside the body. Building on this research from the medical sector, Congdon uses textile techniques to create bespoke architectures that will guide the orientation and patterning of cell growth. Embroidery, lace-making, and crochet enable versatile, complex, and variable scaffolds, which Congdon and scientists seed with cells. To date, she has experimented with growing couture jewelry and fashion trimmings, such as a brooch and bangle bracelet, from skin and bone cells. But more than future fashion applications, Congdon's research points to convergences in design and science that could have practical applications as much as speculative ones. As part of her research, Congdon is developing new tools for designers to use in the laboratory. She has created a small embroidery hoop, about one inch in diameter, to help fasten cells onto a membrane. She has worked with a jeweler to redesign forceps to better manipulate tissue and fabric. And she has redesigned petri dishes to function as tissue molds, growing tissue in the shape of petals, for instance.

Biofabrication

Where Congdon is rethinking the petri dish, other designers working with biology are transcending it altogether. Biofabrication is the process of manufacturing materials with biology as the driving force. Organisms such as bacteria, yeast, mammalian cells, and fungi are harnessed as factories to grow products. As a field of research and study, biofabrication has evolved to integrate not just the life sciences, but collaborations between biology, tissue engineering, technology (such as 3D printing and additive manufacturing), and design. Research and development of biofabricated materials, techniques, and products take years, but ultimately point to a new material age where the objects around us grow, form, and degrade, enabled by design.

How are designers and architects wielding biofabrication? Ginger Krieg Dosier grows cement bricks. The process, which she and her partner Michael Dosier spent years researching and developing, emulates the growth of coral and seashells. Nature created the blueprint, and as Professor Patrick Rand, an advisor to Krieg Dosier's project, said, "She sparked the whole process by imagining that biochemistry could do in days what geological processes have taken millennia to accomplish."[4]

Krieg Dosier had long wondered how something hard and durable, like coral and shells, can grow underwater. As she discovered, a key component is calcium carbonate, the chemical compound that is also found in limestone—itself a primary component of cement. The Dosiers thus developed a process of mixing sand with nutrients and microorganisms—specifically, a strain of *Bacillus* bacteria that is naturally occurring and doesn't cause disease—to create a microenvironment that enables calcium carbonate crystals to grow around and between the grains of sand, hardening into the concrete bricks. Rather than the months or years it takes the process in nature, in the Dosiers' lab, it takes a few days.

Krieg Dosier turned the research she and her partner developed into a company called bioMASON, which offers ecologically sensitive construction materials to the architecture and building community. Traditional concrete bricks and masonry are made by intensively firing clay for days at more than two thousand degrees Fahrenheit, releasing extensive amounts of carbon into the atmosphere—7 percent of global carbon emissions.[5] The Biocement Bricks (2017–ongoing) take just a few days to reach full strength, at room temperature and without burning fossil fuels. Grown in molds, they can take varying shapes, textures, and colors, some resembling traditional bricks and paving materials, and others imbued with bioluminescence. The bioMASON bricks perform in the same way as traditional bricks for use in construction. Krieg Dosier has opened the company's first manufacturing facility, but imagines that in the future, the equipment can be put in shipping containers to allow the bricks to be grown anywhere, given that the process doesn't require much energy or a fuel supply.

Harnessing microbes enables us to synthesize renewable versions of existing materials and to make things in groundbreaking ways without the environmental impact of traditional production. In the hands of Natsai Chieza, microorganisms are collaborators in dyeing textiles, a process that is conventionally water intensive and highly polluting. Compared to the gallons of water used traditionally, only seven ounces of water are needed to dye two pounds of silk with microorganisms.[6] It is a significant difference.

Chieza has degrees in architecture and material futures. She began examining material systems that come from biology in collaboration with John Ward, Professor of Synthetic Biology for Bioprocessing at University College London, seeking to discover a more renewable material future. With the tools and expertise of Ward's lab, she developed methods of dyeing textiles with pigment-producing microbes such as *Streptomyces coelicolor*, a bacteria typically found in plant roots.

To create the bacteria-pigmented textiles, Chieza coats or submerges silk in a bacterial solution for about seven days in laboratory conditions. The bacterial cells act as factories to produce pigments, which Chieza catalyzes using specific nutrient environments. The color palette ranges from red to purple to blue, controlled through variables like time and acidity. The amount of oxygen impacts color proliferation. Patterns are created through targeted bacterial growth, systematically applied through techniques such as folding, silk-screening, twisting, clamping, or dipping the textile in the bacterial solution. Bacterial "glitches" become beautiful byproducts of the process. As Chieza points out, "Variation and adaptation are inherent to biology."[7]

Chieza's recent work, created during a creative residency at the biological engineering company Ginkgo Bioworks, includes experiments with refining techniques and scaling up incubation containment, which increases the cell count in the dyeing process to create larger patterned textiles. She has explored layering bacteria-pigmented colors. For the Assemblage series (2018–19), Chieza is designing the tools and protocols to print patterns on silk crepe and organza for garments whose construction optimizes the dyed patterns on the textiles. The resulting bacteria-dyed garments are ethereal. Their patterning is evocative of marbled landscapes, the colors of dusk and mixed berries.

Project Coelicolor (2018–19) will push Chieza's work further to explore uniform dyeing techniques, achievable only by maximizing the incubation dimensions. Chieza proposes this will lead to discoveries of a new, predictable biological dye process, replete with expanded aesthetics. What new parameters will emerge for facilitating the microbial growth and pigmentation? What new aesthetics and patterning will be possible? How can the bacteria-dyeing process be optimized to enable symmetric patterns and pigment expressions on uniformly dyed textiles? With continued discovery, Chieza is moving from proofs of concept to a scalable system of biofabricating textile dyes.

Assisting Natural Processes

Whereas Western culture is now open to adopting biological growth as a fabrication platform, Modernism sought to keep biological growth at bay, seemingly fearful of its encroachment. Nature, unpredictable and wild, was a force to control. Aesthetics of permeability and porosity were eschewed in favor of protective glazing and smooth surfaces. Yet preventing and abolishing biological growth has altered ecosystems and left a deeper footprint than we intended. Firms like Reef Design Labs, founded by Australian designer Alex Goad, design the material conditions to support growth and biodiversity.

Reef Design Labs works in marine habitats. Existing infrastructure and barriers in coastal environments, such as seawalls and jetties, are inhospitable surfaces for diverse ecosystems, consisting of smooth concrete that braces against waves and allows surface algal growth, but not much more. Organisms prefer crevices and notches, burrows and holes in which to grow and thrive. With this in mind, Reef Design Labs developed Eco-Engineered Seawall Tiles (2017–ongoing), which have varying parametric patterns and are made from marine concrete cast in 3D-printed molds for installation on existing seawalls.

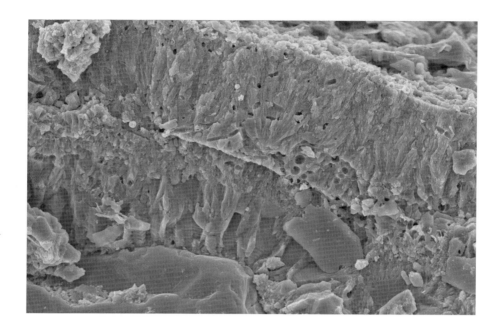

Biocement Bricks, 2017-ongoing; Ginger
Krieg Dosier (American, b. 1977),
bioMASON (Durham, North Carolina, USA,
founded 2012); Aggregate, bacteria,
nutrients, water, nitrogen, calcium;
Each brick: 5.72 × 40 × 1.9 cm (2 1/4 ×
15 3/4 × 3/4 in.)

↑
SEM (Scanning Electron Microscopy) image
of biocement (calcite polymorph) during
the production process

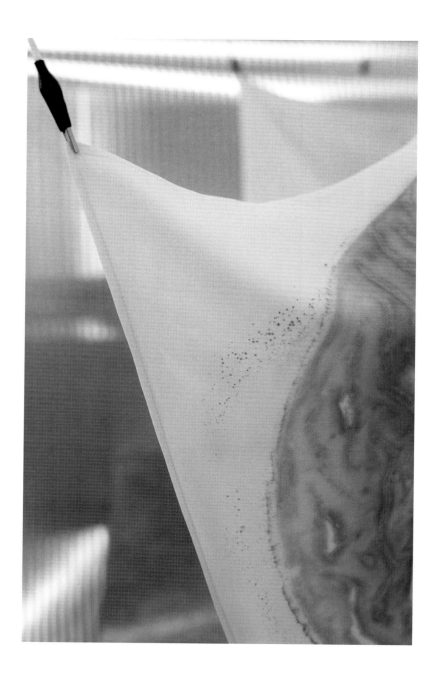

Project Coelicolor, 2017; Natsai
Audrey Chieza (British Zimbabwean, b.
1985), Faber Futures (London, England,
UK, founded 2017) in collaboration
with Ginkgo Bioworks and Professor
John Ward, Department of Biochemical
Engineering, University College London;
Silk, *Streptomyces coelicolor* pigment;
Dimensions variable

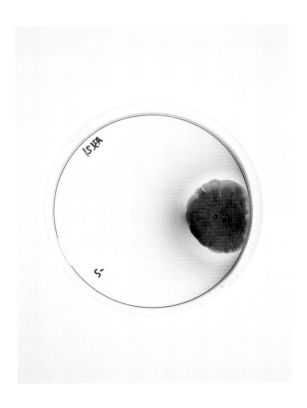

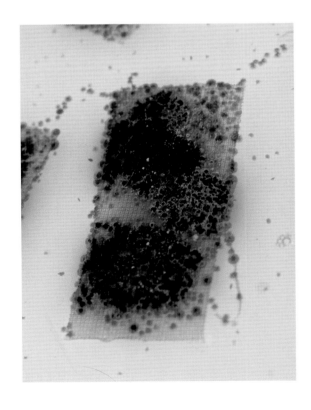

↓
Streptomyces coelicolor bacteria, 2017

Eco-Engineered Seawall Tiles, 2017-
ongoing; Alex Goad (Australian, b. 1989),
Reef Design Lab (Melbourne, Victoria,
Australia, founded 2014); 3D-printed
marine concrete; Each tile: 25 × 25 × 5
cm (9 13/16 × 9 13/16 × 1 15/16 in.)

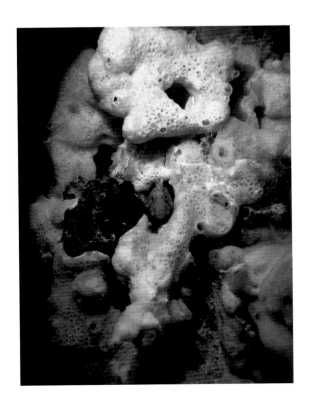

The structural features of the tiles—deep grooves, textures, and ridges, in varying pattern complexities—are important for growth. They promote an area's natural ecology by reestablishing native species populations. As forms, they suggest an aesthetic of permeability and porosity.

Initial tests in Sydney Harbor demonstrated that native species, such as blue gropers, bivalves, seahorses, and other crustaceans and aquatic plants, grew in the gaps and spaces of the Seawall Tiles. The tiles provided food and space to hide from predators, lay eggs, and shelter against storm waters. Reef Design Labs is partnering with the Sydney Institute of Marine Science on further research looking at which patterns attract what species. This way, the structural features of the Seawall Tiles can target organisms suitable to a particular habitat, maximizing the colonization of native species and leading to enhanced biodiversity. Whereas the individual tiles can be installed on existing seawalls, perhaps one day the irregularly shaped, parametric patterning will be applied to the design of the seawall surface itself. As Goad points out, humans will continue building into the marine environment. "How can we do that and build with nature and for nature?"[8]

Working with nature to passively enable its processes is also at the heart of Arturo Vittori's Warka Water Tower (2013–ongoing). The Towers harvest and collect water from the air. They stand more than thirty feet high, with a skirted canopy, each one a beacon in the remote, rural community it serves, where access to potable water is extremely limited. Vittori first installed a prototype Tower in the Ethiopian village of Dorze and named it after an endangered fig tree native to Ethiopia, the Warka. Warka trees are known for their prodigious shade and serve as a gathering spot for the local community. Vittori intended for the canopy of the Warka Water Tower to serve a similar purpose.

The idea of a passive device to harvest water from moist air is not new—modern examples of fog harvesters date to the 1980s—but Vittori's tower is. He and his team have spent years working on the design, iterating and prototyping to ensure its successful installation and implementation. Made of bamboo, a mesh netting, and hemp rope, the Warka Water Tower has a lattice structure and weighs only about 176 pounds, despite its height. It is low cost (approximately $1,000), with local residents erecting it on-site by hand. They need no machinery or scaffolding, which would limit the number of communities in which it could be installed. Once established, village residents use and maintain the Tower independently.

The Warka Water Tower collects rainwater directly in a holding tank. Water from fog and dew is harvested with a hydrophobic mesh textile, akin to a net. Vittori and his team optimized the mesh textile by increasing the number of filaments and decreasing the size of the holes between those filaments, in order to collect more airborne droplets of moisture. The droplets coalesce on the fog nets, just as a spider web catches dew on a cool, moist morning. The net's hydrophobic surface repels the harvested water, which slides off and is directed by a funnel to the holding tank. Important research into optimizing fog nets was undertaken by MIT scientists, the results of which inform designs like Vittori's. As the MIT researchers point out: "Nature has already done the hard work of evaporating the water, desalinating it, and condensing the droplets. We just have to collect it."[9] The water in the container passes through a tube that functions as a faucet, carrying it to those waiting on the ground. The Towers save community members—largely women and children—hours each day that would have been spent gathering potable water. The design enables not just water collection, but life.

Food Facilitators

Whether in remote, rural areas or in urban centers, a central question governing the future is: how will we ensure there is not just potable water, but enough food to eat? Controlled-environment agriculture is one approach, and it manifests in a variety of ways, from massive indoor vertical farms to personal desktop growth chambers. Plants grow hydroponically under photosynthetically optimal pink light, with ideal water levels and nutrients.

The plants need little to no pesticides. They grow three to four times as fast as they grow in traditional outdoor agriculture.[10] The plants and those who farm them don't have to contend with rainy seasons, droughts, or a late spring freeze.

Caleb Harper is pairing advancements in agricultural technology with an open-source ethos. He founded the Open Agriculture Initiative (OpenAg) at the MIT Media Lab to develop collaborative tools and platforms for agriculture. Among the platforms in development is the Personal Food Computer (2018–ongoing), an open-source growth chamber ideal for schools, educators, citizen scientists, makers, and more who are interested in exploring food production through experimentation.

The unit is a modular, twelve-inch cube, designed in collaboration with the OpenAg community to be inexpensive and easily deployable. Users download the blueprints, build, hack, and modify the Food Computer, which consists of sensors, a small fan, LED lights, and a single-board computer set to run open-source data. Those data are what OpenAg calls climate recipes. The "recipes" are developed by and shared among the community. They serve to maintain a climate in a box, controlling environmental variables such as carbon dioxide, temperature, humidity, light level, and dissolved oxygen. The Food Computer can also monitor and modify conditions to optimize plant growth, releasing nutrients and water or altering temperature according to the needs of a plant.

The climate recipes produce unique physical qualities—phenotypes—in the plant, varying color, size, flavor, yield, and nutrient density. OpenAg is aggregating the data and recipes into an open–source digital library. Users can create, download, and run climate recipes to produce desired phenotypes. Climate recipes could then be shared around the world to enable growers to optimally produce food depending on their needs and preferences. In effect, climate becomes decoupled from geography.

Agriculture is the oldest technology that manipulated life. Since the first agricultural revolution, when humans moved away from hunting and gathering to farm crop staples as food sources, we have been modifying crops. Agricultural production today is still largely constrained by industrial-era economics. As Harper explains, "information remains opaque, practices and metrics of production are largely unobtainable, and the ownership of physical and intellectual property is typically restricted to a minute percentage of the population."[11] By democratizing how we grow food and share information about it, OpenAg may help facilitate a new, networked agricultural revolution. Farming could become a digitally-shareable, decentralized activity, led by design.

Warka Water Tower, 2013-ongoing;
Arturo Vittori (Italian, b. 1971),
Architecture and Vision (Bomarzo, Italy,
founded 2003) and Warka Water Inc.
(Petaluma, California, USA, founded
2016); Bamboo, polyester mesh, polyester
cable, hemp rope

Personal Food Computer, 2018-ongoing;
Caleb Harper (American, b. 1982) and
Hildreth England (American, b. 1978),
Open Agriculture Initiative (OpenAg), MIT
Media Lab (Cambridge, Massachusetts, USA,
founded 1985); PVC, polycarbonate, LEDs,
electronics, sensors; Each unit: 30.48 ×
30.48 × 30.48 cm (12 × 12 × 12 in.)

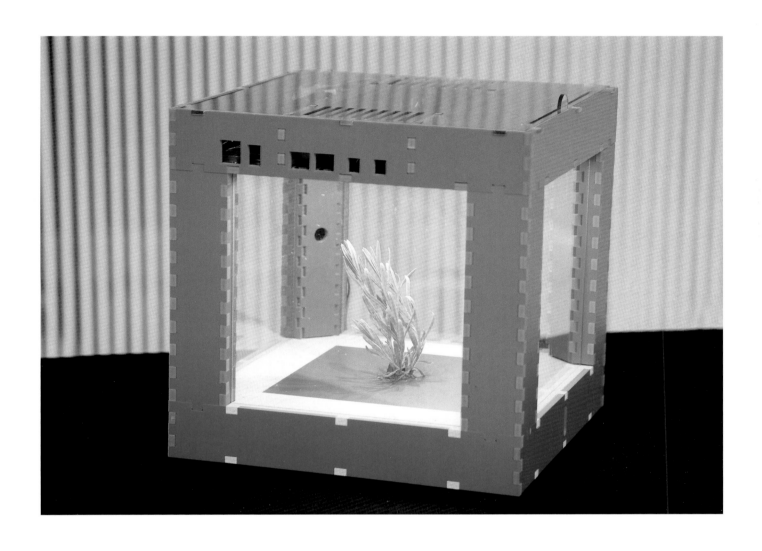

1
Philip Beesley and Sarah Bonnemaison, eds., *On Growth and Form: Organic Architecture and Beyond* (Halifax: Tuns Press, 2008), 7.

2
Annalisa Rosso, "Vegan Design—Or the Art of Reduction," *Domus*, April 10, 2018, accessed October 12, 2018, https://www.domusweb.it/en/design/2018/04/10/vegan-design-or-the-art-of-reduction.html.

3
Amy Congdon, interview by Andrea Lipps and Matilda McQuaid, May 16, 2018.

4
Kevin Ryan, "How This Startup Is Using Bacteria to Grow Bricks from Scratch," *Inc*, January 19, 2016, accessed October 31, 2018, https://www.inc.com/kevin-j-ryan/best-industries-2016-sustainable-building-materials.html.

5
"Cement Technology Roadmap Shows How the Path to Achieve CO_2 Reductions up to 24% by 2050," World Business Council for Sustainable Development, April 6, 2018, https://www.wbcsd.org/Sector-Projects/Cement-Sustainability-Initiative/News/Cement-technology-roadmap-shows-how-the-path-to-achieve-CO2-reductios-up-to-24-by-2050.

6
Christine Stevenson, "Garments of Interdependence: Natsai Audrey Chieza on Fashion, Design, and Synthetic Biology," *SinBioBeta*, June 14, 2018, accessed November 2, 2018, https://synbiobeta.com/news/garments-of-interdependence-natsai-audrey-chieza-on-fashion-design-and-synthetic-biology/.

7
Natsai Audrey Chieza, "Reflections from Ginkgo's First Creative-in-Residence," Ginkgo Bioworks, April 11, 2018, accessed November 2, 2018, https://www.ginkgobioworks.com/2018/04/11/creative-in-residence/.

8
Juliet Childers, "Reef Design Lab is Using 3D Printing to Save the Coral Reefs," Edgy Labs, October 17, 2018, accessed October 25, 2018, https://edgylabs.com/reef-design-lab-is-using-3d-printing-to-save-the-coral-reefs.

9
Gareth McKinley, an MIT professor of Mechanical Engineering who worked on the research, as quoted in David L. Chandler, "How to Get Fresh Water out of Thin Air," *MIT News*, August 30, 2013, accessed October 26, 2018, http://news.mit.edu/2013/how-to-get-fresh-water-out-of-thin-air-0830.

10
"Progressive Plant Growing Is a Blooming Business," NASA, April 23, 2007, https://www.nasa.gov/vision/earth/technologies/aeroponic_plants.html.

11
"Open Agriculture Initiative (OpenAg): Projects," MIT Media Lab, https://www.media.mit.edu/groups/open-agriculture-openag/projects/.

Naturing/ Renaturing

"We are already remaking ourselves and our world, retracing the steps of the original synthesis—redesigning, recoding, and reinventing nature itself in the process."
—George Church[1]

How do nature, synthetic biology, and design intersect? George Church and Alexandra Daisy Ginsberg speculate on the design of living systems and imagine life on Mars, traversing terrains of ethics, evolution, and notions of "better."

Dr. Alexandra Daisy Ginsberg is an artist-in-residence at Somerset House Studios, London, where she is continuing her cross-discipline approach to exploring human values that shape design, science, technology, and nature. Ginsberg has spent more than ten years researching synthetic biology and the design of living matter, resulting in her book, *Synthetic Aesthetics: Investigating Synthetic Biology's Designs on Nature* (MIT Press, 2014). In 2017, she completed "Better," her Ph.D. from the Royal College of Art, interrogating how powerful dreams of "better" futures shape the things that get designed, including in synthetic biology. Ginsberg has exhibited internationally, including at Cooper Hewitt, MoMA, the Museum of Contemporary Art, Tokyo, and the National Museum of China. She has been awarded the World Technology Award for design in 2011 and the London Design Medal for Emerging Talent in 2012.

Dr. George M. Church is Professor of Genetics at Harvard Medical School and Director of PersonalGenomes.org, which provides the world's only open-access information on human genomic, environmental, and trait data. His 1984 Harvard Ph.D. included the first methods for direct genome sequencing, molecular multiplexing, and barcoding, which led to the first genome sequence in 1994. His innovations have contributed to nearly all "next generation" DNA sequencing methods and companies. Church has coauthored 490 papers, 130 patent publications, and one book, *Regenesis* (Basic Books, 2014). In conjunction with the National Institute of Health, he co-initiated the BRAIN Initiative in 2011 and Genome Projects in 1984 and 2005 to provide and interpret the world's only open-access personal precision medicine datasets. His honors include the National Academy of Science Award, a National Academy of Engineering Award, and the Franklin Bower Laureate for Achievement in Science.

Alexandra Daisy Ginsberg   In my work, I investigate human relationships with nature and technology, which often manifest through design, and I'm fascinated by how synthetic biologists speculate about what to design. Among my latest projects is The Substitute, about the extinct northern white rhino— there are just two females left, both too old to reproduce. In the work, we bring a rhino "to life," but it exists only to pace around a virtual cabinet of curiosity. We are exploring the limits of lifelikeness, touching on questions about naturalness and context raised by promises of de-extinction of that species. You are actually exploring de-extinction with your attempts to revive the woolly mammoth. I'm curious: how do you think designing life fits into the practice of synthetic biology?

George Church   Among synthetic biologists, I tend to be more on the evolutionary end of the spectrum. A lot of synthetic biology started with computer scientists who believe that you can make synthetic biology be very deterministic, like computers—that you can program biology and then it does what you want it to do. I'm much more on the end of the highly experimental, where you want to make large libraries and figure out which things in the libraries work best for various purposes. It's a diversity-based goal. I think we should have more cultural diversity, we should have more biological diversity. That may mean we need to set new goals.

We use some sort of computer-aided design (CAD) for all early projects, as well as machine learning and accelerated evolution via large cellular and/or molecular libraries (100K to billion in size). We then select for the best designs, which can be hard to do in some science and engineering fields.

DG   How then do you see nature and humans' role in it?

GC   Humans are part of nature. Nature has renatured/terraformed Earth multiple times—for example, shifting oxygen gas from trace levels (a trillionth of current levels) to a maximum of 35 percent (toxic to most ancient life), then to 21 percent today. Humans have accelerated evolution to include STEM and cultural evolution. We will probably be able to finally move life from Earth to the rest of our solar system.

DG   This leads to a thought experiment I've proposed for our conversation to guide us through some of these questions about nature, synthetic biology, and design: how we might design from scratch a simplified working ecosystem and its components, freed from naturally evolved biology, to replace ecosystems that make Earth's environment livable. We could call this "renaturing." It fits into the instrumentalization of Earth's nature as "ecosystem services,"[2] a trend in policymaking that assigns value to things like air or water quality, soil fertility, and carbon capture by understanding them as services for human benefit.

I was fascinated by your statement from our earlier emails that "'Simplified' [ecosystems] seem rarely (and very temporarily) better or more adaptive, since long-term diversity wins." I'm curious: What does "better" mean when we are designing an ecosystem?

GC   "Better" is context dependent. Take transportation, for instance. Bicycles, oil tankers, rockets, or jets—each is better at transportation depending on what your goals are. I think the same is true for ecosystems. But with ecosystems, the goal is survival. So "better" is proportionate to failure—failure being that the entire ecosystem disappears. I don't think that's too flamboyant to say. So "better" is something that has a lower probability of failing. Maybe we're all going to fail eventually, in ten to the hundredth years from now when there's heat death of the universe, maybe not, but we seek to put that off as much as possible.

DG   That's a difference between biology and design: there is no best in biology; whereas in engineering and design, there is an "optimum." The goal in engineering is to find the best possible solution from what's available. How do you rationalize the process between the human idea of bettering, and biology just trying not to fail?

GC   Maybe I overstated. I don't deny that there is optimization in engineering. I also don't think that there is biological exceptionalism or that biology has a different set of rules than the rest of engineering. So if your engineering goal is to support a certain amount of weight on a bridge without it falling down, then you satisfy those specifications. Optimization might be making it more cost-efficient by reducing long-term wear and tear or reducing initial cost.

I think the same is true for living systems. Often there are short-term goals among living systems, but they are ultimately about long-term ecosystem survival. For example, a short-term goal might be to optimize the amount of biomass that you get per photon, which would be quite valuable to a variety of ecosystems. In practice though, in real ecosystems, it is very often not clear that's what's happening. Take the forest canopy, for instance. Its goal is not to maximize biomass. It is to minimize the number of photons that get down to the forest floor so the trees don't have any competition. Basically the trees are blocking more light than they consume, which means that many plants are more efficient than the trees.

So, if we want to think about ensuring human survival and maybe even well-being and happiness, we probably want to get off the planet so we can do experiments. Because on the planet, we are becoming a smaller and smaller world.

DG   Do you mean because of population growth?

GC   Because of transportation. We're now talking about rockets taking us from one side of the Earth to the other in an hour. Even if it takes twenty hours by plane, that's still remarkably small. We're mixing all the species very rapidly, getting hybrids and invasive species, and we're ending up with a very homogeneous soup. Any disease can spread very quickly. Any invasive species can dominate multiple environments. That's dangerous.

DG   How does humans leaving the planet fit as a goal for the species? Is it a short-term goal or a long-term goal for survival, like the trees in the forest trying to block photons from the forest's floor?

GC   Well, we are not blocking, we are enabling. We're sending seeds out into the wind and the water. The birds are dispersing the seeds, so I think that is a different strategy. There are many strategies, but to me that's a healthy one.

DG   I'm working on another project called The Wilding of Mars, which simulates "seeding" Mars with biology. Mars becomes a repository for the mechanism of life: we can watch life take Mars in a different direction, and Mars perhaps take life in a different direction. The ecosystems will be procedurally generated, like a computer game, and we may see new things created along the way.

It's an extrapolation of probably my favorite experiment, Richard Lenski's Long-Term Evolution experiment. [Lenski split one population of *E. coli* bacteria into twelve samples thirty years ago and, ever since, he has been tracking the evolution in each population, over tens of thousands of generations.] The difference about the world I'm making is that it is not for humans: humans would give the planet to other biology. How would we benefit if we could observe a new planet being biologized, but only from a distance? Do humans need to be on it, to be part of it?

GC   The challenge is that evolution is very, very slow. Lenski's experiments are slow and he is working with the fastest-growing organisms on Earth. If you study standard ecosystems, they barely evolve. The evolution we are seeing right now is a mix of extinction or hybridization. That's most of what is observable on Earth and probably the same sort of thing would be happening on Mars. I think Mars probably needs even more shepherding and farming than Earth because it's a far more violent, or anti-Earth-like environment. It's essentially a cold vacuum with lots of radiation.

DG   You mentioned [in earlier correspondence] that in principle, we could send as few as one species to Mars—humans. What would designing for primarily human habitation on Mars look like?

GC   At a minimum you can build housing that is resistant to the vacuum of Mars. But it would be like a spaceship with gravity that is 40 percent of Earth's gravity, similar to the structures in the book and movie *The Martian*. Those were flimsy compared to what you'd need to keep the vacuum out. But then once you establish what are essentially these terraria or greenhouses, you could raise the internal temperature and pressure and you would have what would be just like a biosphere on Earth.

DG   That's what I find so interesting. When we're talking about terraforming or making terrariums or greenhouses, it's always about replicating Earth elsewhere. This comes back to the thought experiment: how would you replicate Earth on Earth, or create a minimum viable ecosystem somewhere else?

GC   A biosphere isn't necessarily just like Earth. You can make them pretty wild and strange if you want. It's not so much our imagination as our ability to implement our imagination. We can imagine leaves that are black, that capture more wavelengths, but implementing that is a challenge.

DG   I assume that humans can't live alone on Mars. Do we need our microbiome to perform efficiently?

GC   It's not clear we need a microbiome. Many animals including humans can survive without a microbiome fairly efficiently. If you wanted to mimic our microbiome, you probably could with some molecules, as far as we know. But, in any case, the fact that we can survive without the entire microbiome is a proof of concept that we could get better and better. To some extent, we probably don't want human pathogens, so that would be an improvement.

DG   By "better and better," do you mean that we would be improving our efficiency without having to rely on other species?

GC   Well, the reduction or elimination of pathogens would likely be considered an improvement. We might still want to have some kind of struggle, but it could be a struggle that we're in more control of rather than just an arbitrary struggle, like having smallpox.

I think diversity is important to the conversation. Part of the challenge of naturing Mars depends on whether our intellectual creativity is up to the task of creating enough diversity for many generations. Or can we use some of the diversity that's developed through billions of years of evolution? Not because it's the only life that can exist, but because life has already gone through so much trial and error. Why throw it out until we've created additional diversity? We are capable of doing it, but it's not clear how much additional diversity we need, how much we want, and how much we are capable of making.

DG   I can't imagine living without trees, for instance.

GC   You could have trees on Mars—in fact, you might even be able to have taller trees because of the lower gravity. The water would go higher, there'd be less force pulling it down, so you might be able to get trees taller than a giant redwood. They would just have to be in a container that could survive the vacuum on the outside.

DG   If we're imagining ourselves devoid of other species, would we still be a "natural" species? During *Synthetic Aesthetics*, a research project that brought together synthetic biologists, social scientists, and artists and designers, my coauthors and I spent ages debating whether synthetic biology should be defined as designing life, nature, or biology. I'm curious what you think about these distinctions.

GC   I see nature as the entire universe(s) throughout time. It is not specific to biology. Forces of nature can be extreme and can include intelligence.

DG   So if we are a solo species off on Mars, are we still natural? Or do we need to operate in an ecosystem with other organisms to be natural?

GC   I think "natural" is one of these words that's used in many different ways. Natural is sometimes used colloquially to mean the way that things were when my grandparents grew up. That is a historical reference—since we're a changing species, we're always doing something unnatural in the next generation. For example, cars are unnatural. They weren't found in nature when the first human walked on the Earth, but they have become part of nature, in that everything is part of nature.

So if we choose to have a planet that has only humans on it, hopefully we will still have the planet Earth, which has a lot of diversity on it. If we colonize Mars, we've increased diversity, we haven't decreased it, so nature is now bigger, more complex. We now have a set of humans that can somehow survive without anything else. If we then start designing organisms that can replicate without carbon on Mars—let's say we want to build cities faster, and so we make little replicators that take the silicon, iron, and oxygen from the soil and make cities that resist the pressure difference—then we've added a few new species that are wildly different, and therefore have increased the diversity of our solar system. And I suspect that's what we'll do.

There will be many economic and artistic motivations to increase diversity, especially once we get off the planet. On Earth, I think there's a lot of pressure for us to be the same. We're cooped up in this little room, and the more we're bouncing off the walls and doing wacky things, the harder it will be from a social perspective.

DG   Isn't that just human nature? Isn't that how animals behave? Will we do the same anywhere?

GC   It's not bad, it's just that there are different criteria when you are in a small container rather than a large diluted one. When humans migrated to North America over 13,000 years ago, there was vast space without any humans in it. On the other hand, when it's winter and you've got twenty people in one room and there's nowhere to go, you better be more well-behaved than if you're a human that is a hundred kilometers away from the next human, where you can just go do whatever you want. You can set the forest on fire and you are the only one who is going to suffer, you and the animals. There are different rules for different densities of people. Right now, we tend to be at a very high density—it's estimated that somewhere between 57 percent and 84 percent of the world is in what would be called a city—and so we start having the social norms of high-density urban life.

DG   Are there other ways that we could use the design of biology on Earth to mitigate that?

GC   It's very hard to dilute all of us. If we spread the 7.5 billion people evenly all over the planet, it probably wouldn't be a good thing for the environment, or the people. We are, for the most part, a highly gregarious species. We're a lot more social than most species. I think we're kind of in the category of mice and passenger pigeons. They're comfortable sitting on top of each other.

If you go to another planet and this experiment starts to fail, you'd better hope that your rockets still work or that the thing that's failing doesn't also impact your ability to leave the planet, or else the entire colony will die. But the interesting thing about colonies, whether in space or on Earth, is that you could make a colony that is an improvement along one of these engineering axes. For instance, we could make a colony that never gets infectious diseases. That's something that almost nobody on the planet has experienced. Nobody makes it through their life without an infectious disease, but you could make a colony on Earth where there are no sick days.

DG   When we talk about survival of the human species, and if the goal of designing biology is for humans, that means humans are at the top of the hierarchy and we've got to maximize human life above other lives? What are the ethics of this practice?

GC   Ethics can be considered the very long-term safety of our species, or life in general. We may be unsatisfied with "Nature, red in tooth and claw," because life or intelligence could destroy itself (or allow itself to disappear). We might aspire to prevent or delay this.

So it's not just because we are humans, it's not just selfish. It's because we haven't yet found a species that's capable of helping other species get off the planet. For example, even if whales are smarter than we are, which is possible but speculative, they haven't yet shown the ability to help the sequoias get off the planet, while humans could get the sequoias off the planet.

DG   Maybe the whales know the sequoias want to hang out on Earth.

GC   Some of them hang out on Earth where they can get hit by a meteor and go extinct, and some of them can go to Mars where they can escape the meteor. So the whales are just looking at the short-term benefits for the sequoias, they're not actually looking for the long-term benefits of the sequoias. So, even if you don't like humans, pick your species. Save the whales, save the trees, whatever it is. Humans are in the best position to save those species.

DG   A speculation for another day! But I'm still worried about the trees on
Mars not getting to enjoy a livable atmosphere.

GC   They could definitely have a livable atmosphere. We can give them whatever atmosphere they want.

DG   Not without mechanical life support. I feel the same way about humans,
which is why I'm not volunteering to go Mars. I don't like the idea of my
support apparatus suddenly stopping working, and that's it. I've evolved to
work on Earth.

GC   Your apparatus can stop working on Earth as well. A million people die
every year from automobile accidents. Some would argue that's more predictable, but if you went to Mars and there were no pathogens, I would argue that
that's more predictable than on Earth, when you never know what epidemic is
going to wipe you out.

DG   But the radiation? I live in a temperate climate in London which is pretty
livable, whereas Mars would be like scuba diving in a freezer.

GC   Let's take you up on that. Say we built a large terrarium, so large that
you can't actually see the edges of it, and it has London weather. You can have
exactly how much fog you want, or you can get rid of the fog if you're tired
of it. How are you going to know when you are in London or on Mars, aside
from gravity?

DG   Well, I can leave whenever I want.

GC   You can't leave Earth right now.

DG   I feel like I am tethered to Earth, and I like that. But that's a good point.

GC   But, how would you know that you're tethered? Let's say, we've simulated New York, and London, and the airline ride between these. Let's say you
go to sleep, we take you to Mars, and then . . . What's the test to determine
that you are on Mars, other than gravity? Actually, we can even fake gravity, if
need be, with centrifugal forces.

DG   Only if you come against the door . . . then you would know.

GC   I see a door behind you right now. How do you know that outside that
door there's not a vacuum? Somebody moved your house while we were having
this conversation, and I would not recommend that you open that door.

DG   It's a good point. I've become my rhino, trapped in a box, not knowing
it's a box. But I still choose Earth. Maybe I'm unadventurous, or just really like
the trees. Or I feel like I belong here.

GC   It was only recently that people did move around. Most people would die
within a hundred meters from where they were born. There were all these little
communities where you would basically be born, grow up, and die, in a little
town or even just your family hut, with your little tribe. They could have said,
"I'm trapped. I can't go to Egypt, I can't go to Singapore," but they didn't
even know about those. All they knew about was their little village, and they
were pretty happy. They had goats, that was their whole universe.

DG   I'm not antiprogress. I'm not advocating that the past was necessarily
better. But if we're talking about timescales, do you think there is a time frame
that we should aim for when it comes to human ambitions—is it about goals for
benefitting us in our lifetime, or for future generations?

GC   I think an asteroid could hit us any year. It may have a mean time of a
hundred million years, but you have bad scenarios. It could happen sooner
than that. I'm a big believer in having multiple backups. I think we need to
go to Mars, Venus, and ideally have some colonies that are getting out of the
solar system. And soon, because we don't know when a bad scenario is going
to happen.

Erin Freedman (from Cooper Hewitt's curatorial team)   This is such an imag-
inative recreation. How do you literalize what Earth on Mars, or elsewhere,
could look like when you're thinking about wilding a planet? How does that
materialize in experiments that you would do? A lot of people think of design
as a kind of plan. All of the stages and processes in between are malleable and
can shift and move, but there's an intention that's set.

GC   Well, you could start by asking what's wrong with species on Earth. You
might say pathogens are a problem. It's painful to watch animals and humans
get these horrible diseases, so that's something we can try to fix elsewhere.

Making us resistant to pathogens is an enhancement, but you
could go even further. What would it take for us to survive in a different

142

environment, like space, or like Mars? That would be a completely new set of design criteria, where you do your best to design in classical engineering, but you have this advantage with biology that you can make literally billions of different organisms. If they're small, you could make them very inexpensively and see how they do at the new tasks, or at the old tasks. So that could be part of the deal. If you wanted to get more functional diversity—not just geographical, or aesthetic, or genomic diversity—but you actually wanted new functionality, you'd have to dream up new functions.

DG   It's fascinating to consider: How do visions become real; how do different kinds of synthetic biologists dream of different "betters" and how are those different visions manifested in different kinds of biological things? What might a future "renaturing" look like, and what species, apart from humans, would benefit?

GC   There is truly no limit to this conversation, and probably no limit to our minds. I think a hundred thousand words could be a temporary starting point.

1

George M. Church and Ed Regis, *Regenesis: How Synthetic Biology Will Reinvent Nature and Ourselves* (New York: Basic Books, 2012), prologue, accessed at http://www.regenesisthebook.com/?p=4.

2

Millennium Ecosystem Assessment, "Ecosystems and Human Well-Being: Synthesis" (Washington DC: Island Press, 2005), accessed at http://www.millenniumassessment.org/documents/document.356.aspx.pdf.

Remedia
Nurti

Simulate
Salvage
itate

Augment

Remediate
Nurture

erstar

imulate

Sa

aciliate
Augment

Augmentation yields enhancement, making something greater than it was before. How might we push nature's capabilities to enhance objects, buildings, even ourselves, unifying design with the environment? The first Aguahoja (2017–19)[1] pavilion, which stood more than sixteen feet tall, demonstrated such unification, acting as a beacon to what Neri Oxman calls "design-inspired nature." Supported by a white scaffold resembling a leaf's vascular network, the pavilion's skin consisted of panels that were 3D printed from a biocomposite material originating from plant cellulose and chitosan. Chitosan is made from chitin, which is found in the hard outer shells of many invertebrates, including shrimp. Chitin is the world's second-most abundant biopolymer after cellulose. In shrimp and other shellfish, chitin varies in stiffness and elasticity throughout the organism's shell to optimize its functionality in response to environmental conditions. Oxman and her team from the Mediated Matter group at MIT applied this underlying optimization to the computation, design, engineering, and fabrication of the pavilion's panels.

Oxman designs with nature. As she explains, she seeks "the logic of formation rather than the description of form,"[2] with nature not only inspiring and informing her work but embedding it. Oxman studied medicine before training as an architect and earning a Ph.D. in design computation from MIT, where she founded the Mediated Matter group at MIT's Media Lab. Her projects envision a material world in which there is no separation between product and natural environment. Oxman's explorations start with a natural phenomenon—butterfly wings, the undersides of mushrooms, silkworms, or shrimp shells. She and her collaborators might extract a mathematical law that underlies the phenomenon, develop algorithms to replicate it, and calibrate new fabrication tools to construct it.

For the Aguahoja project, the team spent years experimenting with the chemistry of the biopolymer compositions to optimize optical and mechanical properties. Oxman's team developed a 3D-printing extrusion method that could follow a generative surface pattern to vary the stiffness, resiliency, and color in a panel. When the printing process resulted in air bubbles in the output artifacts, they seeded the air bubbles with photosynthetic microorganisms that could capture carbon and convert it to sugar or biofuel, augmenting the natural environment.

Oxman is unlocking nature's material intelligence, integrating it with engineering, computation, and digital fabrication to create, in her own words, "a unity of physical and digital matter."[3] She coined the term "material ecology" to describe this new design paradigm, which marries material properties and expression, environmental context and constraints, and fabrication methods in the creation of responsive forms. How might we recast objects at the product or building scale to become part of their ecosystem? Rather than the industrial era's "world of parts" assemblies, agnostic to their ecosystems and static in their function and performance, how can materials, design, and fabrication for the digital and biological era become more continuous in their properties and performance? How might we augment objects and buildings with biological materials so that they are not just supportive of their ecosystem but enhance their host environments?

Toward a New Paradigm

Humans have long sought to push nature's capabilities in order to enhance and optimize conditions for our existence. Design is a fundamental instrument in these efforts, perhaps among the oldest and most spontaneous of human pursuits. The earliest farmers crossbred wheat plants to enhance pest resistance and longevity. Industrialists resurrected carbon buried deep in the ground in order to power our lives and augment living conditions. As industry displaced nature, the natural world became a source of inspiration for some and a free commodity to be wielded for others. Undoubtedly, the results of unfettered exploitation and disregard for nature underlay the urgency of our current era. Where once we augmented the environment with static products and buildings to enhance our existence, we now seek to augment materials, objects, and the built environment to enhance nature.

The consilience of biology, design, engineering, and technology enables us to harness science and translate technology through design in wholly new ways. Design acts as a connecting point, serving as an interface between abstract ideas in science or technology and real life. The augmentation of nature itself—as material, as biology, and as system—occurs through collaborations with designers, scientists, coders, and engineers. Advances in neuroscience, computer science, and bioengineering enable innovative modes of performance and functionality. But augmentation needn't yield only technological advancement in its pursuits. Augmentation arises as well through the implementation of ancient and historical technologies, which designers put to use in new ways.

For his Tree of 40 Fruit (2008–ongoing), artist Sam Van Aken uses centuries-old grafting techniques to combine multiple fruits in a single tree. Grafting is the fusion of plant parts. A bud is cut from a donor tree, inserted into a slit in another tree, and bound with tape. The slit heals around the bud, which continues as new growth.

Discovered around the first millennium BCE, grafting was a pivotal technology that enabled and likely influenced the movement of temperate fruits across the world—from Central Asia to Europe and eventually to the United States.[4] As industrial fruit production took hold, growers cultivated single-variety fruits like apples or peaches, privileging varieties for how well they shipped and displayed in a grocery aisle. For example, of more than three thousand peach varieties available, only around one hundred are now grown commercially in the United States.[5]

In a single tree, Van Aken preserves dozens of heirloom and rare fruit varieties. He puts more delicate varietals, like cherries and apricots, in the center of the tree, surrounded by more vigorous fruits, like plums and peaches. He maps a tree's grafts with hand-drawn sketches that are color-coded to the blossom seasons.

To date, Van Aken has mapped more than two hundred and fifty fruit varieties. He calls it a "comprehensive timeline of when [the varieties] blossom in relationship to each other. In this way, I can design a tree."[6] Apples, pears, and plums grow and blossom alongside peaches, cherries, and apricots in a gradient of crimson, pink, and white. The Tree of 40 Fruit collapses an orchard of fruit trees into a single tree, wresting fruit production from an ethos of monoculture. Each tree is a beautiful mutant.

DIY Biology

Biology as Technology
CRISPR-Cas9 is perhaps the most disruptive and revolutionary technology today. It is a naturally occurring and programmable biological system that enables us to design genomes at the level of DNA. If a genome is akin to an organism's instruction manual, then the language in which that instruction manual is written is DNA. There are mistakes in our instruction manuals, in our genomes, that manifest as disease, genetic mutations, neurodegenerative or chronic conditions like sickle cell anemia, cancer, AIDS, heart disease, Parkinson's, Alzheimer's, even allergies. With CRISPR-Cas9, we can manipulate, engineer, and design DNA to our choosing to remedy such "errors." CRISPR-Cas9 enables scientists to alter the genome of almost any organism with incredible precision and finesse, potentially ending not just disease, but even hunger and pollution.

Humans have been grafting, selectively breeding, and augmenting nature for millennia to wield oranger carrots, flatter bulldog faces, and vitamin-enriched rice. We have been modifying genes long before we knew what a gene was, albeit the processes and results were slow to materialize, often steered by nature's own rhythms—the growth cycles of plants or the gestation period of animals. Advances in science and technology have quickened the pace of progress. What took nature billions of years to perfect, we may unlock in a generation. We enhance and refine nature, plucking from DNA the characteristics optimal to our survival and preferences.

At the turn of the twenty-first century, the democratization of biology began taking root with the availability of inexpensive equipment and enthusiast communities connected over the Web. With advancements in gene-editing tools, such as CRISPR-Cas9, and the accessibility of DNA and RNA material, DIY biology continues to deepen. Akin to biohacking, the practice takes biology outside conventional sites like universities, institutions, and

Aguahoja, 2017-19; Neri Oxman (Israeli,
active USA, b. 1976), The Mediated
Matter Group, MIT Media Lab (Cambridge,
Massachusetts, USA, founded 2010);
Chitosan, cellulose, pectin, acetic acid,
glycerin, water; Dimensions variable

For full caption information,
see page 239.

Tree of 40 Fruit, 2008-ongoing; Sam Van
Aken (American, b. 1972); Cultivar tree
with grafts; Dimensions variable

↑
Trunk taken from an heirloom plum tree
that shows the transition of graft
and trunk.

The therapeutic results are promising. The possibilities for unintended consequences are vast.

The CRISPR-Cas9 system was introduced to the world when scientists Jennifer Doudna, Emmanuelle Charpentier, Martin Jinek, and their colleagues published their landmark *Science* paper in 2012.[16] While researching archaea (ancient microbes that are descendants of the earliest life forms) and yeast bacteria, they noticed unusual sequences of nitrogen bases (informally A, T, C, G) in the DNA. The odd sequences were palindromes, the same front to back as back to front, and were clustered together in regular patterns. They named the sequences Clustered Regularly Interspaced Short Palindromic Repeats, or CRISPR for short.

Scientists discovered these CRISPR sequences to be one part of an adaptive immune system by which the bacteria fight viruses. Bacteriophages ("phage" comes from the Greek *phagein*, meaning "to eat, devour") are viruses that infect bacteria. The phages attack bacteria in order to insert their own DNA, replicating within the bacteria. Bacteria that survive the attack store part of the phage's DNA in their own genetic code as a DNA archive—these are the CRISPR sequences. When the phage tries to attack again, the bacteria uses the DNA archive to make an RNA copy, known as a guide RNA, which is paired with a CRISPR-associated (Cas9) protein, the second part of the system. The Cas9 protein uses the guide RNA to scan and compare the bacterial DNA against the RNA copy, looking for the phage invader. When it finds an exact match, the Cas9 protein cleaves both strands of the virus DNA, rendering it silent. It is a precise system, akin to a DNA surgeon.

Potently, the CRISPR-Cas9 system is programmable. Scientists can synthesize guide RNA to search for any DNA sequence they choose. Once the CRISPR-Cas9 system locates and cleaves the targeted DNA, it can be left as is—silent—or it can be repaired using a gene editor to introduce a new, functioning sequence. The system allows live cells to be edited across the spectrum of living things—microorganisms, plants, animals, and humans. As its pioneers state, it is capable of "considerable potential for gene-targeting and genome-editing applications." CRISPR-Cas9 is effectively a programming tool that enables human-designed biology.

To date research teams have rendered cells impervious to the HIV virus,[17] developed high-yield and more productive crops,[18] and stored a digital GIF in DNA (Fig. 1).[19] One potential application of CRISPR includes resurrecting extinct species. Harvard geneticist George Church and his lab are using CRISPR-Cas9 technology to create a hybrid elephant-mammoth embryo by adding the genetic material of a woolly mammoth to the genome of an Asian elephant. They will implant the hybrid embryo into an elephant and plan to bring it to term.

The technology has its roots in design. More than an end product, design is a process, a mindset, and an activity. Design is something that humans do to the world, seeking to enhance, optimize, augment, facilitate, and translate nature and advancements. As Church tells us, he considers himself a designer within the medium of synthetic biology.[20] The mechanism and material is biology. The approach is design.

Fig. 1 A still image (left) of the galloping mare from Eadweard Muybridge's 1887 *Human and Animal Locomotion* series is next to a still image (right) taken from information encoded into bacterial DNA and recovered using CRISPR by Seth Shipman et al. at Harvard Medical School in 2017.

industrial research labs and into community and at-home labs where professional and amateur scientists tinker with biology at relatively low cost. For many, it carries the same independent ethos as that of garage tech entrepreneurs from the 1970s and 80s. Community biohacking labs like GenSpace in New York and BioCurious in California, for instance, are self-funded facilities that retain their independence to focus on research of their choosing.

Many biohackers and DIY biologists believe that distributing biological knowledge and technology, rather than centralizing biology in universities or profit-driven labs, can lead to positive results. Among them is Josiah Zayner, a biologist with a Ph.D. in molecular biophysics who worked in NASA's Synthetic Biology program. Zayner is now the Founder and CEO of The Odin, a company that seeks to put genetic design in the hands of consumers. He creates mail-order kits that contain the tools necessary for molecular and genetic engineering, replete with sample experiments and live microorganisms.

Among the kits offered is a basic <u>DIY Bacterial Gene Engineering CRISPR Kit</u> (2015–ongoing) to introduce gene-engineering techniques to beginners. Gene engineering, also referred to as genetic engineering, involves the purposeful modification of an organism's characteristics by manipulating its DNA. The DIY CRISPR kit includes everything from petri dishes and pipettes to nonpathogenic *Escherichia coli* bacteria and Cas9 plasmids. There are enough materials to conduct five experiments, designed to modify the DNA of *E. coli* using the CRISPR-Cas9 system. The aim is to demonstrate how CRISPR can be used to enable *E. coli* to survive and grow in conditions where normally it would die.

The kits act as educational tools, intended for teaching or home environments. According to Zayner, the kits help people become DNA literate.[7] They provide access to the knowledge and materials needed to conduct biological experiments, expanding the number of people equipped to conduct personalized experiments while stoking fears of unintended consequences or misuse.

Augmented Organisms, Enhanced Bodies

In 2017, Zayner injected himself with DNA that he had engineered to give himself bigger muscles. The experiment failed, but it raised the specter of interest in using CRISPR-Cas9 technology for human augmentation.[8] Body augmentation is not new. We have long enhanced ourselves with accessories and clothing, from colored contact lenses and hair extensions to prostheses and sunglasses. But a new wave of CRISPR-enabled augmentation portends an unknown future. Will we one day use genetic design to become smarter, stronger, ageless, or without disability? What does it mean when our immutable characteristics become mutable? For all the ways in which we partner with biology, using its technology to enhance our own nature is perhaps among the most inherently human and potentially destabilizing acts.

Out of these practices emerge artists and designers whose critical and speculative work questions, provokes, and probes synthetic biology and the growing fetishization of technological approaches to life. Oron Catts and Ionat Zurr are leaders in the field, having established The Tissue Culture and Art Project in 1996, hosted by SymbioticA in the School of Anatomy, Physiology and Human Biology at the University of Western Australia. Using biology and living tissues, their work questions the manipulation and commercialization of biological systems, confronting ideas of scientific advancement and the complexities of our relationship to life and nature.

<u>BioMess</u> (2018–ongoing), their latest project, is composed of two parts. The first consists of specimens on loan from natural history museums. Catts and Zurr work closely with museum curators to select specimens based on unusual characteristics that confound traditional notions of bodies, reproduction, or gender. Specimens at a 2018 installation at The Art Gallery of Western Australia, for instance, included sponges, which lack internal organs, a digestive tract, and nervous and muscular systems; several genera of sea stars, whose bodies can lose and regrow limbs, even regenerating a second body from a lost limb; and seahorses, whose males carry and deliver young. The

DIY Bacterial Gene Engineering CRISPR
Kit, 2015-ongoing; Josiah Zayner
(American, b. 1981), The Odin (The
Open Dictionary Institute) (Oakland,
California, USA, founded 2013); Plastic,
glass, rubber, microorganisms

BioMess, 2018-ongoing; Oron Catts
(Australian, b. Finland, 1967) and Ionat
Zurr (Australian, b. United Kingdom,
1970), The Tissue Culture and Art Project
(Perth, Australia, founded 1996);
Incubator, hybridoma cells, taxider-
mied specimens

specimens represent exceptional and peculiar adaptations found in the animal kingdom, their features and functions having evolved in response to specific environmental contexts. As oddities, the specimens illustrate the specificity of nature: life is context dependent.

What does it mean when we construct life independent of context? In the second part of BioMess, Catts and Zurr design a semi-living object in collaboration with local biology labs. Life becomes raw material. The object consists of hybridoma cells from two cross-kingdom species fused into one cell, a practice currently employed in synthetic biology. Dependent on an incubator to sustain them, semi-living objects are liminal life forms that deride the biotechnology used to create them. As Catts tells us, in order for biologists to attain some level of control over living systems, the life forms need to be isolated and reduced to their component parts as much as possible, in essence privileging information over context. As Catts asserts, "it is DNA chauvinism."[9]

The project threads the Enlightenment's quest to understand nature by means of controlling it with today's pursuit to commodify it. Seventeenth-century collectors filled cabinets of curiosities with unusual specimens from exotic locations, signifying an awe of nature, but the assembly and collection of those specimens also evoked ownership and status. With the BioMess semi-living organism, we substitute the cabinet of curiosity for the bioreactor. We push nature to novel and unforeseeable ends.

Biology remains a frontier for exploration. Despite concerns over misuse and unintended consequences, progress in biotechnology and human augmentation has important therapeutic goals as well. Eyeglasses enhance vision. A stent improves blood flow. The promise of gene editing is that it can solve disease and mutation. Advances in science continue to reverberate into design, allowing us to partner with biology in pioneering ways to repair and enhance human faculties. Chuck Hoberman, Richard Novak, Elizabeth Calamari, and Donald Ingber are leading an interdisciplinary team at the Wyss Institute for Biologically Inspired Engineering at Harvard University to explore how the microsystems capabilities of Organs-on-Chips devices can translate to building three-dimensional organs, in this case a kidney.

Organs-on-Chips (Fig. 2) are microengineered devices developed by scientists at the Wyss Institute at Harvard University to recapitulate the function of human organs aimed at better predicting drug safety and efficacy, enabling development of new therapeutics, and advancing personalized medicine. Living cells line the channels of a transparent polymer chip, which is about the size of a computer memory stick. The Wyss team is evolving the ideas and technologies of the Organs-on-Chips to explore three-dimensional organs, but if the surface area of a chip is sixteen square millimeters, the surface area of a kidney is one square meter. A massive change in scale is needed to bring the technology in line with a fully functioning kidney. Hoberman, who has built a career making transformable, functional structures using geometry and origami-like principles, suggested a closed and inflatable origami structure. At its most basic, an origami structure needs "hinges" that are flexible and "panels" that are stiff to enable folding. When inflated, the entire surface area of the Origami Membrane for 3D Organ Engineering (2018–ongoing) would need to fold dynamically as part of its manufacturing process. According to Hoberman, the central challenges to achieving the functionality of a kidney in a meter of surface area are developing a pattern that has enough folds in it, finding a material of the correct thickness, and ensuring the ability to be dynamically folded into position without damaging the delicate biological surface.[10]

The team is designing the piece as an entirely soft device, made of membranes and hydrogels, initially intended for use outside the body. Degradable and porous membranes electrospun from biocompatible materials—like dense fiber nests—encase the kidney cells. The membranes are flexible, with gel panels that are stiff. Initial tests have demonstrated the viability and functional outputs of the kidney cells and membranes.

To test the origami and fabrication method, Hoberman and Calamari are using proxy materials—degradable thermoplastic and UV-cured resin—with mechanical properties similar to those of the biocompatible materials. Calamari, a bioengineer who specializes in fabrication techniques for tissue

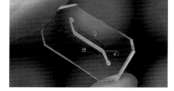

Fig. 2

engineering, adapted a standard industrial laser cutter to seal the degradable thermoplastics. By widening the laser beam to run it purposely out of focus, she heats two sheets of the material so they become fused, rather than cutting through them. The technique allows more versatility to iterate and test the design and patterning than would a stamping method or heated tool application. Demonstration models point to the feasibility of the concept, another promising sign that the research is heading in the right direction.

Recoding and Decoding Materials

We have been optimizing and augmenting materials for millennia, seeking materials that are more robust, durable, pliant, tunable, colorful, and much more. Often this augmentation came through synthetic means. For instance Bakelite, the world's first fully synthetic plastic invented in 1907, gave way to polystyrene and the plastics revolution from which we now seek to unbury ourselves. Designers today are reenvisioning material augmentation. We are returning to nature to source materials, recoding and decoding their structures to push their properties toward augmented applications and aesthetics.

Transgenics is one such approach, in which genes from one species are introduced into the genetic material of another. Transgenics took hold in the final decades of the twentieth century. In materials and organisms, for instance, the discovery and development of the green fluorescent protein (GFP) that makes jellyfish luminesce[11] has wide applications, including to make silk glow, as developed at Japan's National Agricultural and Research Organization (NARO). Scientists there created transgenic glowing colored silk, engineered by injecting silkworm eggs with GFP or with coral DNA to make it glow green or red.[12]

Collaborating with NARO scientists, Japanese designer Hiromi Ozaki, known as Sputniko!, takes augmented materials out of the lab and into the real world. An associate professor at the University of Tokyo, she has degrees in mathematics, computer science, and design and recently served as the Principal Investigator of the Design Fictions group at MIT Media Lab. Throughout her work, she probes developments in biotechnology and their intersection with design.

For the Tranceflora series (2015–19), Sputniko! collaborated with Japan's three-hundred-year-old Hosoo textile manufactory to weave the transgenic silk into a textile. For the first garment in the series, she and designer Masaya Kushino created a contemporary Nishijin kimono and boots using the glowing silk textile. Tranceflora 2.0, the next in the series, will be made using silk engineered by NARO scientists with coral DNA (to glow red) and oxytocin, a key hormone in human bonding. It is a material augmented to induce love, which Sputniko! calls the "love" silk. She and Kushino are designing a dress to be made from the silk, its form to be evocative of connection and bonding.

Silk is an ancient material. Humans have been weaving silk fibers produced by the caterpillar of the silkworm moth, *Bombyx mori*,[13] into textiles for millennia. If recoding silk with genetic material from other organisms is one approach to augmenting the material, another is decoding it altogether. Researchers at the Silklab at Tufts University in Boston, under the direction of Fiorenzo Omenetto, a biomedical engineer and physicist, are extracting the fibroin—a protein found in silkworm cocoons—from silk. As the Silklab team explains, such "structural proteins are nature's building blocks."[14] They give soft biological materials their structure, stiffness, and function. In addition, they are polymorphic, meaning they can exist in different forms.

The silk fibroin extracted by Omenetto and his team is a strong, stable, and biocompatible building block that enables silk to perform in unexpected ways, bridging technological and biological applications. Fibroin can be tuned to fabrication capabilities, easily mixed and transformed for 3D printing, casting, and inkjet or screen printing, exporting its properties into product design.

The silk can range in scale, format, and function, used not just in fashion but in therapeutics, diagnostics, and optics. As part of the Catalogue of

157

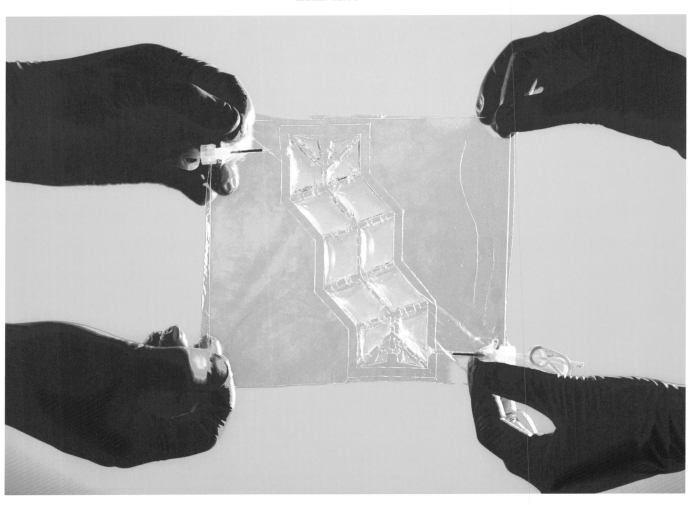

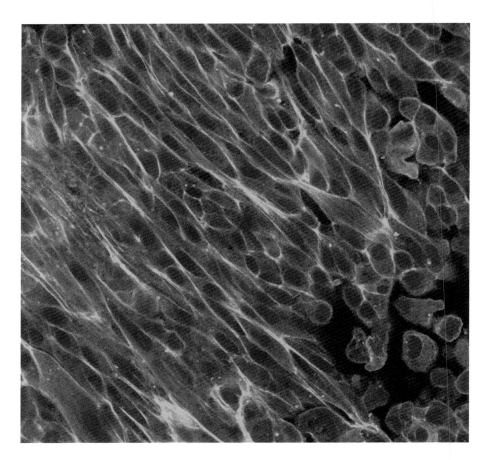

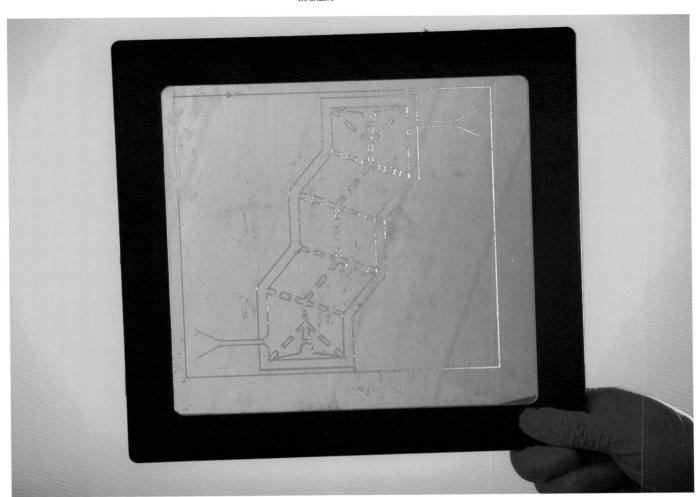

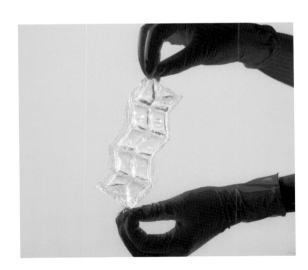

Origami Membrane for 3D Organ
Engineering, 2018-ongoing; Chuck Hoberman
(American, b. 1956), Richard Novak
(American and Czech, b. 1985), Elizabeth
Calamari (American, b. 1991), Sauveur
Jeanty (Haitian-American, b. 1983), and
Donald Ingber (American, b. 1956), Wyss
Institute for Biologically Inspired
Engineering, Harvard University (Boston,
Massachusetts, USA, founded 2009)

Tranceflora, 2015-19; Sputniko! (Hiromi
Ozaki) (Japanese, b. 1985) and Masaya
Kushino (Japanese, b. 1982), Another Farm
(Tokyo, Japan, founded 2018), in collab-
oration with National Agricultural and
Research Organization (NARO) (Tsukuba,
Ibaraki Prefecture, Japan, founded 2006)
and Hosoo (Kyoto, Japan, founded 1688);
Glowing transgenic silk

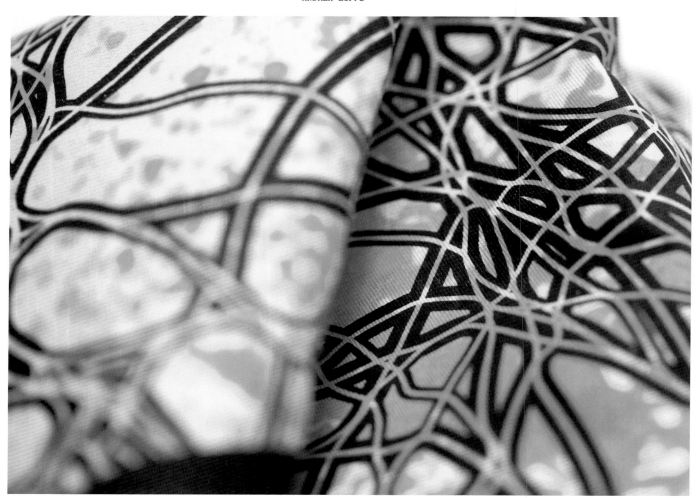

Catalogue of 10 Silk-Protein Derived
Devices at the Interface between
Technology and Life Sciences, 2019;
Living Materials Silklab, Tufts
University Biomedical Engineering
(Medford, Massachusetts, USA, founded
2002); Silk; Dimensions variable

10 Silk-Protein Derived Devices at the Interface between Technology and Life Sciences (2019), the Silklab team has made solid silk screws for use in reconstructive surgeries; biosensors made from liquid silk pigments; optical lenses made from silk; and more. Omenetto and Laia Mogas-Soldevila, an architect and head researcher at the Silklab, are developing digitally derived and biologically sensitive material forms that, through embedded chemistries, interact with their surroundings to change form, color, and function in response to the environment. The versatile range of properties of the silk fibroin demonstrates the possibilities of a naturally derived material to be remade into smart products. More than a material, Omenetto insists, silk becomes "a collection of functions."[15]

Variance and Flux

Parametric design—controlling set parameters—is a strategy used by designers today in material augmentation. Like Oxman's parametrizing the chemistry of Aguahoja's chitosan and cellulose composition mentioned at the outset of this essay, the Chilean-based design collective gt2P experiments with a parametric design process in their work with lava. The designers work with a volcanologist, controlling the parameters of temperature, gravity, firing time, and cooling time of their lava glazes, in many ways replicating the conditions of the Earth. Their Remolten N°1: Revolution Series (2017) of stools are covered in a glaze made from pulverized volcanic stone that, when kiln-fired at a range of temperatures, results in various surface textures and colors.

gt2P's experiments with lava rock have persisted for years. The Less CPP (2018) lighting series anchors the delicacy of porcelain with the resilience of dark lava. The studio casts the bodies of the porcelain lights in a Catenary Pottery Printer they designed to generate analog versions of parametric forms. (A catenary is the curve a hanging rope or cable takes under its own weight when suspended at its ends.) gt2P's Catenary Printer consists of a piece of fabric, such as muslin, hung at multiple points in a wood frame. As liquid clay (the porcelain slip) is poured into the fabric, the muslin arcs under the weight. The slip dries and additional layers are poured in and dry, building up the form's walls with deposited material. The porcelain is more opaque where it pools in the printer—in the ruffles and at the center. Lava reinforces the center of the lights, hiding the mounts. The firing temperature of the porcelain is close to the melting point of the lava stone, bonding the two materials into one.

A landscape in perpetual flux shapes the Chilean imagination. Eighty volcanoes are active in the country. As each erupts, lava and ash from the Earth's core spew to the surface, reshaping the topography each time. In gt2P's Santiago-based studio, the team translates the millennia of lava eruptions and cooling periods that formed the Andes Mountains into expressive design conditions. Nature remains as much a geological resource as a biological resource. Lava meets chitosan and cellulose and microorganisms. Design-inspired natures converge.

1
Neri Oxman, "Bio-inspired Design," presentation at World Economic Forum, Davos-Klosters, Switzerland, January 20–23, 2016, video, February 19, 2016, https://www.youtube.com/watch?v=-nAA0DfAdiIU.

2
Neri Oxman, interview by Ellen Lupton, in *Beauty—Cooper Hewitt Design Triennial*, 222.

3
Neri Oxman, "Towards a Material Ecology," Synthetic Digital Ecologies: Proceedings of the 32nd Annual Conference of the Association for Computer Aided Design in Architecture (ACADIA), October 19–20, 2012 (San Francisco: California College of the Arts, 2012).

4
Ken Mudge et al., "A History of Grafting," *Horticultural Reviews* 35 (2009): 439.

5
Richard P. Marini, "Peach and Nectarine Varieties for Virginia," Virginia Cooperative Extension Publications, Virginia State University, 462–722, February 23, 2015, https://pubs.ext.vt.edu/422/422-762/422-762.html.

6
Sam Van Aken, "The Tree of 40 Fruit," TEDxManhattan, video, March 24, 2014, https://www.youtube.com/watch?v=t9EuJ9QlikY#t=300.

7
Josiah Zayner, interview by Andrea Lipps, July 20, 2018.

8
Others have experimented on themselves by receiving gene-based anti-aging therapies, like Liz Parrish and Brian Hanley. See Antonio Regalado, "A Tale of Do-It-Yourself Gene Therapy," *MIT Technology Review*, October 14, 2015, https://www.technologyreview.com/s/542371/a-tale-of-do-it-yourself-gene-therapy/; and Antonio Regalado, "One Man's Quest to Hack His Own Genes," *MIT Technology Review*, January 10, 2017, https://www.technologyreview.com/s/603217/one-mans-quest-to-hack-his-own-genes/.

9
Oron Catts, interview by Andrea Lipps, June 11, 2018.

10
Chuck Hoberman, interview by Andrea Lipps, July 6, 2018.

11
Professors Osamu Shimomura, Martin Chalfie, and Roger Y. Tsien won the Nobel Prize in Chemistry in 2008 for the discovery and development of GFP. See "The Nobel Prize in Chemistry in 2008," October 8, 2008, https://www.nobelprize.org/prizes/chemistry/2008/press-release/.

12
Tetsuya Iizuka et al., "Colored Fluorescent Silk Made by Transgenic Silkworms," *Advanced Functional Materials* 23, no. 42 (June 12, 2013): 5232–39, https://doi.org/10.1002/adfm.201300365.

13
The *Bombyx mori* caterpillar is the most widely used insect in silk production, although other insects also produce silk fibers. See "Silk," in Encyclopædia Britannica, September 19, 2017, https://www.britannica.com/topic/silk.

14
Tufts Silklab, "Materials at the Interface between Technology and Life Sciences," proposal submitted to Cooper Hewitt, Smithsonian Design Museum, July 2018.

15
Julie Liebach, "The Silk Road's Turn toward Biotechnology," *Science Friday*, June 11, 2015, https://www.sciencefriday.com/articles/the-silk-roads-turn-toward-biotechnology/.

16
Martin Jinek et al., "A Programmable Dual-RNA–Guided DNA Endonuclease in Adaptive Bacterial Immunity," *Science* 337 (August 17, 2012): 816–21, https://doi.org/10.1126/science.1225829.

17
Rafal Kaminski et al., "Elimination of HIV-1 Genomes from Human T-lymphoid Cells by CRISPR/Cas9 Gene Editing," *Scientific Reports* 6, 22555 (2016), https://doi.org/10.1038/srep22555.

18
Daniel Rodríguez-Leal et al., "Engineering Quantitative Trait Variation for Crop Improvement by Genome Editing," *Cell* 171, no. 2 (2017): 470–80, https://doi.org/10.1016/j.cell.2017.08.030.

19
Seth L. Shipman et al., "CRISPR–Cas Encoding of a Digital Movie into the Genomes of a Population of Living Bacteria," *Nature* 547 (July 20, 2017): 345–49, https://doi.org/10.1038/nature23017.

20
George Church, meeting with Matilda McQuaid and Caitlin Condell, February 5, 2018.

Remolten N°1: Revolution Series, 2017;
Guillermo Parada (Chilean, b. 1981),
Tamara Pérez (Chilean, b. 1981),
Sebastián Rozas (Chilean, b. 1981), and
Victor Imperiale (Chilean, b. 1986),
gt2P (Great Things to People) (Santiago,
Chile, founded 2009); Stoneware structure, volcanic lava; High stools: 37 ×
30.5 × 30.5 cm (14.5 × 12 × 12 in.),
low stool: 20 × 28 × 28 cm (7.75 ×
11 × 11 in.)

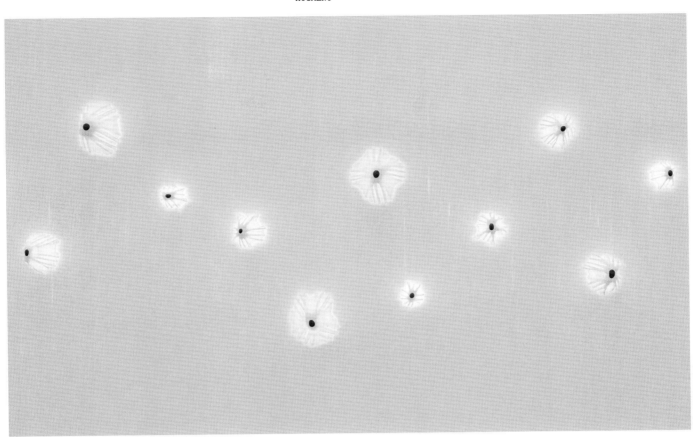

Less CPP N°2: Wall Mural 15C, 2018;
Guillermo Parada (Chilean, b. 1981),
Tamara Pérez (Chilean, b. 1981),
Sebastián Rozas (Chilean, b. 1981), and
Victor Imperiale (Chilean, b. 1986),
gt2P (Great Things to People) (Santiago,
Chile, founded 2009); Porcelain, remolten
volcanic lava, LED lights; Sizes vary, up
to 20.32 × 12.7 cm (8 × 5 in.)

Paracrafting Landscape

To create their Remolten series of furniture and lighting made from volcanic rock, the Santiago-based design firm gt2P sought out geographer Alejandro Vial during their research. Here they reconnect to discuss the project and the impact of the Chilean landscape on their design process.

gt2P (Great Things to People) is a Chilean design, architecture, and art studio established in Santiago in 2009, represented by Friedman Benda. The gt2P designers are in a continuous process of research and experimentation in digital crafting, prompting new encounters between technologies and working with rich traditional materials and techniques. The gt2p work methodology synthesizes the use of systematized knowledge and observation through parametric design with an artistic dimension that connects to the cultural heritage of the designers. gt2P has been featured in numerous international exhibitions, including The Design Museum, London; National Gallery of Victoria, Melbourne; Museum of Arts and Design, New York; Henan Museum, China; MAXXI Museo Nazionale Delle Arti Del XXI Secolo, Rome; and the Denver Art Museum. Their work is in the permanent collections of the National Gallery of Victoria, Denver Art Museum, and Metropolitan Museum of Art.

Alejandro Vial is in his twentieth year at the University of Santiago, Chile, teaching geomorphology, geology, and edaphology with an emphasis on the Earth sciences, the environment, and energy. Prior to this, Vial held management positions at the Chilean Ministry of Health and the Cultural Heritage Unit in San José de Maipo.

169

Paracrafting Landscape   gt2P and Alejandro Vial

Guillermo Parada   Alejandro, you gave us very useful information at the start of our research for the Remolten project concerning remelted volcanic lava. Let's talk about the role of nature, and specifically the landscape of Chile, and its importance in the development of our culture.

Alejandro Vial   I am a geographer, specialized in geomorphology and natural disasters, and I would say that, from a geomorphologic point of view, Chile is a great laboratory. We have different natural processes that have to do with the configuration and evolution of the territory.

GP   You are referring to the laboratory of the Earth.

AV   Well, this is a seismic country and in the national territory there are more than one hundred active volcanoes, of which fifty-some are being monitored permanently by the National Geology and Mining Service.

GP   Currently I think we have four on yellow alert.

AV   That's right. This is a country covered entirely by holes. If one analyzes Chile, it is striking that between the valleys of Huasco or Copiapó and Aconcagua, there are no volcanoes. This is what [has been] called the zone of the transversal valleys because there is geological change. The geological structure of the country in that region ends with the Ojo del Salado that is in the interior of Copiapó, and reappears with the Aconcagua, an ancient volcano. It should never be said that a volcano is extinguished or turned off, because magmatic chambers still exist.

GP   As in the case of Chaitén.

AV   Volcanoes are like the safety valves of boilers. The magmatic chambers are these boilers that are gathering pressure and, at some point, the pressure is released through a volcanic eruption. It happened with Chaitén, and specifically with the Lonquimay, in 1987. The eruption was not produced by the main crater, but a crater ripped the slope of the volcano. Volcanic activity depends on the type of rock that forms the volcano. There can be volcanism of an explosive type, where there is a column of pyroclastic material, burning pieces, which finally results in volcanic ash, pumice, very rich in silica, which is cooled quickly in contact with the atmosphere, and solidifies.

GP   That was the incident you mentioned to us at the beginning [of the Remolten project], the acid eruptions.

AV   Exactly. Those that are rich in silica are acidic. Of the magmas . . . one must say basic or acidic magmas, because acidic magmas do not give lava. Magmas are the melted materials that are inside. Then, they come out as pyroclastics, in the case of acidic magmas, or as lavas in the case of basic magmas. Those with lava, because they have more metallic components, tend to form effusions, because they melt and last longer. The silicon material is refractory, heat resistant; it endures much higher temperatures than the others.
    To speak of volcanic ash is conceptually a mistake because it is not the product of the combustion of anything.

GP   It's pyroclastic material, it's stone.

AV   Exactly, it's stone that exploded in small grains or in small pieces as it happens with the pumice stone, which is practically pure silica.

GP   This discussion is what helped us to launch the Remolten project. [It] allowed us to choose the volcanoes where we could find this lava.

Tamara Pérez   Initially we researched three volcanoes, which were the closest to us—the Chaitén, the Villarica, and the Osorno.

GP   We looked for pieces of volcanic rock. We crushed them in Santiago, at the Geology Department of the University of Chile, where we also had the rocks tested for mineralogical differences. The interesting thing about those tests was that they proved we could make faceted pieces, objects with double curvature, and attempt different shapes.

And another interesting outcome was that, when given more time inside the kiln at the lowest possible melting temperature, more resistance was given to the material. So, if we removed it quickly and let it cool in the air, we created super-weak obsidian. And if we seeped it in a controlled temperature, we created a very resistant stone.

AV   The same thing happens in nature. Solid rock is consolidated in long terms, the strongest rocks are those that are cooled inside the crust.
Planet Earth is a foundry furnace, with a metallic core that is at temperatures above three thousand degrees, and radiates heat towards the periphery in such a way that the rocks, which consolidate at the base of the crust, between fifteen and thirty kilometers deep, cool very slowly.

GP   That makes them very solid.

AV   While volcanic rock, which cools down on contact with the environment, is generally a rock . . .

GP   Crystalline.

AV   Easy to break, because it is like pumice stone, that is not glass. You hit it and it breaks.

GP   We discovered those two possibilities within the world of solidity regarding the resistance of the stone. We realized that if we made pieces completely out of lava, for example, to make a bench, or to make a table, the problem was the weight. For domestic use they would be impractical. So the idea was to look for a collaborative material. This is where the search began to return to its origin, seeking collaboration with other materials, for example, collaboration with porcelain.

AV   And with porcelain, it worked well.

GP   Super well.

AV   You learned with the trial-and-error method.

GP   Exactly. With this project, we had excellent results during the first two months. But after a year we did not have successful results, zero. Imagine the level of frustration.

TP   It happened when trying to transition to larger pieces. They broke.

GP   We realized that the [structural] interior piece [made of porcelain] was shrinking. What we did was burn the structural pieces at a higher temperature, and we put them in the oven as a whole, to prevent another contraction. This research was interesting. It enabled us to systematize our process and generate knowledge that could be replicated. We started to generate our own temperature curves, our burning parameters, without the computer as a mediator, but in an oven with physical parameters. Then we started to yield an array of surfaces on the pieces, some were completely smooth, others more rough, or pieces that were highly polished.

AV   You can see the trickle of the melted material and the vacuoles, which form when the minerals are gasified and then the bubble bursts.
When you talked to me about this [project], I had doubts. What will be the fate of this? Because, according to the experiences in the laboratory, to work with rocks, for example, metamorphism has never been artificially achieved. In general rocks in nature are found in three ways: the rocks we call eruptive, which are those that come from within the landscape, from the inside of the crust. The sedimentary ones are products of erosion and transportation. And in the middle are what we call metamorphic rocks, which are rocks that form by high pressures, high temperatures, and by the movements of the crust and have recrystallized and mineralized, which is what happens with tourmaline.

GP   And also with marble, with lapis lazuli, the tosca stone.

AV   Exactly, in general they are the rocks that bring minerals and that are considered semiprecious stones. They are all metamorphic.
But today technology allows us to use ore that previously had to be disposed of.

GP   In fact part of the reason why we launched the Remolten project was because a client gave us some pieces of volcanic rock and said, "You're creatives, see what you can do with this." The material had a direct relationship with our landscape. For Chileans, nature is so deeply rooted in our everyday life. When you get up in the morning, you see the snowy mountain

171

range, you can even see the mountain range in the desert, the mountains follow you wherever you go.

AV   The border between Chile, Peru, and Bolivia is a volcano, the Tacora volcano. There in the foothills of the Tacora, lies the border, the tripartite landmark. That means that when entering Chile, we immediately encounter a volcano.

We ask our topography students at the university, "How do you orient yourself?"

GP   With the mountain range.

It's interesting because initially, when we were studying to be architects, we had professors who were trained at Columbia University and Harvard, and who were interested in parametric design, computers, and that everything had to be built by robots. When we were finishing the master's degree at the School of Architecture, we thought everything was going to be built by robots.

But [when we left Chile, we] realized that what we looked at all day was something rooted in us. We did not realize what we had. Our value is the mixture of all this ultra-technological and ultra-scientific knowledge, but also the landscape we see every day.

Remediate

Remediate   Matilda McQuaid

It is difficult today to conjure up an image that *isn't* related to the environment when we use the word "remediate." Warnings of eroding coastlines, diminishing species, polluted oceans, and toxic waste sites are omnipresent in every news forum. They have also been rallying cries for many designers as they try to slow, stop, and even reverse the negative impacts of our human footprint on the planet. Their actions express an opportunity for renewal and realignment with nature, and their projects reveal how they have chosen to rehabilitate, reform, and regenerate for future generations.

Rehabilitate

Experiencing nature in a tangible way has physical and mental benefits. When spending time in nature is combined with daily exercise, people have fewer diseases, lower blood pressure and cholesterol levels, and overall less stress.[1] Popular in Japan is forest bathing (*shinrinyoku*), a slow and meditative walk through the woods with participatory interventions along the way, which reduces stress by promoting the natural killer cells, a part of the immune system that fights cancer.[2] The United States Department of Agriculture reports that "breathing in antimicrobial compounds found in the essential oils of trees increases relaxation and improves stress management, resulting in increased vitality and less anxiety."[3]

With clear evidence indicating the positive benefits of spending time in nature, "the medical field has begun to adopt a biopsychosocial model in which mind and body are viewed as inextricably linked."[4] As landscape architect Ulrika K. Stigsdotter explains, "This changing view is encouraging for designers who seek to integrate patient, family, and community-centered care into design."[5]

Stigsdotter's project Nacadia Therapy Forest Garden (2011–ongoing) is a research- and therapy-based garden and an example of how the biopsychosocial model can be used to promote mental rehabilitation. "Entering Nacadia is like entering into another world; it is like a refuge with no demands. You forget time and place in Nacadia," explains a patient who suffers from post-traumatic stress disorder. Designed by Stigsdotter, with input from researchers in landscape architecture, architecture and environmental psychology, as well as medical doctors, psychologists, and therapists with expertise in nature-based therapy, Nacadia shows how designers carefully construct an experience within and using nature to provide healing opportunities for patients suffering from stress-related illnesses.

Nacadia is open year-round and is situated within the Hoersholm Arboretum, forty miles north of Copenhagen, Denmark. It covers two acres of land and is a forest garden of outdoor rooms with plant material creating the floors, walls, and ceilings to encourage immersion in nature and promote healing. The design has six built components: the hut, a wooden elevated deck in a tree, the main wooden walkway, an entrance gate with a pergola, a greenhouse, and an office building (transformed from an existing gardener's cottage) surrounded by a large wooden terrace. Approximately two-thirds of the garden is covered by tree canopies, with the remaining area comprising grass meadows. Water features are also included: a spring, stream, pond, and lake with an island. One of the major goals of Nacadia is to conduct as much therapy as possible outdoors—very different from traditional therapeutic methods.[6]

Stigsdotter and her group designed five outdoor rooms with certain constant conditions—shape, size, and direction—but with fluctuating content. Some rooms have walls of shrubs or green fences, floors of grass, stone, or wood, and ceilings of treetops, pergolas with flowering climbers, or the open sky. Each choice of material and spatial placement relates to the patient's needs and ability, which can change over time and are accounted for in the overall design. Nacadia addresses the mental state initially in an effort to improve physical well-being.

In a project where the situation is reversed, designers have worked to improve compromised motor functions in an effort to enhance mental well-being. The Soft Robotic Grip Glove (2015–ongoing), designed by Conor Walsh's Harvard Biodesign Lab, represents an important new area of soft robotics in assistive devices, using flexible and lightweight materials instead of rigid and heavier components for functionality. It was developed to assist individuals who have limited motor skills in their hands, caused by muscular dystrophy, stroke, and partial spinal cord injury. According to research conducted by the Biodesign Lab, approximately four million chronic stroke survivors with partial paralysis exist in the United States and another six million are found in developed countries globally.[7] In most of these cases, partial or entire loss of motor functions in the hand has occurred, severely reducing basic daily activities. The glove allows the user to perform daily activities, promoting independence and a sense of well-being.

The base glove resembles the dimension and weight of a common padded wheelchair glove and has modular, independent finger actuators comprised of three fabric layers and two airtight bladders placed between each fabric layer. Sensors are used to control the actuators and, when activated, inflate the bladders, causing the gloved hand to open, close, grasp, pinch, and hold an object. The control system, which includes electronics, battery pack, electric air pump, exhaust, and fill air manifold, is contained in a compact box lightweight enough to wear on a belt or attach to a wheelchair. Because user functionality was the primary focus of the design, prototypes were tested on potential users at every step of development. Users discussed the comfort of the glove—that it felt good to have fingers extended—when it was impossible to do this without the glove.[8]

Reform

No other manmade material has had such a longstanding impact on designers and our world than plastic. With a worldwide production of plastic close to three hundred million tons per year, plastic objects are choking the life out of our planet.[9] Plastic has also become a remarkable catalyst for designers, who are collaborating with marine biologists, environmentalists, and concerned citizens to find alternatives that replace it, invent ways to collect it, and thereafter repurpose it (some of which are explained in Salvage, pp. 88–107). One of the largest and most recent (as well as controversial) endeavors for collecting ocean plastic is the Ocean Cleanup, a multimillion-dollar project aiming to clean up the largest accumulation of ocean plastic in the world, the Great Pacific Garbage Patch. Years in development, the Ocean Cleanup uses passive floating cleanup systems to collect marine debris. The first cleanup system was launched in October 2018.

Equally as concerning as the enormous garbage patches are miniscule plastics that pollute our rivers and oceans. Referred to as microplastics, a term introduced in 2004, they are less than 5 millimeters (3/16 inch) in size and result from the breakdown of plastics in the ocean and other bodies of water. They are typically found as pellets, fragments, or fibers. They account for 92 percent of all marine plastics floating in the world's ocean.[10] Microplastics hover like smog on the surface of water and in sediment. The most hazardous characteristic of microplastics is their ability to absorb chemicals.[11] This can render microplastics toxic and, when absorbed by marine life, they become part of the food chain. In order to research microplastic pollution, Max Liboiron, a professor in Geography at Memorial University of Newfoundland, invented BabyLegs (2017–19), "a do-it-yourself monitoring tool for marine microplastic pollution."[12] BabyLegs was "born" at the Civic Laboratory for Environmental Action Research, a "feminist, decolonial, marine science laboratory that studies plastic pollution in Newfoundland and Labrador."[13] Made from babies' tights for a net, plastic soda bottles for pontoons (this insures that costs

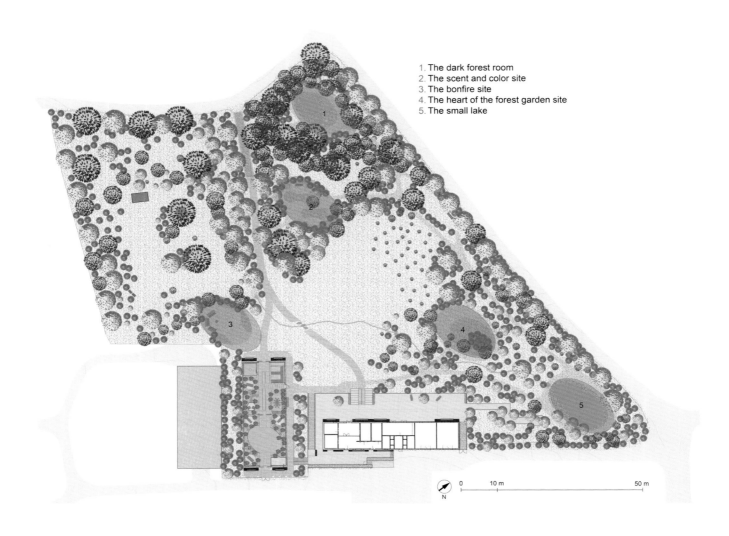

1. The dark forest room
2. The scent and color site
3. The bonfire site
4. The heart of the forest garden site
5. The small lake

0   10 m   50 m

N

Nacadia Therapy Forest Garden, 2011-
ongoing; Hoersholm Arboretum, Hoersholm,
Denmark; Ulrika K. Stigsdotter (Swedish,
b. 1971); University of Copenhagen
(Copenhagen, Denmark, founded 1479)

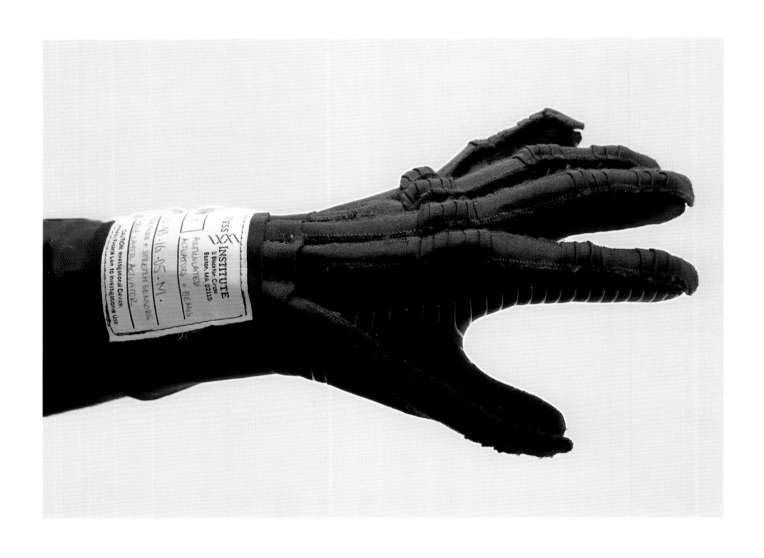

Soft Robotic Grip Glove, 2015-
ongoing; Conor Walsh (Irish, b. 1981),
Diana Wagner (American, b. 1986), Megan
Clarke (American, b. 1995), Dorothy
Orzel (American, b. 1958), Yu MengZhou
(Canadian, b. 1994), and Ciarán O'Neill
(Irish, b. 1991), Harvard Biodesign Lab
(Cambridge, Massachusetts, USA, founded
2012); Knit textile, compressed air

↓
Variety of microplastics

Babylegs, 2017-19; Max Liboiron
(Canadian, b. 1980), CLEAR (Civic
Laboratory for Environmental Action
Research) (St. John's, Newfoundland,
Canada, founded 2015); Plastic bottle,
nylon stockings, rope; 45.72 × 20.32 ×
7.62 cm (18 × 8 × 3 in.)

stay low), and other inexpensive, off-the-shelf materials, BabyLegs attaches to a boat, which drags it along the surface to collect bits of microplastic for study and, if lucky, identification. The design mimics the much more expensive Manta trawler ($3,500, as opposed to BabyLegs' less than $12 solution). BabyLegs is open source, as is its larger version, LADI (Low-tech Aquatic Debris Instrument, pronounced "lady").

Liboiron's research on microplastics focuses on the area around Labrador, which is home to indigenous and aboriginal communities who rely on fish for sustenance. Plastic toxicity, according to Liboiron, results when microplastics are ingested into a hot and acidic climate like the gut, at which point chemicals can leach out of the plastic and move into tissue at crucial times of development in fetuses, children, and women.[14] For Liboiron, this has become an issue of equity, which recognizes that when people start from fundamentally different social, economic, educational, and political positions, treating everyone equally does not overcome those differences.[15] This makes microplastic pollution, especially in communities whose livelihood depends upon fishing, a major crisis economically, socially, and environmentally.

BabyLegs offers an important example of open-source scientific research, where it lives in social space, and of how such research can encourage the development of low-cost community projects for environmental monitoring and assessment. When designers provide the tools and the road map for creation, and allow users to make specific choices with regard to materials and construction, knowledge and empowerment follow, which can change the behavior of an individual and a community.

Similarly research-driven is Charlotte McCurdy's After Ancient Sunlight (2018), which offers an alternative to how we think about our relationship to the sun so that it is in the present rather than focused on the captured carbon from what she refers to as "ancient sunlight." She uses this term in her 2018 master's thesis to describe "everything made from the fossilized remains of the chemical storage of ancient photosynthetic activity."[16] Over millions of years under high pressure and high temperature, the remains of algae, coral, and plants are transformed into today's fossil fuels. McCurdy states that we need to free ourselves entirely of petroleum products and find alternatives. As a proof of concept, McCurdy created a petroleum-free, algae-based (in order to harness present sunlight) plastic to replace traditional waterproof materials. She labelled it Solene™, and described it as a material that uses "young sunlight" because it is made from quickly grown and harvested plant matter (algae).[17] The Solene™ raincoat McCurdy designed underscored the extreme weather events that are linked to climate change.

McCurdy also has created two books that document her research. She printed the first with traditional petrochemical-derived black ink on conventional paper and bound with petroleum-based glue. McCurdy produced the second publication by reading the first book aloud into a double-valve container that splatters bubbles of plant-based soaps and salvaged wood charcoal on vegan watercolor paper. The beauty and creativity in all of McCurdy's elements comprising her thesis—the books, raincoat, ceramic studies, and more—derive from her methodical research and desire to communicate the possibilities, as she explains, of "what it would mean—what it would feel like—to live in a present-tense relationship with the sun."

Even in death, we are polluters. Our bodies emit toxins during decomposition and, when cremated, these ashes continue to release toxins into the soil and water. Studio Nienke Hoogvliet is collaborating with the Dutch Water Authority to introduce a new type of biodegradable alternative to a traditional cremation burial. Several years ago, the Dutch Water Authority produced the first polyhdroxyalkanoate (PHA) using sludge, the leftover material from wastewater treatment. PHA, a type of bioplastic, is made by bacteria as an energy-storage medium (like fat in mammals). The Dutch Water Authority realized that instead of cultivating bacteria to produce PHA, they could use the bacteria already present at wastewater treatment plants, which accumulate PHA and are abundantly available.[18] Hoogvliet then combined PHA with cremation ashes to create Mourn (2017–ongoing), a cone-shaped object that can be buried in soil or water in its entirety. It releases nutrients and toxins gradually, as opposed to the immediacy of scattering ashes, thereby having little impact on the soil and groundwater.

Designer Jae Rhim Lee, founder of the company Coeio, proposes a different way of thinking about death that "moves us toward death acceptance . . . a critical aspect of protecting our environment."[19] She created the Infinity Burial Suit (2016–ongoing), an organic cotton suit with a built-in mix of mycelium and proprietary natural materials that the designer refers to as biomix. Lee's research initially focused on mycelium, and she studied with Paul Stamets, a renowned American mycologist, professor, and author of several books on the extraordinary benefits of mycelium for human and planetary health. One of the super biomaterials of the twenty-first century, mycelium is a network of fungal threads—those fuzzy, cobweb-like growths under rotting logs—which at some point in its life cycle fruits mushrooms, like an apple tree produces apples.[20] Mycelium is fast growing—from ¼ to 2 inches per day— and more than eight miles of these cells can permeate one cubic inch of soil. According to Stamets and other scientific sources, mycelium can absorb or eliminate toxins from the soil—called mycoremediation—while enriching the soil during biodegradation.

From thousands of species of mushrooms, Lee made her selection after consultation with mycologists, who recommended specific types of fungi for the various stages of decomposition and for absorption of chemicals.[21] Lee reports on the Coeio website that according to the Centers for Disease Control and Prevention in the US, there are 219 toxic chemicals in the human body, including tobacco residues, dry-cleaning chemicals, pesticides, fungicides, flame retardants, heavy metals, preservatives, and more. Mycelium can assist in breaking down these toxins. Lee is currently on her third design iteration, all three created in collaboration with zero-waste fashion designer Daniel Silverstein. Lee has designed a shroud version for pets and humans and is working on other mycelium-based products for the funeral industry.

Regenerate

When Dellarobia Turnbow, Barbara Kingsolver's protagonist in *Flight Behavior*, stumbled upon the hibernating grounds of monarch butterflies, she had a transformative experience:

"Unearthly beauty had appeared to her, a vision of glory to stop her in the road. For her alone these orange boughs lifted, these long shadows became a brightness rising. It looked like the inside of joy, if a person could see that."[22] Butterflies are loved by everyone, and within the order Lepidoptera, monarchs are the most famous and popular in North America. They are easily recognizable with their bold orange and black coloring. Although it is still unknown how widely they pollinate, monarchs are a barometer for the sustainability of North America.[23] Their susceptibility to agricultural pesticides, temperature changes, land development, and habitat loss has made them a rallying cry for changes in government policies around the use of pesticides and for the preservation of their native habitats.

New York City is located on one of the migratory paths of the monarch, which travels northward from its winter hibernation in the mountains of Mexico to the Midwest and Northeast United States during spring and summer. Important to the survival of the monarch is milkweed, on which adult females lay their eggs, larvae feast throughout larval metamorphosis, and the pupal form dangles as a chrysalis. Milkweed is especially critical for monarchs during autumn migration, when they require a sustained habitat with nectar and resting spots.[24]

Terreform ONE's Monarch Sanctuary (2018–ongoing), designed for the façade of a commercial building in New York City, is a thirty-thousand-square-foot refuge for the renewal of the local monarch butterfly population. Architect Mitchell Joachim, who founded Terreform ONE as a nonprofit organization, wanted to create a multipurpose façade that contributes to the well-being and diversity of life in the city. He describes his design for the Monarch Sanctuary as "a vertical meadow behind a glass façade that contains living plants and flying butterflies in an environment highly regulated for

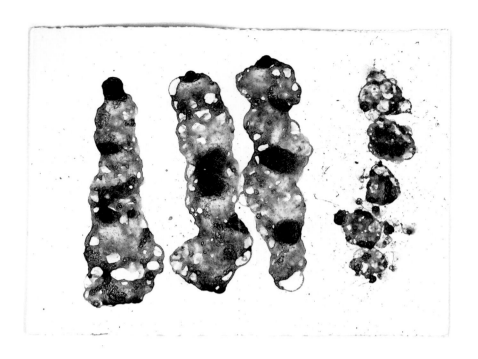

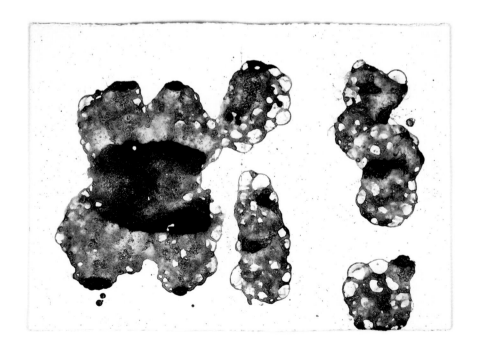

↑
Pages from a petroleum-free book; Vegan
watercolor paper, cotton thread, charcoal, and plant-based soap

After Ancient Sunlight, 2018; Charlotte
McCurdy (American, b. 1989)

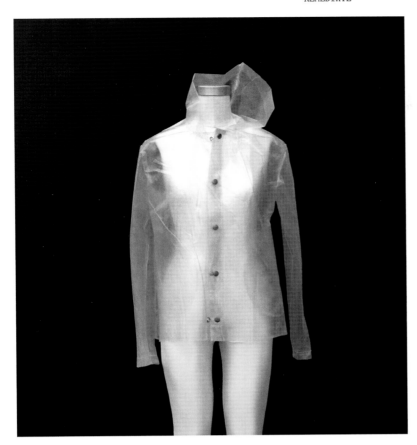

↑
Raincoat: Solene (a novel 100% marine-
algae-derived polymer), rayon thread,
brass fasteners; 91.44 × 63.5 × 30.48 cm
(36 × 25 × 12 in.)

↓
Three species of live marine algae,
salt water

Mourn, 2017-ongoing; Nienke Hoogvliet
(Dutch, b. 1989), Studio Nienke Hoogvliet
(Hague, Netherlands, founded 2013);
Ashes, PHA bioplastic made from waste-
water; 30 × 15 cm (11 13/16 × 5 7/8 in.)

Infinity Mushroom

Infinity Burial Suit, 2016-ongoing;
Jae Rhim Lee (Korean, b. 1975), Coeio
(Mountain View, California, USA, founded
2015); Mycelium spores, organic cotton,
microorganisms; Dimensions variable

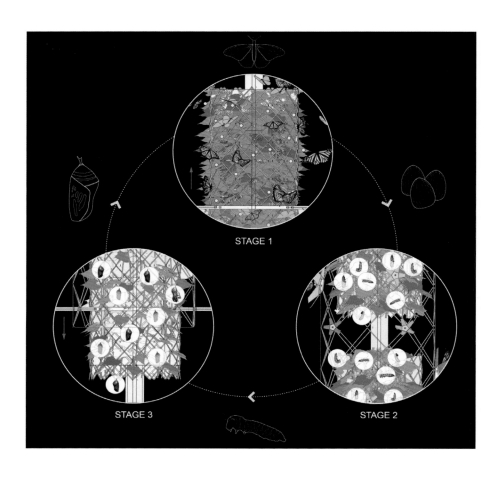

Monarch Sanctuary, 2018-ongoing; Mitchell
Joachim (American, b. 1972) and Vivian
Kuan (American, b. 1966), Terreform ONE
(Brooklyn, New York, USA, founded 2006);
Glass, metal, plastic, milkweed, Monarch
butterflies and larvae

For full caption information,
see page 239.

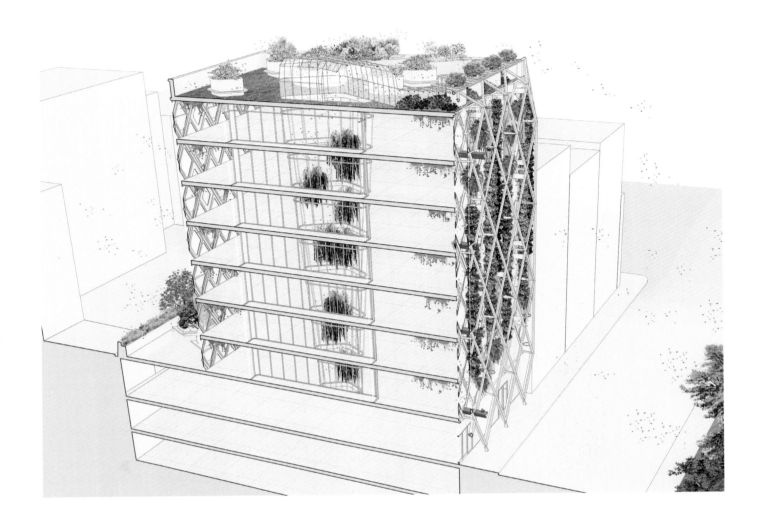

temperature and humidity." By planting milkweed and nectar flowers through-out the exterior of the building (roof, façades, and terrace), he hopes to provide more breeding grounds for wild monarchs, while colonies in the façade will also increase monarch population. Joachim sees the building as an "object lesson in enhancing the urban environment with green technologies, including plant life and other creatures, in designing for other species, and in convey-ing images of new possibilities for the urban environment. This project alone will not save the monarch, but it will crucially raise awareness about our much-loved insect residents."[25]

Stabilizing shorelines against erosion has been accomplished by building jetties and inserting boulders, which are artificial defenses that have to be maintained and replaced over time. Designer Sheng-Hung Lee invented TetraPOT 2.0—The Evolution of Greener Sea Defense (2015–18), a module that works with the surrounding ecosystem. Inspired by the solid concrete water breakers or tetrapods scattered along the shores of Taiwan, Lee adapted this design to contain a mangrove seedling inside the concrete pod. In his prototype, Lee constructed a three-part mold with a central chamber for the mangrove that includes three primary openings. The holes allow the root system of the gradually maturing mangrove to connect to both the adjacent TetraPOT and mangrove roots from other TetraPOTS, creating an interlocking system of roots that will remain long after the pod itself has deteriorated.

Lee also sees this natural breakwater as regenerating mangrove forests, which, according to Smithsonian scientists, are among the most productive and biologically complex ecosystems on Earth. They cover approx-imately fifty-three thousand to seventy-seven thousand square miles globally, providing essential habitats and feeding grounds for thousands of species.[26] They have also been disappearing at an alarming rate. Data shows that between 2001 and 2012, the world lost between thirty-five and ninety-seven square miles of mangrove forest per year due to coastal development, aquaculture, and industrial activities.[27]

Preservation of native species is the essence of Fernando Laposse's project called Totomoxtle (2017–ongoing), or "corn husk," referring to the brilliantly colored veneers made from native Mexican corn that he uses for marquetry in wall coverings, lighting, and furniture. Laposse, who was born in Paris, France, and grew up in Mexico, made a trip when he was six years old to Tonahuixtla to visit Delfino Martinez, a friend of his family.[28] Returning every summer until he was fifteen, Laposse learned farming practices from the Mixtec, an indigenous community inhabiting present-day Oaxaca, Guerrero, and Puebla, where Tonahuixtla is located. He remembers being drawn to the beautiful black, purple, and pink colors of the ears of corn, which also translated into the leaves. This native corn reflected the diversity of maize in Mexico. When Laposse returned to this community thirteen years later, as a product designer and to participate in a residency in Oaxaca related to the corn husks, he could not find native corn in the city markets or in Tonahuixtla. It was a rare commodity, having been replaced with hybrid corn that was industrially grown with herbicides and genetically modified seeds. The land was useless for farming and the community had all but evacuated the town. Laposse found Martinez, however, who was part of a small group of farmers starting a cactus reforestation project to stop erosion on the now barren land. They were also creating an earthworm composting center to fertilize the land with the ultimate goal of replanting their native corn. It was at this point that Laposse, who was so moved by the farmers' plight and determination, decided to expand the scope of his project to achieve Martinez's goal.

Important to Laposse and Martinez's story is the seed. Traditionally when farmers harvested the native corn they would choose the best variety from which to keep the seeds to use for the next growing season. This permit-ted growth of the native species. These seeds were lost when industrialized farming took over. Fortunately, Centro Internacional de Mejoramiento de Maíz y Trigo (CIMMYT), the germplasm bank in Mexico, holds the largest seed collections of maize in the world, with more than twenty-eight thou-sand unique varieties. Laposse and the farmers collaborated with CIMMYT scientists to carefully select seeds that would work with the soil and altitude of

Tonahuixtla. The organization is also training the farmers to preserve the best seeds in the hope that Tonahuixtla will start its own seedbank.

With money received from grants and awards, Laposse moved his studio to Tonahuixtla in order to accelerate the project. In the meantime, the farmers had cleared two hectares of land and planted twelve different types of corn using bull-drawn plows and sowing the seeds by hand. To ensure success, Laposse had two agronomists working with him to monitor growth for the first harvest in 2018. He also designed a system for die-cutting the husks with a manually operated press that uses no electricity. Leftover trimmings are fed to the goats.

What excites Laposse is not only the work that his studio is producing from the native corn husks, but how it is spawning other initiatives related to indigenous farming practices. Restaurants are rescuing traditional recipes and including native corn in the ingredients. Laposse continues to document and quantify the positive impact that the project is having in the community with the hope of replicating this model in other indigenous communities.

TetraPOT 2.0—The Evolution of Greener
Sea Defense, 2015-18; Sheng-Hung Lee
(Taiwanese, b. 1987); PLA; Special
thanks: Tasos Karahalios, LUNAR; Elyssa
He, IDEO; Ji Ke, HAX; Terrence Zhang,
Boio; and Shu-Yan Wang and Lin Shun
Kuang, Puten Model Company

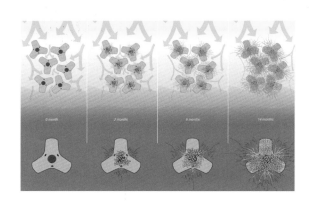

Totomoxtle, 2017-ongoing; Fernando
Laposse (Mexican, b. 1988), with Delfino
Martinez, Lucia Herrera, and Noé Leon;
Corn husks; Dimensions variable

↑
Delfino Martinez with Fernando Laposse
(left) and Sophia Laposse (right)

↓
Die-cutting husks

194

1

"Health and Wellness Benefits of Spending Time
in Nature," U.S. Department of Agriculture
Forest Service, Pacific Northwest Research Station,
Ecosystem Services Team, Portland Oregon, accessed
October 11, 2018, https://www.fs.fed.us/pnw/about/
programs/gsv/pdfs/health_and_wellness.pdf.

2

Clare Cooper Marcus and Naomi A. Sachs,
*Therapeutic Landscapes: An Evidence-Based Approach
to Designing Healing Gardens and Restorative Outdoor
Spaces* (Hoboken: John Wiley & Sons, 2014), 18.

3

"Health and Wellness Benefits," 2.

4

Marcus and Sachs, *Therapeutic Landscapes*, 32.

5

Ibid.

6

Ulrika K. Stigsdotter, project description, emailed to
author, July 5, 2018.

7

"Soft Robotics," Harvard Biodesign Lab, accessed
October 11, 2018, https://biodesign.seas.harvard.
edu/soft-robotics.

8

Ibid.

9

"Our Planet is Drowning in Plastic Pollution,"
United Nations Environment, accessed February 1,
2019, https://www.unenvironment.org/interactive/
beat-plastic-pollution/.

10

Max Liboiron, "Redefining Pollution and Action: The
Matter of Plastics," *Journal of Material Culture*
21, no. 1 (2016): 87–110, https://doi.org/10.1177/
1359183515622966.

11

Ibid, 88.

12

Max Liboiron, "Compromised Agency: The Case of
BabyLegs," *Engaging Science, Technology, and Society*
3 (2017): 499–527, 499.

13

Ibid, 502.

14

Ibid, 503.

15

Ibid, 502.

16

Charlotte McCurdy, "After Ancient Sunlight:
Materials for a Post-Petroleum World" (Master's
thesis, Rhode Island School of Design, 2018), 18.

17

Charlotte McCurdy, interview by Matilda McQuaid,
July 18, 2018.

18

"World first—PHA from Sewage Sludge,"
Bioplasticmagazine.com, October 23, 2015, accessed on
October 6, 2018, https://www.bioplasticsmagazine.
com/en/news/meldungen/20151023-Sewage-based-
PHA-produced.php.

19

Katie Rogers, "Mushroom Suits, Biodegradable Urns
and Death's Green Frontier," *The New York Times*,
April 22, 2016.

20

Paul Stamets, *Mycelium Running: How Mushrooms
Can Help Save the World* (Berkeley: Ten Speed
Press, 2005), 1, accessed October 9, 2018, https://
decroissons.files.wordpress.com/2014/04/paul-
stamets-mycelium-running-how-mushrooms-can-
help-save-the-world.pdf.

21

"Of the estimated 1–2 million species of fungi—
about 150,000 species being mushrooms—we have
catalogued only about 50,000, of which 14,000
have been identified with a species name." See
Paul Stamets, "Helping the Ecosystem through
Mushroom Cultivation," Fungi Perfecti, January 5,
2000, https://fungi.com/blogs/articles/helping-the-
ecosystem-through-mushroom-cultivation.

22

Barbara Kingsolver, *Flight Behavior* (New York:
Harper Perennial, 2012), 5–6.

23

Anurag Agrawal, *Monarchs and Milkweed: A
Migrating Butterfly, a Poisonous Plant, and Their
Remarkable Story of Coevolution* (Princeton: Princeton
University Press, 2017), 29–30.

24

Ibid, 238.

25

Mitchell Joachim, "Monarch Sanctuary New York
City, Terreform ONE," December 2, 2017, accessed
October 10, 2018, https://archinode.blogspot.com/
2017/12/monarch-sanctuary-in-new-york-city-by.
html.

26

Candy Feller, "Mangroves," Smithsonian Ocean,
the Ocean Portal Team, accessed on October 10,
2018, https://ocean.si.edu/ocean-life/plants-algae/
mangroves.

27

Ibid.

28

Fernando Laposse, interview by Matilda McQuaid,
April 11, 2018.

Collaborating With . . .

What are the benefits and challenges of working with an interdisciplinary team? Designer Suzanne Lee and scientist Nadine Bongaerts discuss topics ranging from communication to speculative design and the need for a greater understanding of the ethical complexities of scientific advances.

Suzanne Lee is chief creative officer at Modern Meadow, a company focused on an interdisciplinarian approach to creating animal-free materials. She has over twenty years of experience in design research and fashion. She started growing microbial materials in 2003 and established Biocouture, the first biocreative consultancy. In 2014, Lee founded Biofabricate, the annual summit to unite design, biology, and technology. Lee has received a TED Senior Fellowship and is a Launch Material Innovator, an initiative of NASA, Nike, USAID, and the U.S. State Department.

Nadine Bongaerts is a synthetic biologist and fascinated by engineering life at the smallest scale. She holds a bachelor's and master's degree in Life Sciences from the University of Leiden and TU Delft and is currently finalizing her Ph.D. on synthetic biology at Inserm and the Centre for Interdisciplinary Research in Paris. Next to her scientific work, she actively bridges the world of science with society and business through her work (as vice president) for Hello Tomorrow and science-communication agency Science Matters, which she cofounded in 2011. She has taught biology at the Royal Academy of Arts in The Hague and is currently a faculty member of Singularity University, the Netherlands.

Matilda McQuaid   What are the similarities between scientists and designers?

Suzanne Lee   I find the best of both are deeply creative people, but their creativity manifests in different ways. Designers are energized by solving problems, finding new ways to approach and create a product. We love experimentation—pushing and pulling at ideas. We're happy in an uncertain environment. I'm not sure scientists are as comfortable around so many unknowns.

Nadine Bongaerts   We scientists constantly have to deal with unknowns as well, and creative problem-solving is crucial to making progress. We operate on the basis of what other researchers discovered before, but especially in biology; unexplainable things happen all the time. This doesn't always make me feel comfortable. At the same time, this is exactly what makes research exciting and interesting. Finally, I think both designers and scientists share a high level of curiosity.

MM   What are some of the values and challenges of an interdisciplinary team?

SL   It's challenging for sure to engage in a team where people come at a problem from the opposite direction or with a bottom-up mindset (starting with the molecular). We designers tend to experience and appreciate the world in different ways. Science is hypothesis driven and evidence based. I believe my design expertise is also hypothesis driven and evidence based, but my "data" come in the form of my senses—I have honed my eye, my touch, my experience of making. Where there is synergy it can be very harmonious and you experience an enjoyable flow, but when we get into the subjective it can be impossible at times! One side wants the other to adopt its methodology. There simply aren't satisfactory metrics for things like aesthetics and haptics, for example. So that's where we all get into deeper investigation so we can come to a common understanding. It can be thrilling but also at times maddening for both parties!

NB   I think interdisciplinary teams are the only way for innovation to reach its full potential. When it comes to developing groundbreaking innovative products, researchers can easily focus too much on technological perfection, when this is not always necessary for the end product. Or at times when a certain innovation is so new there might not be proper regulation in place for it to be approved by the authorities. And will society accept this innovation? Innovation happens in a complex environment and teams have to resemble that complexity in order to deal with a broad variety of challenges. Similarly, in research, it is beneficial to work with people with different scientific disciplines. My research is highly interdisciplinary and combines synthetic biology, chemistry, drug design, enzymology, and molecular dynamics simulations, amongst others. I am not an expert in all those fields, so the research can advance much faster by working with others who are.

SL   From the outside, if you're neither a designer nor a scientist, you may not see why there would be challenges. But in fact both are very "other," so the nature of the two coming together is extraordinary and has the potential to set up discomfort and even conflict.

I get frustrated when people think that designers basically come in to "make something look pretty" at the end. Or that the designer will help you communicate your work better, rather than work together in a true collaboration. Our design team members at Modern Meadow are in the lab, working alongside our scientists, all day, every day—that's how we solve problems together.

MM   What is the role of ethics in design and science?

SL   To what extent do you think subjects like ethics, economics, sustainability, the humanities in general should be taught to both scientists and designers as part of their training?

NB   As synthetic biology becomes increasingly powerful, I think a strong focus on ethics in education becomes even more important. This was exemplified by the recent CRISPR babies case, where Chinese researcher He Jankui introduced nonproven mutations in embryos to make them supposedly HIV resistant. An unfortunate example of what happens when innovative research is conducted with a lack of ethics.

Ethics courses are of course taught, at least during my studies. I found them very relevant and interesting, but I could see that a lot of peers felt it to be more of an obligation than something crucial for their academic career. Most preferred classes about science over ethics. I think those university classes are typically too theoretical, they should be taught in more tangible ways and closer to the work of the scientist as well as to society. The international student competition for synthetic biology iGEM is doing a good job at integrating science eduction with ethics.

SL   It reminds me of Red Hook, the neighborhood where I live in Brooklyn, New York. Part of the reason I moved there was because we have a cultural center called Pioneer Works. They have incredible public programming for a general audience. Some of the best events I have been to had two eminent scientists onstage being asked fundamental questions about the motivation and impact of their work. These events are standing room only—they're blockbuster happenings! You can sense that there is a real hunger for people wanting to understand science, to have a public debate. A great facilitator can help tease out the significance of the science to society along with the challenges that were overcome along the way. At their roots these are the amazing stories of individual creative beings. They just happen to be scientists. How/what would you teach designers about ethics in relation to science?

NB   For both scientists and designers it's important to be aware of your own values and those of others and the potential implications that your work can have on society. Like with every technology, innovations from synthetic biology also could be accidentally or purposely used in the wrong way or made available for only a small group of people when they are too expensive or too complicated to be used for ordinary applications. Designers can play an important role in incorporating ethics into the design of synthetic biology-linked products, for example, by taking into account biosafety, cultural, financial, and user aspects. You probably have better ideas than I on how to teach this to designers, but I think that designers should be part of conversations about how we make sure that tech is used for good. And more philosophically, how do you define what is good?

MM   What are the challenges with designers communicating science?

SL   There are designers whose work is investigative or critical but not necessarily lab based. I worry when design tips into the "speculative" and is perhaps even dystopian, without fully engaging with the complexities of the subject.

When design is beautifully executed it can look very convincing. It's easy for a speculative project to be picked up by the media for clickbait without any attempt to communicate nuance and simply be represented as real. This can be genuinely harmful to the field. I have heard frustration from synthetic biologists who find such publicity unhelpful and disruptive, especially in the Trump era of scientific skepticism and fake news. We need greater understanding of the ethical complexities of scientific advances in mainstream media. Design, tech, and lifestyle outlets have a responsibility to not hype, or worse, misrepresent work—people often read only the headline, believe it, and then you're in danger of setting up fearful perceptions around science.

NB   I can't agree with you more. I have found myself frustrated in some art/design exhibitions when seeing speculative design with many scientific errors but so well executed. It looked very real to nonexperts. I saw a project where the artist, dressed as a scientist in a white lab coat, made a video of himself going into a freezer to get some samples and showing how easy it is to make a weird organism with all sorts of genes from other organisms.

SL   In the exhibition, were people asking questions like "Is this real, does it exist?" Or were people accepting it as fact?

NB   Actually, I'm not sure what they believed. But I'm pretty sure that it was not possible for nonbiologists to know if it was fact or fiction. Of course, they were in an art exhibition, so maybe it made them less worried that this was

199

real. But if you isolate it from the museum, then for sure, it is very believable. I wonder what the idea behind such work is. Is it to be provocative or to fuel a debate? I think speculative design can be used for these purposes, but it should not misinform the public about science. What role and responsibility do you think designers have in science communication?

SL It depends on the project. If a designer has been commissioned to work with a scientist to communicate the work of the scientist then it would be poor design not to have helped a visitor gain a better grasp of the science and related issues. You may do that through all kinds of means, including humor, performance, etc. I would argue that a design project that engages with science, even if not initiated by a scientist, still has a responsibility to represent and explore evidence-based science through design thinking. Art, conversely, is not bound by the same restrictions. In fact, art has always served to interrogate our humanity, society, to ask difficult questions, to be machiavellian—art, as you note, however, exists in a context where we can expect to feel uncomfortable and provoked. So being cognizant of context is key.

MM What have been some methods and tools for designers and scientists communicating with each other?

SL At Modern Meadow the design team labored over the creation of a system that breaks down aesthetics, haptics, and manufacturing processes into quantifiable elements to help bring the subjective closer to the objective and therefore help our materials scientists better understand feedback and progress. It's been very successful, but we continually evolve and improve it.

NB It's interesting how you adapt your communication to what scientists are used to. I also adapt my language and word use depending on whom I am talking to. Good communication within a team of different disciplines requires both sides to acquire a basic level of understanding of how the other works and what they can do so you can develop a common language.

MM Give some examples of communication gaps between scientists and nonscientists.

SL A few areas of mismatched understanding are scale, time, and predictability.

NB Sounds very familiar! The complexity, uncertainty, but also how research works and when you can trust it or not. Scientists are trained to check the sources of what an article claims. Who conducted the research? How many times was it repeated? Did other groups of researchers find similar results? Where was the research published? The internet allows anyone to write an article or blog about science and nonscientists should be educated in how to judge that information.

MM Give some examples of how approaching this communication gap differently has enhanced the understanding between scientists and nonscientists.

SL I always refer back to the film and book *Powers of Ten* by Charles and Ray Eames. That is a wonderful attempt to bridge the understanding of scale for designers. Much more work needs to be done here—we need to return to the Renaissance mindset.

NB I believe researchers should be better trained in public outreach. Current science education in academia is generally focused on peer-to-peer communication. This is why for a few years I have been training other scientists in science communication to different audiences.

MM Do you think citizen science has played a role in helping or hindering this communication gap?

SL I think citizen science can play a tremendous role; it's kind of how I started myself. I've had no formal scientific training, and there are many designers and nonscientists discovering the world of synthetic biology, made accessible by affordable tools like those Nadine pointed to previously: Biorealize, Bento, and Amino Labs. The hacker mentality that gave us the Apples and Microsofts of the twentieth century are likely to produce some of the successful biotech companies of the twenty-first century. We're seeing nontraditional, more agile biotech spaces, like OpenCell in London, supported and encouraged by leaders in synbio. That type of initiative brings both worlds together as an innovation community.

NB Experiencing science is probably the best communication that exists. The more tangible you can make science for people, the better.

MM   You also have to communicate a somewhat new vocabulary to a wider audience: investors, educators, and a general public. What are the challenges? What is your strategy?

SL   I'm lucky in that the area of biotech that is my "home" is biofabrication. I think the word says it all. It's about fabricating with biology. When it comes to communicating to a wider audience it's helpful to use analogies, e.g., "our process is like brewing beer, but instead of the yeast cells turning sugar into alcohol, our yeast cells produce collagen." Good design excels at synthesizing and simplifying information and helping present ideas in more accessible ways.

NB   I can relate to that. I always try to put myself in the shoes of the person or people I am talking to. What do they know? What would be relevant to share and why? What is my message and what could be the outcome of the conversation. It's not always easy to answer these questions at the outset, but when you do, it really helps in the final communication.

MM   How do you use the word "design?"

SL   So when you talked about design you immediately went to things like illustration and the presentation of your scientific ideas.

NB   Well, it's a lot broader than that; I also "design" experiments.

SL   Yes, there's so much wrapped up in the word "design." Let's see if we define it the same way? For me an overarching definition might simply be finding solutions to problems, making life easier/better for people (which is what sets it apart from art), and aligning with Dieter Rams's ten commandments of good design. The presentation of ideas would be communication design (e.g., an illustration), but there's also product design, interaction design, experience design, etc. The context and method of design process are key; when you speak about "experiment design," Nadine, aren't you laying out a problem and planning a way to find a solution—to prove or disprove a hypothesis? Design does this too, but frequently it might take the form of something less deliberate. We might start working with materials or methods without a clear end point, we might learn what could be possible by experiencing through our hands, making visual observations, noticing user behavior—all the while acquiring tacit knowledge that we then translate back into an iterative understanding that informs a brief and allows us to improve a design over time.

What we could maybe say is that design for scientists is different from what design means to designers since this word can be used in many different ways. Design as in design of experiments, design of a cell, design of a product, design of graphics, design of graphs, etc. We need to specify what we mean when using this word.

With biofabrication I see design at several levels. Cell engineers "design" organisms like bacteria and yeast to produce protein materials like spider silk and collagen; we take the "product" of that cell factory and "design" fibers and fabrics that we can then "design" into consumer products (a coat, a chair, a car interior, etc). So one huge challenge I have experienced in grappling with how design and science come together effectively is in the understanding of scale. As a designer I've only ever designed things I can see and feel or experience. I work at the macro and perhaps micro scale but not at the nano scale. Biology, and the design of living organisms, happens at that nano (molecular) scale, which is harder to apprehend and translate into a product like a shoe! The second big challenge for designers in working with biology is time. I can prototype with existing materials in the moment and discover a result—there's no way to rapidly speed up life and growth! Small improvements might be achieved to accelerate a process like fermentation, but we're still talking days not minutes. And maybe a third challenge for designers trying to understand a science like biology is its unpredictability.

NB   Exactly. What is interesting about the challenges you are mentioning is that they are similar for scientists. We also prefer organisms that grow fast, produce a product of interest efficiently, behave in a predictable way in different conditions. At the same time, with the introduction of synthetic biology we are finally talking about "designing" living systems. This means that at least our level of knowledge and ability to deal with these challenges has at least improved enough to allow for the design of organisms in the first place. We are maybe far from solving all these issues, but we hope increased progress in understanding of biology will in the end benefit both scientists and designers working with biology (e.g., speeding up the production of a biomaterial production or allowing the precise engineering of its look and feel).

MM   What does GMO mean?

NB   GMO (genetically modified organism) is a word that people know and relate to as something scary. If you ask people in detail what it means, they usually refer to Monsanto, but are often unaware that insulin is made by genetically modified organisms as well.

SL   I always find it amusing in America when you meet a non-GMO advocate but they're most likely wearing a GMO cotton T-shirt. Nearly 100 percent of cotton grown in America is genetically modified. We seem comfortable with GMOs in certain instances but not others. For example, people who eat organic but use skincare products that for sure contain GMO ingredients or were created with a GMO. So it seems not all GMOs are treated equally in the eyes of the customer.

NB   Yes, I also noticed that the label "no GMO" is often used on products in the U.S. as a means to brand them as more natural/healthier, because most people believe GMOs are bad.

SL   I agree with you, and I think it gets even more complicated. A consumer product could be manufactured using a genetically modified organism, but as long as there is no genetic material left in the end product it's legitimate to market it as "no GMO." I don't think most people know that.

NB   What is also quite ambiguous, most European countries prohibit the production of GMOs; however, it's okay to import them. Or, a plant is not called GMO when it has been exposed to a lot of UV radiation that caused many random mutations in its DNA while, at least according to a new law in the European Union, a CRISPR-engineered plant in which a scientist used a precise DNA editing tool (CRISPR-Cas9) to make a specific modification in the DNA (that could also have occurred spontaneously in nature) is considered a GMO. It's as if the GMO label does not depend on the result (a plant with a small DNA change), but more on the level of human activity involved to make the DNA change. Interestingly, in the United States CRISPR-engineered plants are not considered GMOs.

SL   Right.

NB   As GMOs or GMO products will increasingly impact our lives, it is important to have more open discussions about this.

SL   Whose responsibility is that? Is it scientists doing the research? Is it the corporations who are earning the money from the products? Is it governments who endorse those technologies? Is it broader society putting pressure?

NB   Well, it's probably a mix of all of those.

SL   What is the global synthetic biology community doing to guide that conversation?

NB   I think the concept of GMO is abstract and not straightforward to grasp, as it is a generalization of many products. Therefore, it is almost impossible to say that all GMOs are good or all are bad. As a community we need to show how diverse GMOs can be and what it means for people and our societies. In the near future, this conversation will be facilitated by synthetic biology products like spider-silk shoes, lab-grown leather jackets, or therapies based on patient-engineered cells. I also see community members who are developing innovative educational kits like Bento Labs or Amino Labs to teach synbio. On a personal level, I try to proactively engage with and educate the general public, regulators, and high school teachers in my direct environment and support other scientists with the science communication. When talking about GMOs, I think it is important to listen to concerns of people and to be open about potential risks or what we don't know yet. Fact sharing is not enough. First you need to build relationships of trust.

MM   As the area of synthetic biology is rapidly growing, what is the best way to tell the story about its importance and relevance to the general population? (Some people see it as very alien and somewhat freaky.)

SL   What I have found most compelling is creating everyday relatable products (a shoe, a bag, a T-shirt) appealing to people through design and then explaining how it was made. No one is fearful of a pair of sneakers! Design allows us to defuse the fear factor of science like synbio and infuse it with wonder.

NB   Synthetic biology forces us to rethink the relation between nature and technology. We perceive both as opposites, but nature is full of amazing and very useful technology. Synthetic biology helps us to make better use of this natural technology as a solution for all sorts of problems when done in a responsible way.

MM   What has been the structure of the most successful teams you have been involved with?

SL   A balance of people from different disciplines, but most importantly the expertise of each is respected equally. What absolutely doesn't work is designers starting from a position of ego—"you just need to give me this" —or scientists treating designers as lesser beings who don't use "data" they understand.

NB   I totally agree. Diversity can be challenging, but with an open culture and good communication you can get really far.

I feel like hyperspecialization caused disciplines to become more separated over time. Historically, scientists were always mixing different disciplines. Look at Leonardo da Vinci or biologists from the past who made biological sketches or their own instruments for observation. Now it is time to get back together. Synthetic biology, as it mixes many disciplines, is a great example and opportunity of this.

SL   That's so true. Then, are we on the verge of a new renaissance? Where the sciences, and design, technology, and art are once again poised to interact once more to forge a new understanding of the world?

NB   I hope so.

Nurture

Fig. 1   The corner of Jorge Gamboa's
kitchen in Puebla, Mexico.

In the corner of graphic designer Jorge Gamboa's kitchen in Puebla, Mexico, is a water jug, a refrigerator, and a basket with plastic shopping bags balanced on top (Fig. 1). In Puebla, and throughout much of Mexico, tap water is often unsafe to drink. Drinking water is obtained by purchasing plastic water jugs of filtered water, and it is cooled or frozen in plastic-encased refrigerators. Gamboa is one of millions of people living today whose access to clean water and ice is dependent on plastic.

Less than a fifth of all plastic is recycled globally—to date, 6.3 billion tons of plastic has become unrecycled waste.[1] Each year, millions of tons of plastic make their way into our oceans, resulting in the deaths of marine animals and the continued pollution of the world's water sources. Although these statistics about our present are staggering, projections suggest a far more terrifying future. The World Economic Forum expects that by 2050, if we do not change our current consumption of plastic, there will be more plastic than fish in the world's oceans.[2] The plastics in Gamboa's home are a small visible part of a much larger problem that remains hidden from view.

One afternoon, as Gamboa contemplated the tower of objects in his kitchen, he realized that he could reduce them to three "elements"—plastic, water, and ice. Gamboa reached for a plastic bag from the top of the tower. If he angled it just so, it began to look like the form of an iceberg. Gamboa perched the bag on a branch and, after much trial and error, discovered that natural light was essential to capturing the translucent form of the plastic in such a way that suggested an iceberg. He uploaded the photo to his computer and manipulated the image to place the bag floating in the midst of a clear blue body of water, one bright corner jutting above the rippling surface.

Plasticeberg (2017) is deceptively simple. At first glance, there is a majestic beauty to the iceberg glistening in the sun above the waterline. It takes a moment for the eye to focus on what is floating below the surface in the darkened depths of the ocean, where the handles and edges of the plastic bag reveal themselves to the viewer. Perhaps this clever double-take is why, as soon as Gamboa's design was publicized as the first-place winner of the BICeBé 2017 International Poster Contest in Bolivia, Plasticeberg went viral. The image was shared widely on the internet, and by early 2018, Plasticeberg had become the face of National Geographic's "Planet or Plastic?" initiative to reduce single-use plastics, gracing the magazine's cover and commanding attention in supermarkets and bookstores around the world.

The sustained international praise of Gamboa's design is a testament to the power of a single image to capture the essence of a truly global crisis. The plastic bag ethereally floating in the ocean transcends linguistic boundaries and resonates across communities. Plasticeberg, Gamboa says, "speaks for itself, and I would hope that it would spark a light in people and raise awareness."[3]

Plasticeberg is a lyrical, heartbreaking evocation of our harsh reality. It is also a call to arms. Plastic consumption is part of our daily routines throughout the world. Embedded in Gamboa's metaphorical image is the reminder that more than 40 percent of plastic is used just once and discarded.[4] Our recycling systems are not effective enough to combat this crisis (Fig. 2). We need to drastically reduce our dependence on plastics immediately if we want nature as we know it to survive.

Our global crisis extends far beyond the use and disposal of plastics. In 2018, the United Nations scientific panel on climate change detailed a harrowing picture of our world in the coming decades. The continued warming of our Earth has irrefutable dire consequences,[5] but design offers us the power to veer away from this calamitous trajectory. In ways large and small, designers are challenging us to reevaluate the way we live and change our behavior to align with nature.

Fig. 2   A tiny seahorse swims with a
discarded plastic cotton swab off the
coast of Sumbawa, Indonesia, 2017.

Plasticeberg, 2017; Jorge Gamboa
(Mexican, b. 1984)

Our greatest source of illumination, the sun, is the heart of our solar system. Light from the sun does more than illuminate our world. It provides warmth and delivers energy to plants, which engage in photosynthesis to convert carbon dioxide (CO_2) and water into carbohydrates. Humans have always supplemented illumination from the sun with other light sources, but, since the industrial age, we have transformed our world through electroluminescence. At present, nearly 20 percent of worldwide energy consumption is in service of lighting.[6] Our collective dependence on electric forms of light is taking a toll on our planet, and prompting designers to consider a new way of thinking. What if our sources of illumination depended on a symbiotic relationship between humans and other organisms? What if our lamps were alive?

Hanging from a steel cable in Dutch designer Teresa van Dongen's studio is Spark of Life (2016–ongoing), a massive glass bulb that emits light from an unlikely source—electrochemically active bacteria. Embedded between four handblown glass segments is a microbial fuel cell, containing the bacteria, which generates power when it emits electrical currents and exchanges electrons with an electrode. The electrode is in turn attached to a light-emitting diode (LED) that produces a sustained dim glow. It is the living organisms that create the light, and those organisms require regular feeding to survive. Every week or so, van Dongen delivers a teaspoon of acetate to the bacteria via a syringe, which keeps them active. Every month, van Dongen administers tap water, salt, and vitamins to sustain the bacteria's long-term health.

For the past several years, van Dongen has been engaged in "the search for a living lamp."[7] She stumbled upon the potential of electrochemically active bacteria while attending a lecture of Dr. Korneel Rabaey, the head of the Department of Biochemical and Microbial Technology at Ghent University. Dr. Rabaey and his colleagues helped van Dongen find the right bacteria to harness, drawing on research begun decades ago into the deployment of bacteria to clean waste water. As van Dongen describes it, the production of electrons by the bacteria is just a side effect, but it is one ripe with potential. "Scientific experimentation," she says, is often begun to "serve big-scale solutions. But small-scale solutions add up."[8]

The awareness that the light is provided by living organisms is as important as its functionality for van Dongen—she isn't interested in the idea of turning her lamps on and off. The bacteria's process of discharging electrons is similar to our process of exhaling CO_2. To dim the lamp "would be like dimming the sound of someone breathing."[9] Her aim is to produce a light that feels alive. With Electric Life (2018), van Dongen has evolved her design to create a series of floor lamps that suggest living insects through their LED-embedded eyes. Electric Life is designed to encourage "a closer relationship" between the living lights and their owner. The lamp provides illumination, but only if the "creatures" are nurtured.[10]

The future of living lights may not be confined to bacteria. What if our world could be illuminated by plants? That is the question driving an interdisciplinary team at MIT, who have been exploring the potential of nurturing living light sources at a different scale. Scientists Seon-Yeong Kwak and Michael Strano have created living, breathing forms of light, Nanobionic Plant Project: Ambient Illumination (2016–ongoing). In collaboration with engineers and architects, including Sheila Kennedy, "the group's goal is to engineer plants to take over many of the functions now performed by electrical devices."[11]

To make a living plant emit sustained visible light, the Strano Lab infuses it with chemically interacting nanoparticles including luciferin, luciferase (which modifies luciferin so it will glow), and coenzyme A (which enhances the enzyme luciferase's power).[12] The metabolism of the plant then powers the light emission.[13] Initial experiments have focused on hardy mature watercress plants, but ongoing research suggests the potential for successful illumination of larger-leaf plants in the near future. Plants, the Strano Lab has noted, "are adapted for persistence and self-repair in harsh environments," making them "compelling platforms for engineering new functions."[14] The implications of this research suggest the possibility of a radical shift in our dependence on conventional lighting. "Our work," says Michael Strano, "opens up the doorway to streetlamps that are nothing but treated trees, and to indirect lighting around homes."[15]

The importance of plant life in our infrastructure goes beyond the potential to provide illumination. Urban green spaces are essential for human physical and mental health, facilitating everything from oxygen and moderated temperatures to social interaction and physical activity.[16] In Vietnamese cities, where rapid urban development has taken place in recent decades, green space has all but disappeared. The United Nations has recommended that cities provide a minimum of ten square meters of green space per person, yet Vietnam's urban areas average less than three square meters per person.[17] The chronic dearth of Vietnamese urban green space has given rise to architect Vo Trong Nghia's commitment to create a green architecture that resonates with his culture. "For a modern architect," Nghia says, "the most important mission is to bring green spaces back to the Earth. How many green areas and trees can we give back to the Earth when we design a building?"[18]

FPT University Ho Chi Minh City (2016–ongoing)[19] is a new university campus building designed by Vo Trong Nghia (VTN) Architects that seeks to facilitate "harmony between humans and nature." Designed to suggest a growing mountain, the building features staggered floors enclosing a substantial park filled with trees and plants. These green elements extend from the central courtyard to the balconies, terraces, and circulation wells of the building. "A tree is the cheapest sun shade device in Vietnam,"[20] Nghia points out, facilitating shade and cooling while improving air quality and reducing the need for energy-consuming air conditioning. For Nghia, green architecture "helps people live with nature . . . if people can develop a sense of treasuring nature, their way of urban planning and construction will become more eco-friendly."[21] VTN Architects hope that the FPT University Ho Chi Minh City campus will foster a new generation of thinkers who embrace the integration of plants in urban environments. For if "the thinking doesn't change," says Nghia, "people will soon live in concrete jungles."[22]

Some would argue that the concrete jungles that Nghia portends for the future are already in existence in many parts of the world. Concrete is ubiquitous in our built environment, but few realize that the manufacturing of concrete accounts for nearly 7 percent of industrial energy production, and 7 percent of the world's CO_2 emissions.[23] Although the International Energy Agency is collaborating with major cement producers to identify systems to reduce CO_2 emissions, the popularity of concrete as a building material seems unlikely to change in the coming decades.

At the Bartlett School of Architecture, University College London, Richard Beckett and Marcos Cruz established the BiotA Lab (2014–18) to facilitate radical approaches to green architecture through "biologically intelligent agendas."[24] BiotA Lab merged expertise in engineering, architecture, and biology toward a long-term goal: bioreceptive design.[25] In collaboration with Javier Ruis, Beckett and Cruz designed Bioreceptive Concrete Panels (2017–19), magnesium phosphate concrete panels that encourage the growth of rootless cryptogams—moss, lichens, and algae—all resilient microorganisms that conduct photosynthesis and absorb air pollution.

The idea that growth should be encouraged, not cleaned off the surface of buildings, demands a new perspective on the architectural façade. Historically, the "irregular nature of growth patterns" in biocolonization have not resonated with the traditional aesthetic approach of modern architecture, which has been developed to bring light and air in, but keep germs out. Splotches of moss and lichen on the surfaces of concrete buildings have been perceived as eyesores. Yet "any 'empty' surfaces in cities offer the potential opportunity for growth to happen" if we embrace a new aesthetic of bio-ornamentation.[26] By supporting and enhancing growth, bioreceptive design "goes beyond the idea of current green walls" and "allows nature to grow according to its own rules in a reciprocal response to parameters of a biodigital material."[27]

To design the bioreceptive concrete panels, Beckett, Cruz, and Ruis drew inspiration from tree bark, which "allows for growth to happen on the immediacy of the architectural skin."[28] Observation of tree bark enabled the designers to generate "fissures, depressions, and striations" in the concrete that channel rainwater and define areas of growth.[29] These predetermined geometries are not found in nature, but are optimized to be bioreceptive. When concrete is subjected to computer numerical controlled milling, these

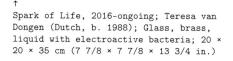

Spark of Life, 2016-ongoing; Teresa van
Dongen (Dutch, b. 1988); Glass, brass,
liquid with electroactive bacteria; 20 ×
20 × 35 cm (7 7/8 × 7 7/8 × 13 3/4 in.)

↓

Electric Life, 2018; Teresa van Dongen
(Dutch, b. 1988); Steel, aluminum, glass,
liquid with electroactive bacteria; 137 ×
90.8 × 78.5 cm (53.9 × 35.75 × 30.91 in.)

Nanobionic Plant Project: Ambient
Illumination, 2016-ongoing; Michael
Strano (American, b. 1975), Seon-Yeong
Kwak (Korean, b. 1983), and Pavlo
Gordiichuk (Ukrainian, b. 1986), MIT
Chemical Engineering (Cambridge,
Massachusetts, USA, founded 1888) and
Sheila Kennedy (American, b. 1959), Ben
Widger (American, b. 1984), Anne Graziano
(American, b. 1993), Jeffrey Landman
(United Kingdom, b. 1988), Karaghen
Hudson (American, b. 1995), Zain Karsan
(Canadian, b. 1991), and Patrick Weber
(German, b. 1994), MIT Architecture
(Cambridge, Massachusetts, USA, founded
1932), and KVA (Boston, Massachusetts,
USA, founded 1990); Nanobionic watercress
plants; Dimensions variable

FPT University Ho Chi Minh City, 2016-
ongoing; Ho Chi Minh City, Vietnam,
expected 2019; VTN (Vo Trong Nghia)
Architects (Ho Chi Minh City, Vietnam,
founded 2006)

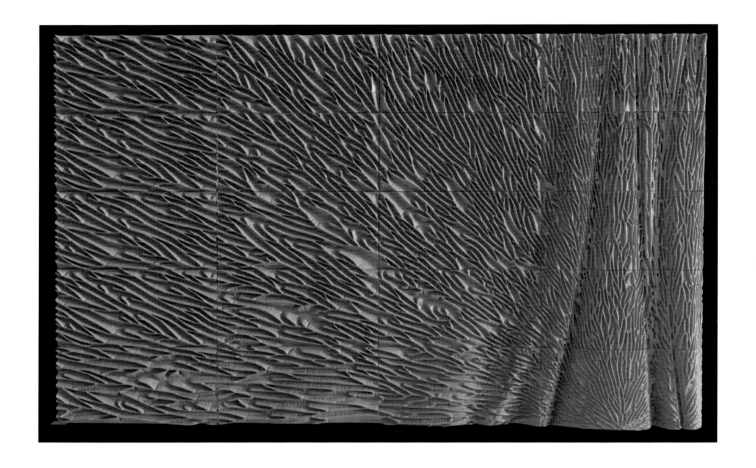

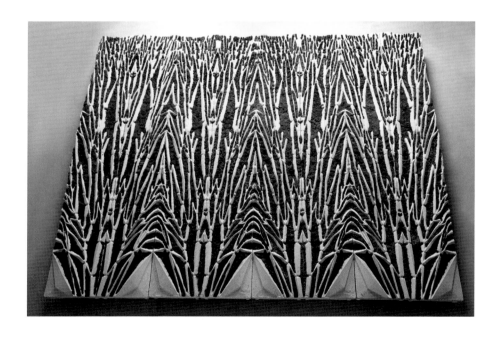

Bioreceptive Concrete Panels, 2017-19;
Marcos Cruz (German and Portuguese,
b. 1970), Richard Beckett (British, b.
1979), and Javier Ruiz (Spanish, b.
1984); Concrete; Dimensions variable

For full caption information,
see page 239.

geometries are incised into the concrete and then seeded, creating a favorable environment for biocolonization.

The idea of choreographing architecture to collaborate with nature has large-scale implications—our urban façades may soon become welcoming hosts for all manner of microorganisms. But it also operates on a site-specific level, as in the work of architect Hiroshi Sambuichi. For Sambuichi, architecture is made up of "moving materials," sun, water, and air. In his practice, Sambuichi "seeks to rediscover the confluence between design and nature," and "to bring out the beauty of a specific place."[30] Sambuichi observes a place during all four seasons before conceiving of his design. This intense investigation allows him to build according to the "moving materials" of the place. "I want to create endemic architecture," says Sambuichi. "Architecture which is adapted to a specific area. If this is well done, and there is a relationship between water and sun, the place will look beautiful." We live in beautiful places, says Sambuichi, and "architecture is meant to make people see that."[31]

For his architectural installation The Water at Cisternerne of Frederiksberg (2017) in Copenhagen, Denmark, Sambuichi reopened the ground that had been covering a series of water cisterns for more than one hundred and fifty years. In doing so, he reconnected the sun and the water for the first time in more than a century. While the original aim of the cisterns was to collect and protect water, Sambuichi's installation is designed to help people think about the changing states of water. As visitors move through the installation, they stroll through the cisterns on wooden platforms that allow them to walk over the water. The platforms run the full length of the space, and as visitors move along they "hear the water" and "feel the air," becoming aware of temperature and humidity. It is only at the end of the installation that visitors come to a top light where the sun enters. Water changes to mist, sunlight reflects in the water, and wind gains and loses velocity. The installation facilitates a meditative engagement with nature, and suggests a different understanding of what architecture might be. "It is important to understand that water can become lighter than air. If people understand that, they will understand the relation between human beings and the Earth."[32]

Understanding the interconnectedness of human beings and the natural world is the ultimate aim of Rwanda Institute for Conservation Agriculture (RICA) (2018–ongoing), designed by the nonprofit architecture firm MASS Design Group. The school campus, which is currently being constructed, has been designed in an effort to improve human, ecological, and animal health in a symbiotic system. In Rwanda, years of inadequate land management has led to soil erosion, which in turn has caused fertility decline in the soil.[33] RICA aims to foster education and training of future leaders in conservation agriculture, who will then implement best practices to improve soil fertility and, by extension, improve health across all living organisms. By nurturing the land, food independence in Rwanda becomes an attainable goal.

In both its built environment and its curriculum, RICA demonstrates the principles of One Health, which is defined by the Centers for Disease Control and Prevention as recognition "that the health of people is connected to the health of plants and the environment."[34] For MASS Design Group, this means promoting biodiversity, ecological conservation, and their relationship to human health. Integrated throughout the campus are woodlands, geological and wellness gardens, areas of agroforestry, and medicinal plantings. The housing facilities are designed to foster teamwork; students live on a small farm that they manage together. The campus structures are built with materials and fabricated with techniques that support One Health principles, including locally sourced and low-carbon options. The architectural plan focuses equally on nurturing social cohesion, providing sites of education, and building back diversity in the surrounding savannah and wetlands.

Just north of Rwanda, in the grasslands and savannah woodlands of several countries in East and Central Africa, lies the natural habitat of the nearly extinct northern white rhino (Ceratotherium simum cottoni). For most of human history, herds of northern white rhinos, the most social of rhinos, roamed these grasslands. Then, in the twentieth century, the subspecies was decimated by poachers who killed the rhinos for their horns. By 2008, the northern white rhino was extinct in the wild. On March 19, 2018, the last male northern white rhino, Sudan, died at age 45. Upon his death, his subspecies was reduced to just two living females, Najin and Fatu, who live at the Ol Pejeta Conservancy in Kenya under armed surveillance. Neither Najin nor Fatu is capable of natural reproduction.[35] As a result, the only hope for the survival of the subspecies is through in-vitro fertilization using sperm and skin samples taken from Sudan, which were extracted while he was living and immediately after his death.

Reports of Sudan's death made international news, in part because they were coupled with accounts of the dedicated, if controversial, efforts to pull the subspecies back from the brink of extinction through expensive and experimental biotechnologies. The intentions of those working to save the northern white rhino from extinction raise a paradox for artist and designer Alexandra Daisy Ginsberg. Humans, Ginsberg notes, are preoccupied with creating new life forms, but fail to value existing ones to the point of extinction. "Will humans protect a resurrected rhino, having neglected an entire species?"[36]

In The Substitute (2019), Ginsberg "brings back to life" a male northern white rhino, informed by a simultaneous development in the human creation of artificial intelligence (AI). Working with visual effects agency The Mill using research from leading AI lab DeepMind, Ginsberg presents a digital model of a northern white rhino performing as an artificial agent, a term used in AI to describe an autonomous entity that can learn from its environment. Viewers of The Substitute stand in front of a life-size floor-to-ceiling projection of the artificial rhino, which is confined to a virtual room. During the course of several minutes, the artificial rhino navigates its way around this box, becoming more "intelligent" over time as it learns from experience. As the artificial rhino habituates to its space, its form and sound toggle from pixilation to lifelike—reminding the viewer that this living, breathing rhino, coming to life without its natural context, is entirely artificial. Its sounds are adapted from rare archive footage of the last northern white rhinos, shared by rhino vocalization expert Dr. Richard Policht.

The Substitute makes use of cutting-edge research into AI's potential, led by Andrea Banino at DeepMind, to develop navigational techniques similar to the specialized brain cells—"grid cells"—naturally evolved in mammals. Efficient navigation is a cognitive challenge for AI. Now, DeepMind has discovered that an artificial agent in a box, learning from experimental data of real rats, developed a grid-like solution to localize itself.[37] In The Substitute, the DeepMind experiment is used to generate paths for the rhino specific to his virtual enclosure: embodying the agent, the rhino begins its life with no "grid cells" and, as it moves around the space, calibrating to markers, it develops them, becoming increasingly "intelligent."

Ginsberg's design practice is experimental—she examines the relationship between design, nature, and the world, particularly the role of design in biology. Preserving an idealized northern white rhino in a digital cabinet of curiosity, The Substitute questions the emphasis put on de-extinction since the death of Sudan, while humans elsewhere strive to develop artificial consciousness. The northern white rhino stands on the brink of extinction not because of evolution, but because of poaching, poverty, war, and human disregard for nature. Experimental science and technology may resurrect the northern white rhino, but the subspecies' survival "requires social, not genetic, engineering," says Ginsberg. She raises parallel concerns around AI.

Humans are discovering ways to resurrect the northern white rhino artificially and biologically. In July 2018, scientists in Italy announced that they had successfully created a group of hybrid white rhino embryos that mixed DNA from two subspecies, the northern and southern white rhino (*Ceratotherium simum simum*).[38] The new embryos are now frozen, awaiting future implantation, and foreshadowing a future where genetic intervention on the part of humans produces new forms of life to replace ones we have abandoned. At the same time, The Substitute demonstrates that we can also bring to life digitally an extinct rhino; divorced from its species and habitat, humans control the inputs from which it learns. "What errors in reproduction may arise as we recreate life artificially?" asks Ginsberg. "Will ever we manage to control ourselves, or our designs?"[39]

The Water at Cisternerne of
Frederiksberg, 2017; Copenhagen, Denmark;
Hiroshi Sambuichi (Japanese, b. 1968)

Rwanda Institute for Conservation
Agriculture, 2018-ongoing; Karama
district, Rwanda, expected 2020; MASS
Design Group (Boston, Massachusetts, USA,
founded 2008)

↑
Sudan, the last male northern white
rhino, is comforted by Joseph Wachira
moments before he passed away on
March 19, 2018.

The Substitute, 2019; Alexandra Daisy
Ginsberg (British and South African, b.
1982), with The Mill (London, England,
UK, founded 1990); Sound by: Chris
Timpson (British, b. 1980), Aurelia
Soundworks (London, England, UK, founded
2015); Maya, Unreal Engine, Illustrator,
Aftereffects, Reaper ProTools, Blue
Ripple, Universal Audio; Each video, 3:00
minutes; Commissioned by Cooper Hewitt,
Smithsonian Design Museum and Cube design
museum; Special thanks to: Andrea Banino,
DeepMind, and Dr. Richard Policht

1
Laura Parker, "We Made Plastic. We Depend on It. Now We're Drowning in It," *National Geographic*, June 2018, https://www.nationalgeographic.com/magazine/2018/06/plastic-planet-waste-pollution-trash-crisis/.

2
"The New Plastics Economy. Rethinking the Future of Plastics" (Geneva: World Economic Forum, January 2016), http://www3.weforum.org/docs/WEF_The_New_Plastics_Economy.pdf.

3
"Jorge Gamboa: La portada viral tiene un nombre y es latinoamericano," LATAM_D (Latin American Design Project), May 17, 2018, https://latamd.com/2018/05/17/jorge-gamboa-la-portada-viral-tiene-un-nombre-y-es-latinoamericano/.

4
"10 Shocking Facts about Plastic," *National Geographic* photo essay, 2018, https://www.nationalgeographic.com/environment/plastic-facts/.

5
Coral Davenport, "Major Climate Report Describes a Strong Risk of Crisis as Early as 2040," *The New York Times*, October 7, 2018, https://www.nytimes.com/2018/10/07/climate/ipcc-climate-report-2040.html.

6
Anne Trafton, "Engineers Create Plants that Glow," *MIT News*, December 12, 2017, http://news.mit.edu/2017/engineers-create-nanobionic-plants-that-glow-1213.

7
Teresa van Dongen, interview by Caitlin Condell, September 17, 2018.

8
Ibid.

9
Ibid.

10
Alice Morby, "Teresa van Dongen Uses Living Organisms to Power LED Light," *Dezeen*, November 2, 2016, https://www.dezeen.com/2016/11/02/teresa-van-dongen-night-light-powered-living-organisms-spark-life-dutch-design-week-2016/.

11
Trafton, "Plants That Glow."

12
Seon-Yeong Kwak et al., "A Nanobionic Light-Emitting Plant," *Nano Letters* 17, no. 12 (2017): 7951-61. doi:10.1021/acs.nanolett.7b04369.

13
Trafton, "PlantsThat Glow."

14
Kwak et al., "A Nanobionic Light-Emitting Plant."

15
Trafton, "Plants That Glow."

16
"Health as the Pulse of the New Urban Agenda: United Nations Conference on Housing and Sustainable Urban Development, Quito, October 2016" (Geneva: World Health Organization, 2016), http://www.who.int/iris/handle/10665/250367.

17
Thanh Mai, "Vietnam Lacks Green Spaces, Suburbs Expand to Fill Need," *VietNamNet Bridge*, July 2, 2018, https://english.vietnamnet.vn/fms/environment/194955/vietnam-lacks-green-spaces--suburbs-expand-to-fill-need.html.

18
Nick Ahlmark, "Greening the City," Al Jazeera Media Network, Rebel Architecture Series, video, September 9, 2014, https://www.aljazeera.com/programmes/rebelarchitecture/2014/06/greening-city-2014630864198550.html; "Vo Trong Nghia: 'Living Close to Nature,'" Al Jazeera Media Network, Rebel Architecture Series, August 2, 2014, https://www.aljazeera.com/programmes/rebelarchitecture/2014/08/vo-trong-nghia-living-close-nature-20148511487251222.html.

19
"FPT University Ho Chi Minh City," Vo Trong Nghia Architects, accessed January 31, 2019, http://votrongnghia.com/projects/fpt-university-ho-chi-minh-city/.

20
Ahlmark, "Greening the City."

21
Ibid.

22
Ibid.

23
"Cement Technology Roadmap Shows How the Path to Achieve CO_2 Reductions up to 24% by 2050," World Business Council for Sustainable Development, April 6, 2018, https://www.wbcsd.org/Sector-Projects/Cement-Sustainability-Initiative/News/Cement-technology-roadmap-shows-how-the-path-to-achieve-CO2-reductions-up-to-24-by-2050.

24
"Professor Marcos Cruz," in *Biosalon Catalogue*, edited by Carole Collet and Karen Gaskill (London: Futuro House, Central Saint Martins, December, 2015): 13–15.

25
BiotA Lab operated from 2014 to 2018, but the research into bioreceptive concrete has continued at the Bartlett School of Architecture under the leadership of Richard Beckett, Marcos Cruz, and Javier Ruis.

26
"Professor Marcos Cruz," in *Biosalon Catalogue*.

27
Richard Beckett and Marcos Cruz, "Bioreceptive Design: A Novel Approach to Biodigital Materiality," *Architectural Research Quarterly* 20, no. 01 (2016): 51–64. https://doi.org/10.1017/S1359135516000130.

28
Ibid.

29
Ibid.

30
"Sambuichi Interview: Building with Sun, Water and Air," video, June 7, 2017, https://www.youtube.com/watch?v=kmxoeKU8wbM.

31
Ibid.

32
Ibid.

33
Alphonse Nahayo, Genxing Pan, and Stephen Joseph, "Factors Influencing the Adoption of Soil Conservation Techniques in Northern Rwanda," *Journal of Plant Nutrition and Soil Science* 79, no. 3 (2016): 367–75, https://doi.org/10.1002/jpln.201500403.

34
"One Health," Centers for Disease Control and Prevention, https://www.cdc.gov/onehealth/index.html.

35
Fatu is infertile due to a uterine infection. Najin is unable to carry a pregnancy to term because of damage to her hind legs as a result of spending years in a zoo standing on concrete. See Mary Holland, "Can the Northern White Rhino Come Back from the Edge of Extinction?" *Condé Nast Traveler*, September 22, 2018, https://www.cntraveler.com/story/can-the-northern-white-rhino-come-back-from-the-edge-of-extinction.

36
Alexandra Daisy Ginsberg, "The Substitute," proposal submitted to Cooper Hewitt, Smithsonian Design Museum, July 20, 2018.

37
Ian Sample, "Google DeepMind's AI Program Learns Human Navigation Skills," *The Guardian*, May 9, 2018, https://www.theguardian.com/technology/2018/may/09/googles-ai-program-deepmind-learns-human-navigation-skills.

38
Helen Thomson, "Hybrid White-Rhino Embryos Created in Last-Ditch Effort to Stop Extinction," *Nature*, July 4, 2018, doi:10.1038/d41586-018-05636-6.

39
Ginsberg, "The Substitute," 5.

Glossary

Researched and edited by
Margaret Simons

Acetic acid
A clear, corrosive liquid produced
when airborne bacteria react with
alcohol. When diluted in water, vine-
gar results, and it is the acetic acid that
produces the familiar, pungent odor.
Occurring naturally in the human
body and plant fluids, acetic acid may
also be synthesized.
View *Aguahoja*
Source:
Brown, William H. "Acetic Acid."
    In *Encyclopædia Britannica*,
    September 26, 2018. Accessed
    October 31, 2018. https://www.
    britannica.com/science/acetic-acid.

Actuator
A device that prompts a specific move-
ment or reaction upon contact with an
intended subject.
View *Cilllia* and *Soft Robotic
    Grip Glove*
Source:
"Actuator." In *Merriam-Webster
    Dictionary*. Accessed October 17,
    2018. www.merriam-webster.com/
    dictionary/actuator.

ATP (adenosine triphosphate)
An energy-carrying molecule found
in the cells of all living things. ATP
captures chemical energy obtained
from the breakdown of food molecules
and channels it to fuel other cellular
functions. Although cells continuously
break down ATP to obtain energy,
ATP is assembled simultaneously in
a process called cellular respiration.
During this process, the enzyme ATP
synthase catalyzes the combination
of adenosine diphosphate (ADP) and
phosphate. ATP synthase is located in
the inner membrane of mitochondria.
In plant cells, the enzyme also is found
in chloroplasts.
View *Choreography of Life*
Source:
"Adenosine triphosphate (ATP)."
    In *Britannica Academic*.
    Accessed September 20, 2018.
    https://academic.eb.com/
    levels/collegiate/article/
    adenosine-triphosphate/3722.

Bacterium (pl. bacteria)
A microscopic, single-celled organism
that may live independently or as a
parasite (dependent on a host for life).
The presence of parasitic bacteria may
be detrimental or beneficial to their
hosts. Bacteria populate most environments including water, soil, organic
matter, and multicellular animals.
Bacteria can metabolize almost any
organic compound, and some inorganic compounds, enacting chemical
change such as decay.
View *Metagenomic Data Visualization,
    Project Coelicolor, Biocement Bricks,
    Mourn*, and *Spark of Life*
Sources:
"Bacterium." In *OED Online*. July
    2018. Accessed October 18, 2018.
    http://www.oed.com.
"Bacterium." In *Merriam-Webster
    Dictionary*. Accessed October
    9, 2018. https://www.
    merriam-webster.com/dictionary/
    bacterium.

Biodegradable
Capable of decay when broken down
by living organisms such as bacteria
and fungi. Biodegradable substances
(for example, food and sewage) release
nutrients during the decomposition process that can be recycled by
the ecosystem. Nonbiodegradable
substances such as glass, heavy metals,
and plastics create global, long-term
disposal issues.
View *Department of Seaweed,
    Infinity Burial Suit*, and *Visionary
    Concept Tire*
Sources:
"Biodegradable." In *The Hutchinson
    Unabridged Encyclopedia with
    Atlas and Weather Guide*. Oxford:
    Helicon, 2018. https://search.
    credoreference.com.
Thain, M. and M. Hickman,
    "Biodegradable." In *Penguin
    Dictionary of Biology*, 11th ed.
    London: Penguin Books Ltd.,
    2004. https://search.
    credoreference.com.

Biodiveristy
The variety and variability among
living organisms on Earth, including
terrestrial, marine, and freshwater
ecosystems. In addition to differences
within a habitat, biodiversity may
apply to an examination of variation
within species, between species, and
among ecosystems.
View *Rwanda Institute for Conservation
    Agriculture, TetraPot 2.0—The
    Greener Sea Defense, Eco-Engineered
    Hexagonal Seawall Tiles*, and
    Metagenomic Data Visualization
Source:
"Article 2. Use of Terms." *Convention
    on Biological Diversity*. United
    Nations Environment Programme.
    Accessed October 3, 2018. www.
    cbd.int/convention/articles/default.
    shtml?a=cbd-02.

Bioengineering
The wide-ranging field that
encompasses the activities where
technology and living things intersect.
Bioengineering describes research
as diverse as medically engineered
artificial human limbs to genetically
engineered DNA of a bacteria sample.
View *Nanobionic Plant Project:
    Ambient Illumination, Origami
    Membrane for 3D Organ Engineering*,
    and *Sea Slug Bandages*
Source:
"Bioengineering." *National
    Geographic Science of Everything:
    How Things Work in Our World*.
    Washington DC: National
    Geographic Society, 2013.

Biofabrication
The designing and building of
products utilizing living things. The
process harnesses a range of organisms such as bacteria, yeast, algae,
mycelium, and mammalian cells to
grow and cultivate the raw material for
design objects that includes fashion,
footwear, and furniture.
View *Project Coelicolor, Tissue
    Engineered Textiles*, and *Zoa*
Source:
"Biofabrication?" Accessed October 3,
    2018. https://www.biofabricate.co/.

Biohacking

Independent, biology-based experiments performed outside the confines of academic or corporate laboratories. Biohacking may be interchanged with do-it-yourself biology, community biology, and amateur biology. Many independent biologists steer away from the term "biohacking" because the term "hacking" has been associated with electronic trespassing and bioterrorism.

View *DIY Bacterial Gene Engineering CRISPR Kit*

Source:

Baumgaertner, Emily. "As D.I.Y. Gene Editing Gains Popularity, 'Someone Is Going to Get Hurt.'" *New York Times*, May 14, 2018. https://www.nytimes.com/2018/05/14/science/biohackers-gene-editing-virus.html.

Bio-inspired design

Application or adaption of biological knowledge in the research, development, and fabrication of objects produced across disciplines that include but are not limited to design, medicine, and engineering. Also referred to as biodesign, bio-inspired design includes biomimicry, where natural forms are emulated for new purposes, and the development of new technologies based on the adaption of these natural principals to create original hybrids.

View *Bamboo Theater, Curiosity Cloud, Petrified River*, and the vast majority of objects included in the exhibition

Sources:

Farzaneh, Helena Hashemi and Udo Lindemann. *A Practical Guide to Bio-Inspired Design*. Berlin: Springer Vieweg, 2019.

Myers, William and Paola Antonelli. *Bio Design: Nature Science Creativity*. New York: Thames & Hudson USA, 2014.

Biomass

The total weight or quantity of biological material in a specified area during a period of time. Biomass may also refer to components of a specified area, such as animal, plant, or species biomass. Biomass may be compared between different strata in the environment (e.g., subterranean versus forest canopy) or within the food chain (e.g., herbivore versus carnivore). Measurement of biomass over time is helpful in determining the health of a habitat.

View *Monarch Sanctuary* and *Rwanda Institute for Conservation Agriculture*

Sources:

"Biomass." In *Britannica Academic*. Accessed September 7, 2018. https://academic.eb.com/levels/collegiate/article/biomass/79265.

"Biomass." In *The Encyclopedia of Ecology and Environmental Management*, edited by Peter Calow, 1st ed. Oxford: Blackwell Science Ltd., 1998. doi:10.1002/9781444313253.

Bioplastic

Moldable plastic created from renewable sources that is biodegradable, in contrast to traditional plastics made of petroleum, which are nonbiodegradable. Substances used to create bioplastic range from potato starch to algae to crab shells.

View *After Ancient Sunlight, Algae Lab*, and *Mourn*

Sources:

"Bioplastic." In *Macquarie Dictionary*, edited by Susan Butler, 7th ed. Sydney, Australia: Macquarie Dictionary Publishers, 2017. https://www.macquariedictionary.com.au/.

Zhang, Cici. "Slime Science." *Science World/Current Science*, April 23, 2018. https://scienceworld.scholastic.com/.

Bioreceptive design

The production of substrates designed to promote biocolonization, the fruitful reproduction of plants and simple organisms in or on the object itself.

View *Bioreceptive Concrete Panels* and *Eco-Engineered Hexagonal Seawall Tiles*

Sources:

Cruz, Marcos and Richard Beckett. "Bioreceptive Design: A Novel Approach to Biodigital Materiality." *Architectural Research Quarterly*. 20, no. 01 (2016): 51–64. richard-beckett-architecture.tumblr.com/post/147746552945/article-bioreceptive-design-a-novel-approach-to.

Eveleth, Rose. "The Future of Architecture: Moss, Not Mirrors." *The Atlantic*, December 7, 2015. www.theatlantic.com/technology/archive/2015/12/bioreceptive-buildings/418620/.

Cellulose

A long string of glucose molecules, linear in nature, that serves as the primary component of cell walls in plants and wood. As one of the most abundant compounds on Earth, cellulose is eaten by humans and animals and can serve as a raw material in many goods such as paper, rayon, and cellophane.

View *Aguahoja*

Sources:

"Cellulose." In *Penguin English Dictionary*, edited by R. E. Allen, 3rd ed. London: Penguin, 2007. https://search.credoreference.com.

Schwarz, C. M. "Cellulose." In *Chambers Dictionary*, 13th ed. Edinburgh, Scotland: Chambers Harrap Publishers, 2015.

Chitosan

A derivative product when chitin is chemically or enzymatically broken down. Chitin is an abundant polymer that derives strength from its fibrous molecules. This substance is found most commonly in the exoskeletons of shrimp, crabs, lobsters, insects, and the cell walls of fungi.

View *Aguahoja*

Sources:

Elieh-Ali-Komi, Daniel and Michael R. Hamblin. "Chitin and Chitosan: Production and Application of Versatile Biomedical Nanomaterials." *International Journal of Advanced Research*. U.S. National Library of Medicine: March 1, 2016. www.ncbi.nlm.nih.gov/pmc/articles/PMC5094803/.

Hale, W. G., V. A. Saunders, and J. P. Margham. "Chitin." In *Collins Dictionary of Biology*, 2nd ed. New York: HarperCollins Publishers, 2005.

Coevolution

The reciprocal, adaptive changes occurring in two or more species due to their interaction in a particular environment. The relationship between predator and prey presents a familiar example of coevolution. Adaptive changes may occur across kingdoms as well, such as the relationship between insects and plants.

View *Monarch Sanctuary* and *Rwanda Institute for Conservation Agriculture*

Sources:

Barber, Keith. "Coevolution." In *Dictionary of Physical Geography*, edited by David S. G. Thomas and Goudie Andrew, 4th ed. Oxford: Blackwell Publishers, 2016.

Thompson, John N. "Coevolution." In *The Princeton Guide to Ecology*, edited by Simon A. Levin, et al., 1st ed. Princeton, NJ: Princeton University Press, 2012.

Collagen

The most abundant protein in the animal kingdom, comprising the connective tissues found in skin, muscles, tendons, and blood vessels. Characteristically elastic, fibrous, and strong, a microscopic view reveals twisted strands, and yet collagen converts to gelatin when exposed to boiling water.

View *Zoa*

Sources:

"Collagen." In *Gaither's Dictionary of Scientific Quotations*, edited by Carl C. Gaither and Alma E. Cavazos-Gaither, 2nd ed. New York: Springer Science+Business Media, 2012.

Larrañaga, Michael D., Richard J. Lewis, Sr., and Robert A. Lewis. "Collagen." In *Hawley's Condensed Chemical Dictionary*, 16th ed. Hoboken, NJ: Wiley, 2016.

Youngson, R. M. "Collagen." In *Collins Dictionary of Medicine*, 4th ed. Glasgow: Collins, 2005.

CRISPR-Cas9 (Clustered Regularly Interspaced Short Palindromic Repeats and CRISPR associated protein 9)

CRISPR works in conjunction with the Cas9 protein to edit DNA in a process commonly referred to as gene editing. Cas9 can be guided to specific locations within a DNA strand by a short search string. The Cas9 protein then slices the subject DNA, in order to replace a segment or shut down a portion of the DNA entirely, to enact a desired result.

View *DIY Bacterial Gene Engineering CRISPR Kit* and *BioMess*

Sources:

Lauerman, John. "CRISPR, the Tool Giving DNA Editing Promise and Peril: QuickTake." *Bloomberg QuickTake: Hard-to-explain topics, explained simply.* November 26, 2018. https://www.bloomberg.com/quicktake/gene-editing.

National Institutes of Health. *What Are Genome Editing and CRISPR-Cas9?* NIH Genetics Home Reference. Bethesda, MD: *U.S. National Library of Medicine.* Accessed October 9, 2018. ghr.nlm.nih.gov/primer/genomicresearch/genomeediting.

DNA (Deoxyribonucleic Acid)

Existing in every living thing, DNA carries the genetic indicators on its long, double-helix strands that determine how organisms grow, develop, function and maintain themselves. Housed in the nucleus of cells, DNA resembles a twisted ladder where the rails are comprised of sugars and phosphates and the rungs are pairs of bases bonded with hydrogen; the base adenine pairs with the base thymine, and the base guanine pairs with the base cytosine. The specific order of the bases on the ladder equates to the genetic code for every organism.

View *DIY Bacterial Gene Engineering CRISPR Kit, Metagenomic Data Visualization, Resurrecting the Sublime,* and *Tranceflora*

Sources:

Parker, Steve. *The Human Body Book: An Illustrated Guide to Its Structure, Function and Disorders.* New York: Dorling Kindersley Publishing, 2013.

Schefter, Jim. "DNA Fingerprints on Trial." *Popular Science*, November 1994.

Electrospinning

A natural or synthetic liquid polymer solution pulled toward highly electrocharged metal plates, creating uniform, nanoscale fibers. A multitude of applications incorporate electrospun fibers, including tissue engineering, protective clothing, filtration, biomedicine, pharmaceutical products, optical electronics, biotechnology, defense and security, and environmental engineering.

View *Origami Membrane for 3D Organ Engineering*

Sources:

Bhardwaj, Nandana and Subhas C. Kundu. "Electrospinning: A Fascinating Fiber Fabrication Technique." *Biotechnology Advances*, 28, no. 3 (2010): 325–47. doi:10.1016/j.biotechadv.2010.01.004.

McQuaid, Matilda, et al. *Extreme Textiles: Designing for High Performance.* Hudson, NY: Princeton Architectural Press, 2005.

Wendorff, Joachim H., et al. *Electrospinning: Materials, Processing, and Applications.* Weinheim, Germany: John Wiley & Sons, Inc., 2012.

Enzyme

A biological molecule that acts as a catalyst in living organisms, regulating the rate of chemical reactions. Primarily made of proteins, enzymes also reduce the amount of energy needed to start reactions. Enzymes are specific; a particular enzyme catalyzes only a single reaction or set of closely related reactions. Enzymatic reactions range from human digestion to wine fermentation to wound repair.

View *Choreography of Life*, *Infinity Burial Suit*, *Nanobionic Plant Project: Ambient Illumination*, and *Resurrecting the Sublime*

Sources:

"Enzyme." In *Encyclopædia Britannica*, October 26, 2018. Accessed October 31, 2018. https://www.britannica.com/science/enzyme.

Berg, J. M., J. L. Tymoczko, and L. Stryer. "Enzymes Are Powerful and Highly Specific Catalysts." In *Biochemistry*, 5th ed. New York: W H Freeman, 2002. https://www.ncbi.nlm.nih.gov/books/NBK22380/.

Fermentation

A chemical change induced by a living organism or enzyme, typically involving bacteria, yeast, mold, or fungi, usually converting sugar into acids, gases, or alcohol. Fermentation of particular raw materials can produce cellulose, a material used in biofabrication.

View *Project Coelicolor* and *Zoa*

Source:

Larrañaga, Michael D., Richard J. Lewis, Sr., and Robert A. Lewis. "Fermentation." In *Hawley's Condensed Chemical Dictionary*, 16th ed. Hoboken, NJ: Wiley, 2016.

Fibroin

The moist substance manufactured in the glands of a silkworm that produces silk thread when mixed with a small amount of wax and air-dried. The biocompatibility and mechanical properties of fibroin make it uniquely qualified to serve in a variety of functions currently under research, including acting as an interface between soft, wet biological tissues and technological implants.

View *Catalogue of 10 Silk-Protein Derived Devices*

Sources:

Brenckle, Mark A., et al. "Methods and Applications of Multilayer Silk Fibroin Laminates Based on Spatially Controlled Welding in Protein Films." *Advanced Functional Materials* 26, no. 1 (2015): 44–50. doi:10.1002/adfm.201502819.

"Silkworm." In *Columbia Encyclopedia*, edited by Paul Lagasse, 8th ed. New York: Columbia University Press, 2018.

Fossil fuels

Organic matter in the Earth transformed by natural processes into substances that can be used as a source of energy. Plants primarily provide the organic raw material, although marine plankton and other microbes may also serve as sources that convert to fossil fuel through a variety of heat, pressure, and time. Fossil fuels include coal, petroleum, natural gas, oil shales, bitumen, tar sands, and heavy oils.

View *AIR-INK*, *After Ancient Sunlight*, and *Algae Lab*

Sources:

Kopp, Otto C. "Fossil Fuel." In *Britannica Academic*. Accessed May 3, 2018. https://academic.eb.com/levels/collegiate/article/fossil-fuel/35002.

"Fossil Fuels." *Economist*, October 25, 2003. Accessed October 31, 2018. Academic OneFile. https://www.gale.com/c/academic-onefile.

Gene

A segment of DNA, occupying a specific place on a chromosome, that is the basic unit of heredity. Physical traits are determined by genes.

View *DIY Bacterial Gene Engineering CRISPR Kit*, *Metagenomics*, and *Resurrecting the Sublime*

Source:

"Gene." In *American Heritage® Dictionary of the English Language*, 5th ed. Accessed January 21 2019. https://www.thefreedictionary.com/gene.

Genetic engineering

The modification of an organism's DNA in order to alter inherited traits. Genetic engineering once included artificial selection techniques where animals and plants were bred to promote desired characteristics in the progeny. The modern interpretation of genetic engineering focuses on laboratory procedures where the DNA is directly manipulated, such as transgenic engineering and CRISPR-Cas9 gene editing. The term "GMO" (genetically modified organism) is employed primarily in the agricultural realm to describe the final result of genetic engineering.

View *DIY Bacterial Gene Engineering CRISPR Kit*, *Totomoxtle*, and *Tranceflora*

Sources:

"Genetic engineering." In *Britannica Academic*, February 24, 2017. Accessed October 10, 2018. https://academic.eb.com/levels/collegiate/article/genetic-engineering/36395.

"GMO." *European Food Safety Authority*. www.efsa.europa.eu/en/topics/topic/genetically-modified-organisms.

Hydrogel

Hydrogels are water-swollen, water-insoluble materials that maintain a distinct 3D structure. They were the first biomaterials designed for use in the human body.

View *Origami Membrane for 3D Organ Engineering* and *Sea Slug Bandages*

Sources:

Kopeček, Jindřich. "Hydrogel Biomaterials: A Smart Future?" *Biomaterials* 28, no. 34 (2007): 5185–92. doi:10.1016/j.biomaterials.2007.07.044.

Taubert, Andreas, João F. Mano, and Jose Carlos Rodriguez-Cabello. *Biomaterials Surface Science.* Weinheim, Germany: Wiley-VCH, 2013.

Hydroxyapatite

An inorganic compound having a crystallized lattice-like form composed of calcium, phosphate, and hydroxide. Found in bones and teeth, hydroxyapatite gives these structures rigidity.

View *3D-Painted Hyperelastic Bone*

Source:

"Hydroxyapatite." In *Mosby's Medical, Nursing, & Allied Health Dictionary*, edited by Kenneth N. Anderson, 6th ed. Philadelphia, PA: Elsevier Inc., 2001.

Luciferase

An enzyme that catalyzes the chemical reaction of the organic molecule luciferin with oxygen, producing light in a process known as bioluminescence. Both luciferase and luciferin are found in a variety of life forms including jellyfish, glowworms, and fireflies. Fireflies carry the genetic code to produce luciferase and luciferin, whereas jellyfish acquire the substances through their diet of small, bioluminescent crustaceans.

View *Nanobionic Plant Project: Ambient Illumination* and *Tranceflora*

Sources:

"How the Jelly Got Its Glow." American Museum of Natural History. https://www.amnh.org/explore/science-bulletins/bio/documentaries/jellies-down-deep/how-the-jelly-got-its-glow.

Larrañaga, Michael D., Richard J. Lewis, Sr., and Robert A. Lewis. "Luciferin." In *Hawley's Condensed Chemical Dictionary*, 16th ed. Hoboken, NJ: Wiley, 2016.

Material ecology

A design approach inspired by nature that integrates the environment into all phases of development, made possible by advances in raw materials, technology, and fabrication.

View *Aguahoja*

Source:

Oxman, Neri, Christine Ortiz, Fabio Gramazio, and Matthias Kohler. "Material Ecology." *Computer-Aided Design* 60 (2015): 1–2.

Membrane

A thin, outer boundary layer of a cell, organ, tissue, or object (natural or synthetic) that may be permeable or semipermeable.

View *Origami Membrane for 3D Organ Engineering*

Source:

"Membrane." In *American Heritage Dictionary of Medicine*, edited by Editors of the American Heritage Dictionaries, 2nd ed. Boston, MA: Houghton Mifflin, 2015.

Metabolism

The biochemical processes involved in fueling the operation of living things. Constructive metabolism, known as anabolism, is the synthesis of complex substances, whereas destructive metabolism, known as catabolism, is the breaking down of complex substances. Enzymes serve as catalysts to both processes, controlling the rate of reaction.

View *Biocement Bricks, Nanobionic Plant Project: Ambient Illumination,* and *Spark of Life*

Source:

"Metabolism." In *The Columbia Encyclopedia*, edited by Paul Lagasse, 8th ed. New York: Columbia University Press, 2018.

Metagenomics

The study of the sequenced DNA taken from an ecosystem sample in order to identify, understand, and evaluate the organisms present and the impact of their interactions.

View *Metagenomic Data Visualization* and *Mourn*

Sources:

Sell, Rebecca, Mikel Rothenberg, and Charles F. Chapman. "Metagenomics." In *Dictionary of Medical Terms*, 6th ed. Barron's Educational Series, 2012.

Rodenbeck, Eric. "New Images of Complex Microbiome Environments Visualized by Berkeley Metagenomics Lab and Stamen." *Medium.* Stamen Design, September 26, 2016. hi.stamen.com/uc-berkeley-metagenomics-lab-releases-new-images-of-complex-microbiome-environment-discovered-a80000770c93.

Microbiome

A community of microorganisms, including bacteria, fungi, and viruses, that inhabit a particular environment; the term is employed extensively to describe the collection of microorganisms living in or on the human body.

View *Metagenomic Data Visualization*

Source:

"Microbiome." In *Merriam-Webster's Medical Dictionary*, 1st ed. Springfield, MA: Merriam-Webster, 2016.

Microorganisms

Small-scale organisms requiring a microscope for observation. This identifier may include single-celled organisms such as bacteria, protozoa, and viruses, as well as fungi and algae if diminutive in size.

View *Metagenomic Data Visualization, Bioreceptive Concrete Panels,* and *Electron Micrographs*

Source:

Stanier, R. Y. "What Is Microbiology?" Institut Pasteur. From the UCLA Biochemistry Department website. http://www.chem.ucla.edu/dept/Faculty/merchant/pdf/microbiology.pdf.

Microplastics
The small pieces of plastic created when large plastic items degrade. Due to their small size, microplastics present a particular threat to aquatic life when eaten unintentionally.
View *BabyLegs*
Source:
Liboiron, Max. "Redefining Pollution and Action: The Matter of Plastics." *Journal of Material Culture* 21, no. 1 (2016): 87–110. doi:10.1177/1359183515622966.

Mycelium (pl. mycelia)
The network of fungal threads in soil that interface between plant roots and nutrients. The fruiting body or reproductive structure of mycelia is mushrooms.
View *Infinity Burial Suit*
Source:
Stamets, Paul. *Mycelium Running: How Mushrooms Can Help Save the World*. Berkeley, CA: Ten Speed Press, 2005.

Mycoremediation
The process of deploying fungi to degrade or detoxify an environment. Enzymes secreted by the fungi break down the complex molecular structures of some toxins into simpler compounds, or with heavy metals, the fungi absorb and channel the substances to their mushroom caps for disposal.
View *Infinity Burial Suit*
Source:
Stamets, Paul. *Mycelium Running: How Mushrooms Can Help Save the World*. Berkeley, CA: Ten Speed Press, 2005.

Natural selection
An evolutionary theory proposed by Charles Darwin positing the traits of organisms enhancing the chances for survival and procreation will increase across generations while less optimal traits face extinction.
View *BioMess*, *Monarch Pavilion*, *Resurrecting the Sublime*, *The Substitute*, and *Totomoxtle*
Source:
Brandon, Robert. "Natural Selection." In *Stanford Encyclopedia of Philosophy*, June 7, 2008. Stanford, CA: Stanford University. plato.stanford.edu/entries/natural-selection/#NatSelEvoThe.

Organic
A wide-ranging descriptor for all living things. When applied broadly, organic may describe substances originating from an unpolluted, natural world. However, in the realm of science, organic refers to compounds that contain carbon, a widespread element found throughout the universe from distant stars and planets to microscopic cell walls.
View *Nacadia Therapy Forest Garden*, *Tree of 40 Fruit*, and *Visualizing the Cosmic Web*
Sources:
"Carbon (C)." In *The Encyclopedia of Ecology and Environmental Management, Blackwell Science*, edited by Peter Calow, 1st ed. Oxford: Blackwell Science Ltd., 1998. doi:10.1002/9781444313253.
"Organic." In *Merriam-Webster Dictionary*. Accessed October 11, 2018, www.merriam-webster.com/dictionary/organic.

Parametric design
The creation of objects based on a set of data variables. The advent of advanced fabrication and computational technologies such as 3D printing and computer-aided design programs significantly increases the opportunities to exercise parametric design. However, manually constructed objects may incorporate parametric design as long as the variables or parameters are implemented in a consistent fashion.
View *Biomimicry Collection*, *Bionic Partition*, *Less CPP N°2*, and *Remolten N°1*
Sources:
Messina, Rab. "gt2P: How to Sit on a Chilean Volcano." *TLmagazine*, May 12, 2018. tlmagazine.com/gt2p-manufactured-landscapes/.
Woodbury, Robert Francis. *Elements of Parametric Design*. New York: Routledge, 2010.

Pectin
A complex carbohydrate found in certain plant cell walls and tissues. In fruit, pectin encourages structural integrity and shape retention by joining adjacent cell walls. Its thickening properties and water solubility have inspired a variety of applications ranging from food, pharmaceuticals, and design.
View *Aguahoja*
Source:
"Pectin." In *Britannica Encyclopedia*. Accessed October 10, 2018. https://www.britannica.com/science/pectin.

Phenotype
The observable traits of an organism, including size, color, and behavior, that result from genetic composition and environmental interaction. A phenotype may change through time due to environmental changes and age.
View *Personal Food Computer*, *Resurrecting the Sublime*, and *Totomoxtle*
Sources:
"Phenotype." In *Britannica Encyclopedia*. Accessed October 10, 2018. https://www.britannica.com/science/phenotype.
"Phenotype." In *Mosby's Medical, Nursing, & Allied Health Dictionary*, edited by Kenneth N. Anderson, 6th ed. Philadelphia, PA: Elsevier Inc., 2001.

PHA (Polyhydroxyalkanoate)
Biodegradable polymers produced in open, mixed microbial environments, and naturally generated as a byproduct of wastewater treatment. If a cost-effective production cycle can be conceived and manufactured, PHAs could serve as the raw material for a commercially viable alternative to petroleum-based plastics.
View *Mourn*
Sources:

Morgan-Sagastume, Fernando, Francesco Valentino, Markus Hjort, Dores Cirne, Lamija Karabegovic, F. Gerardin, Peter Johansson, et al. "Polyhydroxyalkanoate (PHA) Production from Sludge and Municipal Wastewater Treatment." *Water Science and Technology* 69, no. 1 (2014): 177–84.

Zou, Huibin, Mengxun Shi, Tongtong Zhang, Lei Li, Liangzhi Li, and Mo Xian. "Natural and Engineered Polyhydroxyalkanoate (PHA) Synthase: Key Enzyme in Biopolyester Production." *Applied Microbiology and Biotechnology* 101, no. 20 (July 2017): 7417–26. doi:10.1007/s00253-017-8485-0.

Polymer
A macromolecule made of five or more simple, identical molecules called monomers. A polymer may be organic (DNA, cellulose, silk) or synthetic (plastic and glass). Abundant in organisms, organic polymers serve as basic structural materials and contribute to important life functions.
View *Algae Lab*, *Cilllia*, *Sea Slug Bandages*, and *Soft Robotic Grip Glove*
Sources:

Larrañaga, Michael D., Richard J. Lewis, Sr., and Robert A. Lewis. "Polymer." In *Hawley's Condensed Chemical Dictionary*, 16th ed. Hoboken, NJ: Wiley, 2016.

"Polymer." In *Britannica Encyclopedia*. Accessed October 10, 2018. https://www.britannica.com/science/polymer.

SEM (Scanning Electron Microscope)
A microscope that uses an electron beam instead of light (as with a traditional microscope) to form an image. In operation since the 1950s, SEMs benefit from a greater depth of field and higher resolution than traditional microscopes. The use of electromagnets in the place of traditional lenses allows for a greater control over the degree of magnification.
View *Electron Micrographs*
Source:

"Scanning Electron Microscope." Radiological & Environmental Management. Purdue University Division of Environmental Health and Public Safety. www.purdue.edu/ehps/rem/laboratory/equipment safety/Research Equipment/sem.html.

Synthetic biology
Field of research focused on the creation of new living systems through deliberate design. Synthetic biology research primarily focuses on the reengineering of genes to create new biological components or systems that would not occur if left in an original, untouched state. Once reprogrammed, the systems acquire new functions, leading to advances such as sustainable chemicals and next-generation materials.
View *BioMess* and *Resurrecting the Sublime*
Sources:

"Center for Synthetic Biology." Center for Synthetic Biology, Northwestern University. Evanston, IL: Northwestern University. https://syntheticbiology.northwestern.edu/.

Church, George. *Regenesis—How Synthetic Biology Will Reinvent Nature and Ourselves*. New York: The Perseus Books Group, 2014.

Davies, Jamie A. *Synthetic Biology: A Very Short Introduction*. Oxford: Oxford University Press, 2018.

Tissue engineering
The growth and development of a biomaterial by seeding cells on a supportive structure called a scaffold. Typically employed to create an organ or part of an organ, tissue engineering has been adapted to create biomaterials for the disciplines of fashion and design.
View *Tissue Engineered Textiles*
Source:

Dye, Frank J. "Tissue engineering." In *Dictionary of Developmental Biology and Embryology*, 2nd ed. Hoboken, NJ: Wiley-Blackwell, 2012.

Transgenic organisms
Organisms in which genetic material has been modified in a way that could not occur naturally, and the resulting traits are heritable.
View *Tranceflora*
Source:

"Transgenic organisms." *The Encyclopedia of Ecology and Environmental Management*, edited by Peter Calow, 1st ed. Oxford: Blackwell Science Ltd., 1998. doi:10.1002/9781444313253.

Tree of life
A graphic depiction of the evolutionary relationships between all forms of life. Sometimes called a phylogenetic tree, the trunk represents the earliest form of life and the branches symbolize the emergence of traits or characteristics among descendants that differentiate them from the trunk and other branches.
View *Metagenomic Data Visualization*
Sources:

Archibald, J. David. *Aristotle's Ladder, Darwin's Tree: The Evolution of Visual Metaphors for Biological Order*. New York: Columbia University Press, 2014.

"Tree of Life." American Museum of Natural History. https://www.amnh.org/exhibitions/darwin/evolution-today/how-do-we-know-living-things-are-related/tree-of-life.

Index

234

Acknowledgments
Andrea Lipps, Matilda McQuaid, and Caitlin Condell

Nature has been a three-year journey of cross-continental collaboration between the curatorial teams of Cooper Hewitt and the Cube design museum. Cooper Hewitt's counterparts in the Netherlands—Hans Gubbels, Gène Bertrand, and Madeleine van Daele—have been precious partners in this adventure. Our ideas, insights, and discoveries were thanks to endless discussions with them and a broad network of colleagues, friends, formal advisors, and accidental consultants who helped us shape this book and the Triennial exhibition. To all of them we are indebted.

This book and the Triennial exhibition highlight sixty-two projects. Behind these projects is the inspiring and tireless effort of hundreds of designers, scientists, architects, engineers, artists, technologists, and activists who are collaborating to bring work into the world that is more integrated with nature. We thank each of these teams, and their manufacturers, fabricators, gallerists, collectors, assistants, friends, and partners, for their enthusiasm and participation, and for parting with their work while it is on view in the show. It is your practice and vision that we celebrate in these pages.

Caroline Baumann, Cooper Hewitt's Director, was an early and steadfast champion of our project, crucial to its realization. We are grateful to individual project sponsors, including the Tippet Rise Fund of the Sidney E. Frank Foundation, which supported Ensamble Studio's Petrified River, BASF Corporation and RNR Foundation in support of Terreform ONE's Monarch Sanctuary, and Esquel Group and NOE, LLC that supported the Aguahoja project by Neri Oxman and The Mediated Matter Group at MIT Media Lab. Your generous support made these visionary projects possible.

The craft of publishing is a team effort. The clarity of this volume was guided by Pamela Horn, Cooper Hewitt's Director of Cross-Platform Publishing. Matthew Kennedy, Cross-Platform Publishing Associate, applied his meticulous eye to the details and images in these pages. We are grateful to graphic designers Neil Donnelly and Ben Fehrman-Lee from Neil Donnelly Studio, whose brilliant, perceptive design and typographic treatment captured the show's essence. Donna Wenzel rigorously edited every word with scientific insight.

Exhibitions like a Triennial are challenging to design, but Studio Joseph proved yet again to be incomparable partners. They created a conceptual synthesis of the show's ideas, matched by care and attention that enable each work on view to sing. It is our great pleasure to work with their team, especially Wendy Joseph, Monica Coghlan, Jose Luis Vidalon, Alexios Bacolas, Joseph Parrella, Ellen Wong, and Shuo Yang. Their counterparts at Cube, Studio Van Eijk & Van der Lubbe, excelled in their interpretation of the exhibition design concept and layout for Cube's galleries.

The installation itself was a challenge even for Cooper Hewitt's heroic staff. We wish to thank Yvonne Gómez Durand, Head of Exhibitions, who was a stalwart and invaluable collaborator and led a crew that built everything to perfection: Milo Mottola, Kristi Cavataro, Michael Sypluski, Laura McAdams, Carl Baggaley, Nathaniel Joslin, Marcy Chevali, and Chris Moody. She was assisted by Molly Engelman, Exhibitions Coordinator, who kept us all on target. Our registrars, Steve Langehough, Kim Hawkins, Rick Jones, Antonia Moser, and Larry Silver ensured all of the work was shipped and received on time and, together with their crew of art handlers, Paul Goss, Peter Baryshnikov, Ted Kersten, and Joel Holberg, they installed the show safely. The resourceful and creative Mathew Weaver drove our team on the floor to ensure the show was expertly mounted. Jody Hanson lent her magic touch to our mounts. Conservators Sarah Barack, Jessica Walthew, and Kira Eng-Wilmot rigorously tested materials, treated and installed objects, and provided critical maintenance during the run of the exhibition to make sure the galleries were safe for both visitors and objects. Digital components of exhibitions are becoming more herculean with each endeavor. We are indebted to Shamus Adams, Mary Fe Alves da Silva, Adam Quinn, Nolan Hill, and Carolyn Royston for their technical prowess and creative solutions that ensure a robust digital experience for our visitors. At Cube design museum we acknowledge the manufacturers and fabricators of the exhibition design. Special thanks to Cube's logistic partners and their staff in the internal logistics department.

As they say, it takes a village. Dozens more colleagues at Cooper Hewitt made the exhibition possible. Cara McCarty, Curatorial Director, originally had the idea for an exhibition on nature, and she inspired the team to act creatively and think deeply. Our expert communications and marketing team—Laurie Bohlk, Alexandra Cunningham Cameron, Alix Finkelstein, Hannah Holden, and Ann Sunwoo—messaged and promoted the exhibition to get the press and visitors irresistibly enticed. The education team helped us expand on the ideas in the show: special thanks to Halima Johnson, Ruki Ravikumar, Kim Robleda-Diga, and Ruth Starr. We are grateful to Christina de Leon, who proposed designers and acted as an exceptional moderator and translator. Wendy Rogers provided essential help in navigating the bowels of The Museum System. Chris Gauthier worked his magic with the videos in the show. The Cooper Hewitt Shop extended the reach of the show into the retail realm, led by Cat Birch. And key to all our efforts, our Development team, Julia Clark, Deborah Fitzgerald, Milly Egaua, and Laura Meli, secured funding, a critical feat that enables books and exhibitions like *Nature* to be realized.

At Cube, Fion Sanders, fundraiser, created a strong fundraising message that appealed to donors. And Cube's communication and marketing team—Valérie Hoekstra, Carola van 't Hof, Karin van den Bergh, and Noud de Greef—was instrumental in messaging the show and promoting it across Dutch media and beyond.

A special acknowledgement goes to Cooper Hewitt's curatorial assistant Caroline O'Connell, who shouldered the brunt of the Triennial and kept us humming along to bring this massive ship to port. We are thankful for her meticulousness, patience, and good cheer throughout. Erin Freedman, curatorial assistant, got the Triennial off the ground with crucial research and organization. We were joined by a stellar Capstone curatorial fellow, Margaret Simons, and two brilliant interns, Margaret Gaines and Hanna Kaeser, whose research and assistance were essential on a project of this scale. Cube's project coordinator, Madeleine van Daele, oversaw the organization of the exhibition at Cube and interfaced with myriad internal and external stakeholders to bring the show to fruition. Vivian van Slooten provided her with invaluable assistance.

Finally, no project like this can be accomplished without the unwavering support and sounding board of our partners and families. To Andrea's husband, Ryan Heiferman, and young children, Luca and Liv Heiferman, my deepest gratitude to you for once again enduring my late nights and weekends. To Matilda's husband, Craig Konyk, for his eternal good cheer. And to Caitlin's partner Matthew Grill and parents Sarah Whitham and Henry Condell, thank you for your enduring patience, curiosity, and love.

Author Bios

GÈNE BERTRAND has been the Program and Development Director of Museumplein Limburg since 2007; there he shares responsibility for program and exhibition development at the Continuum Discovery Center, the Cube design museum, and the Columbus Earth Center. He has worked for more than thirty-five years in museums and science centers and has a background in culture, media, education, and public relations/marketing. Bertrand has extensive experience in international programs and cooperation. He worked on the development and expansions of the different institutions at Museumplein Limburg that led to the opening of the Cube design museum and the Columbus Earth Center in 2015.

CAITLIN CONDELL is the Associate Curator and Head of Drawings, Prints & Graphic Design at Cooper Hewitt, Smithsonian Design Museum, where she oversees a collection of nearly 147,000 works on paper dating from the fourteenth century to the present. She has organized and contributed to numerous exhibitions and publications, including *Nature—Cooper Hewitt Design Triennial* (2019), *Fragile Beasts* (2016), *Esperanza Spalding Selects* (2017–18), *Making Design* (2015), and *How Posters Work* (2015) at Cooper Hewitt, and *Making Room: The Space Between Two and Three Dimensions* (2012–13) at the Massachusetts Museum of Contemporary Art (MASS MoCA). She has lectured widely on topics of art and design history.

ANDREA LIPPS is Associate Curator of Contemporary Design at Cooper Hewitt, Smithsonian Design Museum, where she conceives, develops, and organizes major exhibitions and books. Most recently, Lipps has authored and edited publications and curated exhibitions on *Nature—Cooper Hewitt Design Triennial* (2019), *The Senses: Design Beyond Vision* (2018), *Joris Laarman Lab: Design in the Digital Age* (2017), and *Beauty—Cooper Hewitt Design Triennial* (2016). Additionally, she is developing a collection plan and wish list for acquiring born-digital work at the museum. Lipps is a regular visiting critic, lecturer, and thesis advisor, participates on international design juries, and frequently moderates and speaks at events, symposia, and academic conferences on contemporary design and curatorial practice.

MATILDA MCQUAID is Deputy Director of Curatorial and Head of Textiles at Cooper Hewitt, Smithsonian Design Museum. She has organized acclaimed exhibitions and publications nationally and internationally, including *Josef + Anni Albers: Designs for Living* (2004), *Extreme Textiles: Designing for High Performance* (2005), *Color Moves: Art and Fashion by Sonia Delaunay* (2011), *Tools: Extending Our Reach* (2015), and *Scraps: Fashion, Textiles, and Creative Reuse* (2016). She led a major collection digitization project at the museum with more than two hundred thousand objects photographed and available online. Formerly at the Museum of Modern Art (NYC) for fifteen years where she curated more than thirty exhibitions, she is also an accomplished author and editor on art, architecture, and design, with many books, exhibition catalogues, and articles to her credit.

MARGARET SIMONS serves as Capstone Curatorial Fellow at Cooper Hewitt, Smithsonian Design Museum, a position bestowed to an outstanding student in the Master's Program of Design History and Curatorial Studies offered jointly by the museum and Parsons School of Design. In her studies, she specializes in international contemporary design, concentrating on furniture, textiles, and ceramics. Simons holds an MBA from New York University's Stern School of Business, giving her the unique combination of skills to research the intersection of art, society, and economics. She also contributes articles to journals, including *Objective*.

Photo Credits

Introduction
9: © Charles Reilly 2018; 10 left: Courtesy of Giorgia Lupi and Kaki King; 10 right: © Tim Bowditch (Photo). Thomas Thwaites, Goatman; 11 top: © USC Game Innovation Lab; 11 middle: Photo by J. Li, B. Freedman, and the Wyss Institute for Biologically Inspired Engeering at Harvard University Media Team; 11 left: Graviky Labs and Tiger Campaign; 11 right: Photo by Alan Boom © Shahar Livne; 12 top: Photo by Han Dan © DnA_Design and Architecture; 12 left: Immatters Studio; 12 right: © bioMASON, Inc.; 12 bottom: Courtesy of Mediated Matter, MIT Media Lab; 13 top: © The Tissue Culture & Art Project (Oron Catts & Ionat Zurr); 13 middle: Photo by Femke Poort © Studio Nienke Hoogvliet; 13 bottom: Max Liboiron, CLEAR; 14 top: Courtesy of VTN Architects; 14 bottom: Courtesy of Alexandra Daisy Ginsberg

Understand
20–21: © Banfield Labs; 22–23: Kim Albrecht, Barabasi Lab; 24–25: © Charles Reilly 2018; 28–29: Courtesy of Giorgia Lupi and Kaki King; 30–31: © James C. Weaver; 32 top left: Photo by Lonneke van der Palen © Aliki van der Kruijs; 32 top right, 33 bottom: © Aliki van der Kruijs; 32 bottom: Photo by Femke Hoekstra © Aliki van der Kruijs; 33 top: Photo by Pim Leenen © Aliki van der Kruijs; 36: © Iwan Baan; 37: © 2015 Tippet Rise; 38–39: Photo by Kabage Karanja © Cave; 40–41: Ed Reeve; 42–43: © Tim Bowditch (Photo). Thomas Thwaites, Goatman; 46–47: © USC Game Innovation Lab

Simulate
59 top: Alexandra Daisy Ginsberg; 59 bottom: Grace Chuang, Gray Herbarium of Harvard University; 60–61: Images by Felipe Ribon / Courtesy of Carpenters Workshop Gallery; 64: Alexandra Kehagalou Studio, originally commissioned by the National Gallery of Victoria; 65: Alexandra Kehagalou Studio; 66–67: Photo by Phillip W. Hyatt © threeASFOUR; 68–69: Courtesy of The Living, Airbus, Autodesk, and APWorks; 70–71: Michelin; 72–75: © Festo AG & Co. KG, all rights reserved; 78–79: Photo by J. Li, B. Freedman, and the Wyss Institute for Biologically Inspired Engineering at Harvard University Media Team; 80–81: © Adam E. Jakus; 82–83: © 2012 Tangible Media Group / MIT Media Lab, licensed under a Creative Commons Attribution-NonCommercial-NoDerivs 3.0 Unported License; 84–85: Courtesy of Modern Meadow

Salvage
88: Photo © Edward Burtynsky, courtesy Greenberg Gallery and Wolkowitz Gallery, New York / Metivier Gallery, Toronto; 90 top & bottom, 91 bottom: Photo by Alan Boom © Shahar Livne; 91 top: Photo by Ronald Smits © Shahar Livne; 92 & 93 bottom: Blickfänger; 93 top: Mike Roelofs; 96 top & bottom, 97 top right & bottom: © Kirstie van Noort; 97 top left: Photo by Anneke Hymmen © Kirstie van Noort; 98–99: Graviky Labs and Tiger Campaign; 100 top: adidas; 100 bottom: Parley for the Oceans; 101: © adidas; 102, 103 top & 105: Photo by Antoine Raab © Luma Arles; 104 top: Photo by Victor Picon © Luma Arles; 104 bottom: Photo by Florent Gardin © Luma Arles; 108–109: Pierre-Yves Dinasquet, Department of Seaweed; 110–111: Photos by Femke Poort © Studio Nienke Hoogvliet

Facilitate
115: Photos by Matt Flynn © Smithsonian Institution; 116: Photos by Han Dan © DnA_Design and Architecture; 117: Photos by Wang Ziling © DnA_Design and Architecture; 118–119: © Friedman Benda and Erez Nevi Pana; 120–121: Amy Congdon; 124–125: © bioMASON, Inc.; 126–127: Immatters Studio; 128–129: © Alex Goad; 132–133: © Architecture and Vision (Arturo Vittori); 134–135: Courtesy Open Agriculture Initiative, MIT Media Lab, licensed under CC-BY-NC-SA 4.0

Augment
148–149: Courtesy of Mediated Matter, MIT Media Lab; 1150–151: Courtesy of Sam Van Aken and Ronald Feldman Fine Arts; 152: Seth Shipman, Harvard Medical School, and Gladstone Institutes; 153: Courtesy of The ODIN; 154–155: © The Tissue Culture & Art Project (Oron Catts & Ionat Zurr); 156: Wyss Institute for Biologically Inspired Engineering at Harvard University; 158–159: Courtesy of Chuck Hoberman and Richard Novak, Wyss Institute for Biologically Inspired Engineering at Harvard University; 160–161: So Morimoto; 162–163: Tufts Silk Lab; 166–167: Photo by Aryeh Kornfeld © Friedman Benda and gt2P

Remediate
176 & 177 top: Ulrika K. Stigsdotter; 177 bottom: Ulrik Sidenius; 178–179: © Wyss Institute at Harvard University and Harvard Biodesign Lab; 180 top: Dave Howells, MEOPAR; 180 bottom, 181: Max Liboiron, CLEAR; 184–185: © Charlotte McCurdy; 186: Photo by Femke Poort © Studio Nienke Hoogvliet; 187: © Coeio, Inc./Jae Rhim Lee; 188–189: © Mitchell Joachim, Terreform ONE; 192–193: Sheng-Hung Lee; 194–195: Fernando Laposse

Nurture
206 top: Courtesy Jorge Gamboa; 206 bottom: © Justin Hofman; 207: © Jorge Gamboa, first presented at La Bienal del Cartel Bolivia (BICeBé) and first published in *National Geographic*; 210 left: A courtesy of Palazzo Clerici; 210 right: Hans Boddeke © Teresa van Dongen, 2019; 211: Strano Research Group; 212–213: Courtesy of VTN Architects; 214 bottom: Rendering by Javier Ruiz © Bio-ID / The Bartlett, UCL; 214 top: Photo by Sara Lever © Bio-ID / The Bartlett, UCL; 215: Photo by Marcus Cruz © Bio-ID / The Bartlett, UCL; 218–219: Jens Markus Lindhe, Cisternerne; 220–221: MASS Design Group; 222: Ami Vitale/National Geographic Creative; 223: Courtesy of Alexandra Daisy Ginsberg

LONG CAPTION INDEX

Resurrecting the Sublime, 2018-19; Christina Agapakis (American, b. 1984), Alexandra Daisy Ginsberg (British and South African, b. 1982), and Sissel Tolaas (Norwegian, b. 1963), with support from IFF Inc. and Ginkgo Bioworks, Inc.; Paleogenomics: Joshua Kapp and Beth Shapiro, Paleogenomics Lab, University of California, Santa Cruz; DNA Synthesis: Twist Bioscience; Alexandra Daisy Ginsberg: Ana Maria Nicolaescu, Johanna Just, Ness Lafoy, Ioana Mann, Stacie Woolsey, and Nicholas Zembashi; With thanks to: Michaela Schmull, Harvard University Herbarium; Aluminum, plywood, neoprene, plasterzote, LEDs, diffuser, motion sensor, smell solutions, limestone boulder; Courtesy of the designers

Bioreceptive Concrete Panels, 2017-19; Research and Design Team: Bartlett School of Architecture (London, England, UK), Principal Investigator, Conception and Design: Professor Marcos Cruz (German/ Portuguese, b. 1970), Computational Design: Javier Ruiz (Spanish, b. 1984), Conception: Richard Beckett (British, b. 1979), Collaboration: Nina Jotanovic and Anete Salmane Biology consultancy: Rushi Mehta, University of Utrecht, Engineering: Manja van de Worp, NOUS Engineering; Client / Partnership: Transport for London, Lambeth Council, St Anne's Catholic Primary School; Manufacturing / Industrial Partnerships: Pennine Stone Limited with B-MADE / UCL; Sponsorship: University College London, Transport for London; Concrete; Dimensions variable

Aguahoja, 2017-19; Research and Design: Neri Oxman (Israeli, active USA, b. 1976), the Mediated Matter Group, MIT Media Lab (Cambridge, Massachusetts, USA, founded 2010); Contributing Team Members: Jorge Duro-Royo, Joshua Van Zak, Yen-Ju (Tim) Tai, Andrea Ling, Christoph Bader, Nic Hogan, Barrak Darweesh, Laia Mogas-Soldevilla, Daniel Lizardo, João Costa, Sunanda Sharma, James Weaver, Matthew Bradford, Loewen Cavill, Emily Ryeom, Aury Hay, Yi Gong, Brian Huang, Joseph Faraguna, and Neri Oxman; Chitosan, cellulose, pectin, acetic acid, glycerin, water; Dimensions variable; We wish to acknowledge MIT Media Lab, GETTYLAB, Robert Wood Johnson Foundation (RWJF), Autodesk BUILD Space, TBA-21 (Thyssen-Bornemisza Art Contemporary), and the Wyss Institute at Harvard University

Monarch Sanctuary, 2018-ongoing; Mitchell Joachim (American, b. 1972) and Vivian Kuan (American, b. 1966), Terreform ONE (Brooklyn, New York, USA, founded 2006); Contributing Designers: Christian Hubert, Nicholas Gervasi, Maria Aiolova, Anna Bokov, Kristina Goncharov, Yucel Guven, Zhan Xu, Larissa Belcic, Shahira Hammad, Deniz Onder, James Leonard, Zack Saunders, Xinye Lin, Sabrina Naumovski, Daniel S. Castaño, Aidan Nelson, Rita Wang, Michael Brittenham, Aleksandr Plotkin, and Anouk Wipprecht, Theo Dimitrasopoulos, Jules Pepitone; Glass, metal, plastic, thermometer, milkweed, monarch butterflies and larvae; Sponsors: BASF Corporation, RNR Foundation, Intel, and Jackie Jangana

CUBE DESIGN MUSEUM

Published by Cooper Hewitt,
Smithsonian Design Museum
2 East 91st Street
New York, NY 10128
USA
cooperhewitt.org

This book is published in conjunction with the
exhibition *Nature—Cooper Hewitt Design Triennial*.
Simultaneously presented at Cooper Hewitt,
Smithsonian Design Museum, New York City, and
Cube design museum, Kerkrade, Netherlands,
May 10, 2019–January 20, 2020.

Nature—Cooper Hewitt Design Triennial is made
possible by support from The Ainslie Foundation.
Funding is also provided by Amita and Purnendu
Chatterjee, the August Heckscher Exhibition Fund,
the Esme Usdan Exhibition Endowment Fund,
the Creative Industries Fund NL, and the New
York State Council on the Arts with the support of
Governor Andrew M. Cuomo and the New York
State Legislature, and at Cube with support from
the government of the Province of Limburg, the
Creative Industries Fund NL, Fonds 21, and Prins
Bernhard Culture Fund.

ISBN 978-1-942303-23-7
2019 2020 2021 2022 / 10 9 8 7 6 5 4 3 2 1

Distributed in North America by
ARTBOOK | D.A.P.
75 Broad Street, Suite 630
New York, NY 10004
artbook.com

Distributed Worldwide by
Thames & Hudson UK
181A High Hilborn
London WC1V 7QX
UK
thamesandhudson.com

Names: National Design Triennial (6th : 2019 :
New York, N. Y.; Kerkrade, Netherlands),
organizer. | Bertrand, Gène, author. | Condell,
Caitlin, author. | Lipps, Andrea, author. |
McQuaid, Matilda, author. | Cooper-Hewitt
Museum, issuing body, host institution. | Cube
Design Museum, host institution.
Title: Nature : collaborations in design / Cooper
Hewitt Design Triennial, co-organized with Cube
Design Museum ; authors, Gène Bertrand, Caitlin
Condell, Andrea Lipps, Matilda McQuaid.
Description: New York, NY : Published by Cooper
Hewitt, Smithsonian Design Museum, [2019] |
Published in conjunction with an exhibition at
Cooper Hewitt, Smithsonian Design Museum and
Cube Design Museum, May 10, 2019–January
20, 2020. | Includes bibliographical references
and index.
Identifiers: LCCN 2019005247 (print) | LCCN
2019007443 (ebook) | ISBN 9781942303244
(epub) | ISBN 9781942303251 (.mobi) | ISBN
9781942303237 (pbk. : alk. paper)
Subjects: LCSH: Design—Environmental aspects—
Exhibitions. | Sustainable design—Exhibitions. |
Human ecology—Exhibitions. | Climatic
changes—Exhibitions.
Classification: LCC NK1520 (ebook) | LCC NK1520
.N38 2019 (print) | DDC 745.4—dc23
LC record available at https://lccn.loc.gov/2019005247

Director of Cross-Platform Publishing
Pamela Horn

Cross-Platform Publishing Associate
Matthew Kennedy

Copy Editor
Donna Wenzel

Book Design
Neil Donnelly and Ben Fehrman-Lee

Printer
PieReg Druckcenter Berlin GmbH

Type
News Plantin, Maxima, and Computer Modern

Paper
Chromolux 200 FSC®-Mix 250 g/m², Magno
Satin FSC®-Mix 135 g/m², EnviroTop FSC®-
Recycle 100 g/m²

Printed in Germany

Inside cover image: Choreography of Life, 2019;
Charles Reilly (New Zealander, b. 1983), Wyss
Institute for Biologically Inspired Engineering,
Harvard University (Boston, Massachusetts, USA,
founded 2009); Video, 4:00 minutes; © Charles Reilly

Climate neutral
Print product
ClimatePartner.com/11728-1903-1002

MIX
Paper from
responsible sources
FSC® C139577

Designers' Statement
Hybridity—of nonhuman species and humans, of
evolution and design—is a concept underpinning the
work throughout this book and in *Nature—Cooper
Hewitt Design Triennial*. These designs expose a
blurring of boundaries, the push and pull between
humans and nature. The design of this book and
exhibition reflects this relationship between discrete
yet mutually dependent entities.

The graphic identity for *Nature* uses
two typefaces with similar structures, Plantin and
Maxima, in always-mutating layers. These layers
reveal themselves throughout this book: on the cover,
on the title pages for each section, and within the
essays, where image locations on one spread trigger a
typeface switch on the previous one, in a constantly
evolving display.

The tension between the natural and the
artificial extends to the production processes used in
making this book. We replaced the standard inks used
in four-color process printing with their fluorescent
equivalents, imbuing the images with a hyperreality
and visual energy that would be impossible to achieve
through standard offset printing.

Neil Donnelly
Ben Fehrman-Lee

Smithsonian Design Museum